THE GOOD, THE BAD, AND THE ECONOMY

LOUIS PUTTERMAN

THE GOOD, THE BAD, AND THE ECONOMY

DOES HUMAN NATURE RULE OUT A BETTER WORLD?

Langdon Street Press
212 3rd Avenue North, Suite 290
Minneapolis, MN 55401
612.455.2293
www.langdonstreetpress.com

ISBN-13: 978-1-938296-01-7
LCCN: 2012934609

Distributed by Itasca Books

Printed in the United States of America

Table of Contents

For those who seek a better world

and aren't satisfied

with easy answers.

Preface

Social reformers, from Confucius and the biblical prophets to Gandhi and Martin Luther King, have dreamed of a world in which peace, justice, and harmony would reign. And viewing the record of humanity from antiquity to the present, we might cautiously pick out glimmers of progress towards that dream. The presumption of absolute rule by an autocrat of one kind or other, under which most people lived for more than three thousand years, has given way to the notion of democracy, an ideal that's been approached in reality in more than a few countries. Legal systems providing relatively equal and unbiased protection have emerged and held sway in considerable parts of the world. The statuses of women, of minorities, and of lesbian, gay, bi-sexual and transgender individuals have been raised in many, though by no means all, countries. Even schemes for the economic protection of those less able to provide for themselves have grown up and shown resilience in some prosperous countries.

And yet we find ourselves living in a world in which the two richest people are worth as much as the poorest one billion, in which the income gap between the richest and poorest countries is roughly a hundred to one. While the open slavery known from ancient times until the nineteenth century is almost universally condemned and outlawed, millions remain enslaved in all but name, with tens of thousands sold into prostitution and trafficked across international borders every year. As for the dream of peace, more than two generations after the devastating global wars that scarred the first half of the twentieth century, half a million people still die each year in wars, civil wars, and war-induced famines. Peace and order are relatively well-established in and among richer and more politically-stable nations, yet their people's sense of well-being is frequently threatened by financial insecurity, stress, and sudden swings of the economic pendulum. Moreover, concern is widespread that economic growth as we've known it and as it continues today may be rendering our planet incapable of sustaining future generations.

On the face of it, such concerns seem surprising. After all, twentieth century science has allowed massive gains in crop yields, unprecedented growth in life expectancy, rapid increases in the speed of communications and travel, dramatic expansion of the size, variety, and accessibility of intellectual and cultural resources, and the sprouting up, with astounding speed, of gleaming cities on what only yesterday were fields, marshes, and deserts. In less than a century, the world has leapt from the horse and buggy and the telegraph to jet travel and video chatting across continents. Diseases that cut down our great-grandparents in their forties and fifties are easily kept at bay now, and once-difficult medical procedures are routinely performed these days on an out-patient basis. With such astounding mastery of raw materials and technology, what is it that's stopping us from also building a more just and peaceful world?

As an adolescent and young adult, I wondered why a world of evident material abundance and scientific prowess was filled with so much suffering and inequality, along with the ever-present danger of nuclear conflagration that then passed for normalcy. It all seemed so completely unnecessary, given that basic physiological needs appeared readily within reach of our productive capacities and that the ultimate needs for love and affiliation don't even require the expenditure of additional resources.

After years of trying to understand these questions by studying the social sciences and pursuing a career of research and teaching, my sense of the tragedy of our current human condition remains as acute as ever. But I now believe that the social and life sciences have begun to make real progress towards formulating answers to the questions that thoughtful people of goodwill have been asking for so many years. Our chances of actually making the world a better place depend, as I see it, not only on our horror at the scale of human misery and waste and on our passion for change, but also on grounding our efforts in a better appreciation of just why a more just, peaceful, and nurturing world has so far proven to be so difficult to construct. That's why I've chosen to write this book for general readers, rather than address another technical paper to my professional colleagues.

Beating the dismal rap

I know. It seems out of place to find an economist, of all people, taking seriously the notion of making the world a better place. My profession boasts of armies of "realists" who remind us at every turn that "there's no free lunch." And there are plenty of reasons why economics has been called "the dismal science."

That epithet arose first in response to the late eighteenth century writings of the Reverend Thomas Robert Malthus, who argued that population growth would inevitably leave the vast majority of the world's people living in poverty. The prediction wound up looking ever further from the mark as the industrial world achieved unprecedented increases in average living standards, so the term "Malthusian" is today applied not to the analysis of modern economies but instead to preindustrial ones. Still, Malthus's pessimistic and skeptical spirit has been at home within the economics profession in every generation since his own.

As the story is oft recounted, Malthus's father had been a friend and admirer of the social reformers Jean-Jacques Rousseau and William Godwin. But the younger Malthus thought that both his father and the men his father admired were guilty of wishful thinking. He argued that neither equality nor the elimination of poverty could ever be realized, thanks to iron laws of physical and human nature. In working out his theory of population, Malthus laid important foundations for later economic theory—especially the concept of diminishing returns to labor. But it would be his assumption of self-interest, his emphasis on scarcity, and his skepticism about social improvement schemes, a skepticism grounded in the belief that competition, inequality, and poverty are necessities of human existence, that would most color economics in later generations.

The views I'll stake out in this book aren't immune to a disciplinary sense of realism or to the belief that what makes humans tick includes a healthy dose of self-interest. "Incentives, incentives, incentives" remains the theme of recent popular books by economists. But where many economists see the pursuit of self-interest as the only motivation worth thinking about when attempting to understand human behavior and the organization of economic life, I argue for a more nuanced approach that leaves considerable room for the more socially-minded side of the human psyche and spirit, a side increasingly well-documented by studies both within and outside of my field. It's only by understanding a wider range of motivations, as well as the different balances among motivations exhibited by different individuals, that we can come to a more realistic appraisal of how individuals and societies operate. Based on such an understanding, we might make better guesses about what is and isn't possible for humans in this rapidly changing world.

A brief roadmap

In a sense, this book is a meeting ground for three ways of thinking about society that rarely, if ever, intersect. The first, naturally, is the approach of economics, with its emphasis on incentives and self-interest. The second, combining the lenses of numerous disciplines, entails an evolutionary understanding of human nature and behavior and a long-period view of human origins and progress. Over the last decade or two, there've been encounters between economics and these other approaches, but little of the light generated has reached a broad reading public.

The third lens that defines my project lies beyond the boundaries of either economics or its sister sciences. Unlike academic fields that seek as objective as possible an understanding of the subjects they study, I want to take seriously the yearnings that gave rise to the social sciences in the first place, yearnings of social philosophers like Rousseau and Godwin and of activists like Gandhi and King. I aim to use the insights of the sciences, including economics, to answer the question of the philosophers and activists: Why can't we build a better world?

In the book's initial chapters, the stage will be set by viewing the massive ripples of the eighteenth century Industrial Revolution in today's India and China, then locating the stirrings of the utopian quest in the almost quaint industrializing world of early nineteenth century England and America. To get us started on our attempt to answer the "Why not a better world?" question, we'll then consider whether a focus on material scarcity à la Malthus Jr. or paying more attention to human interaction and motivation, as in the intersection of my first two lenses, is the more promising route. No surprise—I'll argue for the latter.

With our main characters (ourselves) under the microscope, we'll be ready to interrogate human nature. Are we fundamentally selfish, or are we also concerned for others and responsive to ideals? We'll pile up the evidence on one side of the scale, then on the other, and we'll consult the insights of evolutionary behavioral science to arrive at a reasonable balance. We humans are overwhelmingly predisposed towards looking out for ourselves and for our immediate kin, say both evidence and theory, but we're also highly social animals with predispositions towards empathy, towards positively and negatively reciprocating the helpful and harmful actions of others, towards caring about what others think of us, and towards wanting to think well of ourselves. We're preadapted to being social, and cooperating towards common goals is part of what we do.

One of the most exciting areas in which economics and the behavioral sciences have made contact of late is the experimental economics lab. Here, the complexity of human nature has come to be better understood by asking participants to make decisions under structured constraints in group interactions. I'll illustrate this with emphasis on my own and closely related research. I'll then invite you to travel with me back in time to apply this understanding of complex human social nature to the growing body of archeological, anthropological, and historical knowledge that helps us to understand why the material and social organization of preagricultural bands evolved into today's economic systems built on private property and market exchange.

Finally, we'll look again at the evolution of modern economies, but this time with an emphasis on differences in the pace of change among the world's regions and societies over the space of ten thousand years. It's these differences, I'll argue, that led not only to the vast inequalities between the developed and developing countries that we see today, but also to the equally vast differences in the rates at which countries similarly poor a generation or two ago have been catching up to the world's economic and technological frontiers, or failing to do so.

Wanted: Idealists not satisfied by easy answers

When setting out to write this book, my hope was that I could reach out at least as much to readers inclined, like Malthus Sr., to feel that we should, must, and can better our world as to readers who, like his more famous son, are skeptical about any talk of making the world a better place. Clearly, my aim was a daring one, since most idealists are unlikely to seek wisdom from economists. By drawing on the emerging understanding of human nature that's informed by evolutionary reasoning, I might further risk turning off this audience due to the lingering association of evolution with social Darwinism. But I see no alternative to the meeting of idealism with the hard-nosed appreciation of the constraints to be overcome. To readers who'd rather avoid such a rendezvous, I say: if you're satisfied with criticizing what is and with avoiding investigations of unpleasant realities that might actually help move society towards your professed ideals, by all means do go ahead and ignore the facts to be discussed here.

To those still with me, I state again that I aim to acknowledge unpleasant truths not to carry on the younger Malthus's goal of pouring cold water on idealism, but with the precisely opposite hope of contributing to the body of knowledge that might allow us to make more of our dreams realities. Yes, the evidence that most people act at least somewhat selfishly most of the time is overwhelming, whether we look at the historical record, at recent experimental studies, or simply at our everyday experience. We have to acknowledge it if we're to account for the use of incentive systems that raise society's productivity but promote inequality, insecurity, and stress. And we need to acknowledge both self-interest and the demonizing of the other (the ugly converse of group solidarity) in order to understand why, when unevenly matched societies encountered each other in the past half-millennium, the usual outcome was for the strong to exploit rather than to peacefully offer help to the weak.

But there's also plenty of good news to be found in our growing scientific understanding of ourselves. The caricature of the human as an utterly selfish being is clearly just that, with the evidence for more sociable, fair-minded, empathetic, and potentially cooperative sides of human nature being abundant even in the experimental studies of we dismal scientists. There's evidence that these more nuanced aspects of human nature account for much that makes our society livable. If properly appreciated, I'll contend, these sides of ourselves hold the potential to help us further reduce the negative byproducts of using ego-centered incentives to power our economies.

Similarly, evidence that our largest global inequalities began with gaps in technology and organization that started opening up thousands of years ago will doubtless strike as unpleasant some ardent believers in human equality. They might prefer to attribute the gaps to differences in greed, and they may understandably fear that such lasting inequalities will be seized upon by believers in innate "racial" differences.

But there's abundant good news here, too, starting from the fact that the initial differences are adequately explained by geography, climate, and distributions of animal and plant species, with no evidence whatsoever for genetic inequality of ability (or of moral fiber). Fans of castigating the villains for their greed will find more than enough of it in the story I tell, but I'm likely to stray from their preferred choice of evil-doers. (Almost every militarily and technologically superior group that's ever existed, whether Bantu, Han, Mongol, Maori, or Japanese, has treated brutally at one time or another those groups which it could readily push aside or exploit).

More importantly, forces at work over the past century have for the first time begun the building of a global society in which the exploitation of technological laggards is becoming less excusable and less excused and where the institutional, as well as technological, capacities of the leaders are slowly beginning to be shared. These trends may still be sadly in their infancy, but the overall direction of change is clear, and the more light we shed on our situation, the faster the pace of progress is likely to be.

Part of that progress will come from the realization that while getting conventional economic policies right has been one ingredient in recent success stories like China's, it's by no means the only ingredient. No country has succeeded in jump-starting modern economic growth without a significant governmental input in infrastructure, education, and other domains. Long-standing cultural advantages, including not only the social capacities that undergird effective government but also overseas diasporas providing skills, connections, and investment funds, have played their parts, as well. If social prerequisites for success are properly understood, the least advantaged nations will receive not only economic policy guidance but also help in building human and institutional capabilities to get economic modernization off the ground.

In the end, economic growth is urgently needed to lift the poorest from their poverty, but its urgency is not an excuse for perpetuating the worst byproducts of market-based economic life. Strong property rights, markets, and competition are likely to be needed for the indefinite future as operating systems of the world's economic engine, but they can be put at the service of the goals and values we aspire to. This means denying the market system the opportunity to make us into consuming machines forever stressed by work and career competition. And it means according the challenge of environmental sustainability the high priority it needs to have if our successes are to last.

Conclusion

People react in different ways to the world's all-too-obvious ills. The gospels of Matthew, Mark, and John quote Jesus as saying "The poor you will always have with you." Hinduism views the ups-and-downs of the world as an endless wheel, sharing with Buddhism the notion that the best hope is to liberate oneself from it. And while one often hears claims that Western religions differ from Eastern ones in viewing history as goal-directed rather than cyclical, the Bible's book of Ecclesiastes proclaims that "nothing is new under the sun."

But none of these traditions absolve people of responsibility for their actions. "It is not your obligation to complete the work, but neither are you free to desist from it," reads a famous passage of the compilation of Jewish commentaries called the Mishnah (Pirkei Avoth 2:19). "Right livelihood," or supporting oneself in a manner that does not harm others, is upheld in the Eightfold Path of Buddhism.

Calls to responsibility for the world's moral failings can be found in every religion, as well as among humanistic atheists. A 1993 Parliament of the World's Religions, attended by eight thousand Buddhist, Catholic, Hindu, Jewish, Muslim, Protestant, and other religious leaders, issued a "Declaration Toward a Global Ethic," in which the attendees declared, "The world is in agony. The agony is so pervasive and urgent that we are compelled to name its manifestations so that the depth of this pain may be made clear." They went on to write, "We affirm that a common set of core values is found in the teachings of the [world's] religions, and that these form the basis of a global ethic . . . We must strive for a just social and economic order, in which everyone has an equal chance to reach full potential as a human being. We must move beyond the dominance of greed for power, prestige, money, and consumption to make a just and peaceful world."

The premise of this book is that, as ancient and familiar as are this world's imperfections, and as well set each of us may be in our own personal mixtures of world-weariness and aspiration for change, there's still something to be gained by revisiting the question "Why not a better world?" with the benefit of recent insights into human nature and its various contradictions. I'll argue that the most important obstacles to the project of world improvement can be usefully understood in terms of the old conflict between self-interest and social cooperation, a conflict that has been a key topic in the behavioral social sciences, including my own field of economics, as they've progressed in recent years. More generally, this book argues that understanding the economics of everyday life—how we respond to our own needs, to nature's scarcities, and to the continuous tensions between the need to work with others and the desire to grab and defend whatever we can get for ourselves—is critical to understanding what stands between us and the sort of world we'd like to see.

Notes:
1. Scholars will find non-technical discussions drawing on my research in Chapters 5 – 9.

CHAPTER 1
Why Not a Better World?

What's wrong with our world? Is there anything we can do about it?

Let's begin discussing the first question (What's wrong?) by looking at a rapidly changing region of the world that shows signs of economic growth along with a heavy dose of the ills that have accompanied modernization around the world. We'll then begin to discuss the second question (What can be done?) by considering an early attempt to replace industrial society with something radically different.

Poor, rich, and in between (a Delhi sandwich)

In one of the poorer neighborhoods of India's capital, twenty-eight-year-old Dharmesh Pakkur lives with his wife, Bhagvati, and their three children in a tiny but relatively permanent dwelling that they spend half their earnings to rent. Driven to the city by hunger in their home village, the Pakkurs at first found a way to survive by combing trash barrels for scraps of cloth that they could sell to middlemen who bulk them into larger lots for which there's a ready market. Just after Bhagvati gave birth to the couple's third child, though, the unlucky Dharmesh was stricken with tuberculosis, nearly wasting away before a charity helped him to buy needed medications. Recently, all three children have been chronically ill with diarrhea and respiratory problems, but the couple can't afford to take them to a clinic or buy them medicine.[1] Within the square mile that their shack and others like it occupy, virtually no dwelling has its own plumbing, and there are only six or seven latrines to serve eighty thousand people. The narrow pathways are lined with sewage, and it's not uncommon to find plastic bags filled with fecal matter tossed onto the tin roofs for lack of better alternative.

Shortly after Bhagvati serves warm tea and bits of stale chapati to her husband and children, she heads to the alley beside a shopping mall, a half hour's walk from their home, to do some scavenging. Inside the mall, Annapurna Rajadhani is perusing the display cases of an upscale jewelry store. The thirty-something

1

wife of a successful entrepreneur, she'd entered with the thought of buying a watch. But just now her attention is attracted to a locked display case containing expensive pens, some selling for eighteen thousand rupees (about four hundred dollars) and upwards. Seeing her lingering over this case, and surmising from her fashionable sari and jewelry that she might be able to afford such things, the store clerk, Vishal Narayan, asks if she'd like him to open the case for a closer look. "Not really," she responds. She continues to peer at the case, though, so the clerk tries again. "If you're interested in fine pens, madam, there are some nicer ones than these that we keep locked up in the back of the store. We can get you a Tibaldi for a little under two million rupees"—about forty-three thousand US dollars—"and several others in that price range and above. I have photographs here." He motions to a book atop the display case. Mrs. Rajadhani raises her eyebrows and looks at the clerk quizzically. "Who would spend such an amount on a pen?" she asks. "My dear lady," he replies, "those pens I mentioned are some of the finest in the world, fashioned from white gold with an eighteen karat gold nib, very much coveted, and I give you my word that I've sold two of them just this month, and one last month, as well."

Narayan is eager for a sale because, as a mere employee of the storeowner, his grip on middle-class status is tenuous. He shares a one-bedroom apartment in a run-down neighborhood with his wife, Kalyani, and their five children. The Narayans' hearts are set on seeing at least some of the children achieve real economic success, so the children are under considerable pressure to excel in school. Yet, somewhat uncharacteristically, Vishal has been worrying today about his oldest son, Sunil, who seems exhausted and dispirited from spending four hours after school every day attending a class to boost his chances of scoring well on the higher secondary exam, a class Vishal and Kalyani have paid for with difficulty. Sunil's pale appearance had been making a faint but inchoate impression on the father before it blossomed into a conscious worry when he noticed an article in the morning paper about government efforts to reduce the number of suicides that occur each year among the exam-takers.

Boom and dust

Surging economic growth, yawning income gaps, tense competition for positions in the ranks of the upwardly mobile: these elements would not be hard to find also in Shanghai, Kuala Lumpur, or Bangkok. China, once considered a model of equality, is now a rival in inequality with the likes of Brazil. A recent academic study reports that even though average income in China more than doubled between 1990 and 2000, the average Chinese survey respondent was less likely to report being satisfied with life at the end than at the beginning of that decade. The study's authors mainly attributed this puzzling juxtaposition of rising income with falling self-reported happiness to the fact that although the typical individual's income had risen, it had risen far less than had that of top income-earners.[2] Similar contrasts of riches and rags are found widely in Latin America, as well as elsewhere in Asia and even Africa. And scenes of adolescents enduring fourteen- or fifteen-hour days of study to prepare for examinations are commonplace, especially in industrializing Asia.

In this same perplexing world in which tens of thousands of construction cranes tower over rapidly growing cities on several continents, almost half of the world's 7 billion people are farmers. A billion of these eke out the barest of livings from marginal soils and herds, with little access to modern technology. The rural poor are widely scattered around the world, from Nicaragua, Peru, and Brazil to Senegal, Chad, and Tanzania to Afghanistan, India, Bangladesh, Laos, and China to Indonesia, Papua New Guinea, and the Philippines. They and the slightly less poor help to account for the fifty million plus migrants from countryside to city each year, most of whom will end up living at least for a time little better than before in slums like Dharmesh Pakkur's and worse.

The rural poor themselves vary widely in their degree of interaction with the world of economic growth and technological dynamism. Many villages in China and India are plugged into urbanism and modernity by being home bases for temporary migrants to their country's cities or to construction jobs abroad. The workers return home on annual holidays or send remittances that account for the occasional village family having a fancier house or owning a television set and a DVD player. Others seem to live light years from the modern world, as manifested for instance by the frequent honor killings of women suspected of "improper" relations with men in rural Pakistan or Yemen. It's not uncommon for a village resident in a poor region to own a cell phone and to supply market pricing information that helps local farmers to time their crop sales. Yet villages without electricity, with no telephone reception, and having the nearest bus route a day's walk away can still be found in many countries.

Aside from inequality, economic insecurity, and stress, growing urbanization and industrialization have brought with them the sort of environmental harms familiar from the great industrial episodes of the past. The infamous "dark

Satanic Mills" of nineteenth-century England belched so much soot into cities like Manchester that the trunks of urban trees blackened, producing the classic example of environment and evolution in high school biology textbooks. In 1845, ninety-eight percent of the moths in Manchester were lightly colored, providing near invisibility to predatory birds against a lichen-covered background. So blackened by soot did the trees become thereafter that in 1895 only black moths were well hidden, accordingly evolving to fill almost the whole population of moths in the city.

Today, developing world megacities vie for the unwanted distinction of having the world's most polluted air, with China's Chongqing (population 6.4 million) and Tianjin (7 million) high on the list at about 124 micrograms of particulate matter per cubic meter of air, but India's Delhi (population 15 million) besting them at 150. Old time favorites Los Angeles and Manchester itself are left in their dust with puny readings in the 30–35 micrograms per meter range, thanks to years of clean-up efforts helped along by deindustrialization. In the first decade of the 2000s, rapid economic growth and an abundant supply of coal helped China to surpass the United States as the world's leading emitter of greenhouse gases.

Industrial utopianism—version 1.0

Poverty, inequality, conspicuous consumption, the struggle to get ahead, explosive pressures on the environment—where should we look to explain, and to judge the necessity or otherwise, of these byproducts of industrialization? Since there's little that's completely new in the story playing out in Asia's largest countries on a grander scale these many years after the industrial revolution began in Britain, it's interesting to go back to an earlier, simpler time to view the discontent brewed by the process. What alternatives seemed possible at the time that industrialization was stirring up its first major batch of naysayers?

When a young Welshman named Robert Owen began his climb up the ranks of management in the cotton mills of late eighteenth-century Manchester, that city's population had yet to reach one hundred thousand, less than one percent the size of today's Delhi or Beijing. Less than a quarter of a century had passed since the first factories running coal-powered steam engines began producing what for the times were massive quantities of yarn and cloth. Waterpower was still a common industrial energy source.

Resented for rendering untenable the previously common lifestyle of cottage-based production, the factories of Manchester were decried as under-ventilated dungeons in which an industrial workforce was employed in fourteen-hour shifts with only brief, regimented breaks. Wages were so low that few workmen were willing to take up factory jobs, which were accordingly considered suitable only for children and young women. The factory working conditions of the time would be excoriated in the damning descriptions of Friedrich Engels, who for years supported himself and his friend Karl Marx on his earnings as a Manchester factory manager. The duo's writings describe the same conditions that moved Charles Dickens to evoke pitying emotions in his own readers. The 1809 poem by William Blake that introduced the phrase "dark Satanic Mills" became for a time a socialist anthem, though these days "Jerusalem" is sung without overtones of class warfare at English cricket and rugby matches.

To Engels and Marx, the mills were the inevitable expression of the "laws of motion" of capitalism. The pair discounted attempts to undo the mills' excesses through legislation or social reforms, arguing that the only solution to capitalism's "internal contradictions" lay in a working class revolt that would be hastened by factory misery.

But our Welshman Owen was of a different mindset. Perhaps he was just too well established on the businessman's side of the social divide to be drawn to thoughts of class warfare. He had, in any case, his own social theory, one that emphasized that humans are creatures of their environment and education. After becoming a partner in the industrial enterprise founded by his father-in-law David Dale in New Lanark, Scotland, he helped to convert it into what was in its day an astonishing example of humane factory labor, one that attained fame throughout Britain and beyond.

Dale had already seen to the construction of housing of comparatively good quality in the small industrial village near the picturesque Falls of Clyde. Owen took matters further by ending the use of child labor and corporal punishment. He afforded the factory's workers a higher living standard by selling them their basic necessities at reasonable prices (foregoing the customary monopoly mark-ups of company stores), took effective measures to improve the cleanliness of the workers' housing and of the village as a whole, promoted their physical exercise and education, and established schools for their children. As his theory of human nature evolved, he applied it towards productivity improvement, encouraging the workers to excel at their jobs by hanging colored cubes above each workstation with colors denoting the worker's quality, thus allowing pride in good work to serve as a motivator. Defying Marx's inevitabilities, Owen's New Lanark mills were highly profitable. A steady flow of visitors, including social reformers and intellectuals, politicians, and even royalty, made pilgrimages to the site and pronounced it impressive.

Owen's personal fame as the man behind the New Lanark model was such that when he came to the United States in 1824–25 and lectured on his ideas about social reform, he was received—remarkably!—by both the outgoing president, James Monroe, and the incoming president, John Quincy Adams. In February 1825, he addressed a packed house of Congress with both presidents and many of their cabinet members in attendance. If they expected to hear more about the humane and profitable factory he'd created at New Lanark, however, they may have been disappointed. For by this time, Owen had set his sights on change of a more radical character. He was intent on founding communities that would combine manufacturing and agriculture with child-rearing, life-long education, and cultural activity, all in a setting free of class distinctions—no owners, no employers, no employees. An initial prototype was to be established almost immediately, and once it had been proven a success, the world would awaken to its virtues and follow suit—no class war and no violence required.

New Harmony

A site had already been identified. A property in southern Indiana that had housed a religious community, called Harmony, had been put up for sale by its owners, and on January 3, 1825, Owen inspected it and signed a contract to purchase its twenty thousand acres and 180 buildings. In a land of dreams, what would probably become the most famous utopian experiment of nineteenth-century America was about to begin. It would be known as New Harmony.

Not only the real estate, but also those prepared to populate the new society, were ready for Owen's bold experiment. For years, Robert Owen had been writing and publishing essays about his emerging ideas. Although his full-blown social radicalism was less known to the general public than his successful reforms, his ideas had already captured the imaginations of some well-read Americans, and this following was awaiting his arrival in the United States, ready to join the adventure. They included respected intellectuals, such as Thomas Say, called by some "the father of American entomology." There was also the French naturalist, Charles Lesueur, and enough others for the band to be dubbed the "Boatload of Knowledge" as they made their way to Indiana.

Foremost among Owen's scientific enthusiasts was the geologist, William Maclure, then president of the prestigious Academy of Natural Sciences of Philadelphia. Not only did he serve as the group's leading recruiter and booster, but he also helped Owen to finance New Harmony and for a time shared in its leadership. Even some business people, such as Thomas Pears, a Pittsburgh-based industrial manager with experience in glass manufacturing and other industries, were won over by Owen's ideas and joined the pilgrimage to New Harmony.

By the summer of 1825, the community had about eight hundred members from almost every state of the then extant (mostly eastern) United States. Soap, glue, candle, and shoe factories were in operation, as was a hotel for visitors coming "to see with their own eyes Robert Owen's famous social experiment."[3] The community boasted a rich cultural life, including its own newspaper, frequent lectures on science and social theory, a weekly dance, and a weekly performance by an orchestra of resident musicians. A school registering two hundred students was established along similar lines to the one at New Lanark, with education, board, and clothing costs covered by the community.

Owen was away much of the time on a lecture tour, through which he hoped to drum up enthusiasm for his communal ideas, and the community was in actuality limping along under the temporary leadership of his son. Yet a spirit of optimism prevailed in its initial months.

Well into its first year, the commune was attracting fresh expressions of interest and having to turn some applicants away due to limited housing space. In a letter dated June 2, 1825, Pears wrote to his friend and former employer: "New Harmony now presents to the world a novel and, I think, a sublime spectacle—an assemblage of people meeting together to try to do the utmost good for each other; and my hope is that we shall act as though the eyes of the world were upon us."

But running an economically complex society, even on the small scale of New Harmony, was impossible without some sort of leadership or organizational structure and without laying down principles of job assignment and compensation. Initially, the community adopted a vague and expressly transitional system based on the declaration by Owen, in April 1825, that it would be "forced to admit for a time, a certain degree of financial inequality." Then, returning from his lengthy lecture tour in early 1826 and without sufficient study of New Harmony's actual situation, he spearheaded the drafting of a new communitarian constitution, under which all members would be equal in consumption, with no system of accounting for work performed or for its quality.

Dream and reality

How did the scheme of perfect equality work out at New Harmony? We can't say for sure because the new constitution had barely been unveiled when the balance sheet from the community's first year of operation was completed and published. Like a bucket of cold water poured over the heads of sleepers, it woke even the most fervent Harmonists from their reveries. Suddenly, it was clear that New Harmony had been operating at a large deficit.

Without enough skilled farmers to feed itself, and with most of those having skill in one craft or another being occupied in community services that generated no income, New Harmony was far from covering operating costs. Indeed, keeping it afloat was rapidly soaking up Owen's personal savings and the limited financial support he'd managed to attract from outside backers.

A true believer could argue that the full egalitarianism of the 1826 constitution was never really tried out, so concluding that it was egalitarianism that posed a threat to the experiment may be unfair. But the actions of the Harmonists suggest that they at least saw the lack of material rewards and the accounting system required by them as a core problem. It was, apparently, the leading members of the community who advised Owen that pushing the new ideas too quickly would be taking a further step in the wrong direction. Judging the state of the project to be a dire one, members who had left ostensibly successful and comfortable lives behind to stake all on it begged Owen to stop touring and to take personal command of New Harmony's affairs. They also urged him to eliminate, as impracticable, the utopian elements of the short-lived constitution.

Owen accepted their request. But the magic touch that he had brought to the management of New Lanark (his earlier venture) seemed to have evaporated, or at least to have become incapable of turning around the Indiana commune. Indeed, as much as anything, the experiment's impending collapse might be attributed to the increasingly self-deluding outlook with which Owen approached it. It was he, for example, who ignored the advice of the son who had managed New Harmony in his absence that he should go slow in changing to a more radically egalitarian structure. He also wrongly imagined great enthusiasm, where there had been relatively little, on the parts of the press and of the audiences that he had addressed during his tour. Sensing that it was rudderless, New Harmony began to splinter into competing factions. In the end, it was only the educational and scientific work of those attracted to the venture by Maclure that would survive. Thanks to their efforts, New Harmony, Indiana, was to be a significant scientific center for the next century and a half. The communal experiment itself had essentially reached its end when Owen returned to England in 1827.

Apart from problems of leadership, what else had gone wrong with the experiment at New Harmony? Almost everything, it would seem. Of the 800 original settlers at New Harmony, only 140 had skills useful to its industrial and craft needs, and only 36 had farming experience. Despite the cadre of intellectuals attracted from the urban centers of the east by the appeal of Owen's ideas, most of those who came were young, local, unskilled, and without financial resources. No effort had been made to set standards for membership. Goodwill reigned at the outset, and a sense of peace and physical security generally prevailed—in the faint praise of New Harmonist Josiah Warren, "We had enacted the French Revolution over again with despairing hearts instead of corpses as a result." Yet even the rhetoric of classlessness failed to match the reality. In one of her letters, Thomas Pears's wife, Sara, wrote:

> Oh, if you could see some of the rough, uncouth creatures here, I think you would find it rather hard to look upon them exactly in the light of brothers and sisters, I am sure! I cannot in sincerity look upon these as my equals, and if I must appear to do it, I cannot either act or speak the Truth.[4]

A visitor from Germany, Duke Karl Bernhard, noted that he attended social functions in New Harmony and always "noticed members sticking to their own former social classes" including "upper-class girls refusing to dance with lower-class men." Bernhard concluded that "in spite of all the talk about equality, these people would never mix with their 'inferiors.'"[5]

Getting along with others seemed difficult even for the affable Mr. Owen. In New Harmony, he had festering public disputes with Maclure and another break-away leader, Paul Brown. Business frictions with his erstwhile partners in New Lanark, in which he maintained an interest, were also rife. When finally ending his connection with the New Lanark mills in 1828, he is reported to have uttered to long-time business partner, William Allen, the famous words: "All the world is queer save thee and me, and even thou art a little queer." Strange words from a famous philanthropist, humanist, and utopian!

The good and the bad of it

A generous interpretation of the New Harmony saga would point out that it illustrates how ideals can stir intelligent and practical men and women into action. In the end, Maclure, Say, and Lesueur went on to establish the Indiana town as the home of an important educational and scientific center. Influenced by Maclure, Owen's son David Dale Owen became the official geological surveyor of Indiana and two neighboring states, while son Richard Dale Owen became a natural scientist and university professor, and Robert Dale Owen became a state and US legislator who played a role in promoting public schooling and equality for women. It was this Owen who introduced the bill that created the Smithsonian Institution.

Robert Owen Sr. has his admirers, too. The documents nominating New Lanark, Scotland, as a UNESCO World Heritage Site in 2001 stated that here "Robert Owen created a model for industrial communities that was to spread across the world in the nineteenth and twentieth centuries" and that "the name of New Lanark is synonymous with that of Robert Owen and his social philosophy in matters such as progressive education, factory reform, humane working practices, international cooperation, and garden cities, which was to have a profound influence on social developments throughout the nineteenth century and beyond."

But less generous interpreters of the New Harmony experiment might argue that Owen "went off the rails" when he jettisoned the practical humanism of his innovations at New Lanark for the more radical communitarianism of New Harmony. By this interpretation, Owen's mistake was the same as that of all utopians: underestimating human selfishness. Harmonist Warren wrote of the community's demise: "Our 'united interests' were directly at war with the individualities of persons and circumstances and the instinct of self-preservation . . ." The fact that Owen owned the lion's share of the Indiana colony's assets as his personal property was one glaring contradiction of the spirit of New Harmony that seems to illustrate Warren's point. While Owen was affable and inspiring to some, he was prone to blindness about how his ideas were received and to the consequences of their implementation. Nor is it clear how well suited he himself was for community living: for all of his professed belief in the perfectibility of humankind, his "thee and me" remark fits perfectly with Warren's suggestion of a "war with the individualities of persons."

During the nineteenth century, dozens of New Harmony-like schemes inspired by Owen's ideas, most on a smaller scale, were launched. In the end, each fared as badly or worse. So did similar utopian efforts spawned by the French philosopher Charles Fourier. Unlike those shorter-lived experiments, Israel's pioneering kibbutz settlements survived for decades in the twentieth century under rules of strict egalitarianism, scoring successes also in transitioning from mainly agricultural to substantially industrial production in the 1960s and '70s, before most abandoned their strict communal character in the face of a changed financial environment. Small, voluntary egalitarian societies have continued to be formed since Owen's time, including a spate of commune formation in the United States that began in the 1960s and saw the founding of some communities that persist to the present.

What happened when radical egalitarian creeds were embraced by all-powerful states is a very different story. Recall that Karl Marx, who fancied himself an objective scientific observer and rejected Owen and Fourier as utopians, judged the suffering of his generation's working class to be a necessary precursor of revolution. While he never wielded a weapon besides his pen, and while he might well have lacked the steel of the despots who gave homage to his ideas, Marx's spirit of readiness to accept that some would be sacrificed on the way to the millennium translated after his lifetime into an ideology used to justify some of the worst horrors of the twentieth century, including Stalin's bloody purges of his own political associates, his starvation of more than four million Ukrainian peasants, and his gulag prison labor system. China's Mao Zedong fell into megalomaniacal self-delusion after his success as a revolutionary strategist in the mountains gave way to the problems of managing economic modernization on a national scale. Whipping sycophantic followers and frightened bureaucrats into a frenzied campaign of rural commune building, he caused at least twenty million famine deaths in 1960 and 1961, after which he rebounded from the political sidelines to terrorize China's educated urban population from 1966 until his death a decade later. And before the facts of China's famine would be fully known to the world, Cambodia's Pol Pot would try to out-Mao Mao, succeeding in that perverse effort by causing the deaths of one in five Cambodians through politically induced famine, overwork, and punishment for the slightest suspicion of bad class leanings. In the late 1970s, you risked being executed in Cambodia if you wore glasses, since it raised the suspicion that you were an intellectual.

To be sure, neither the failures of the voluntary utopias nor the horrors wrought by those bent on building their preferred worlds on involuntary labor and blood-letting prove that our own world of fabulous economic growth mixed with fabulous poverty, insecurity, environmental destruction, and lack of social purpose is the best we can hope for. But both warn us that we'd best be prepared to think long and carefully as we consider what futures are and what are not both desirable and actually within reach.

Is nothing new?

One benefit of the chronological "double vision" we've employed in this chapter is the possibility it offers of gauging whether the world's been changing for better or for worse or perhaps just breaking even in these two plus centuries of industrialization. If we compare the world of Owen's time to that of today, we can find discouraging scenes like those of the Pakkurs and the Narayans, from which we might conclude that the spread of industrial society has mostly meant more urban poor, more inequality, and more stress. But we can also find signs of significant progress.

In the 1860s, writers like Marx argued that the factory system was making working people poorer. But careful analysis of the evidence has demonstrated beyond dispute that the average real wages and the purchasing power of wage-earners in developed countries have risen several times over during the last century and a half. Though many economists would attribute the gains to the fact that the average worker has more education and works with a larger quantity of more sophisticated tools and infrastructures—industry in the 1860s operated without electricity, trucks, and telephones, much less lasers, computers, and the Internet—there has been at least some social progress, as well. For example, workers have gained rights to organize, and in many countries the right to vote has become nearly universal, a situation without parallel in Marx's time.

In the early twentieth century, a handful of European empires controlled most of the world's territory, but the early twenty-first century features a world of more than two hundred sovereign states, including recently independent ones like East Timor, Montenegro, and South Sudan. While in the early twentieth century there was at most one country outside of Europe and its direct offshoots that could be classed as industrialized or economically modern (i.e., Japan), today several east Asian, Middle Eastern, and arguably a few Latin American countries have achieved that status, and others are progressing not far behind. Successful economic growth in China and India would mean that more than half the population of what was recently the less-developed world join the industrialized world in relative prosperity.

It would also be unreasonable to mark humanity's scorecard as an unrelenting failure when recent decades have seen dramatically rising life expectancies, falling levels of illiteracy, and hundreds of millions pulled from poverty by successful economic growth. And one can certainly see the sixty-five years of peace and prosperity in most of Europe since the disasters of two World Wars as a sign of genuine progress. Even with respect to our physical environment, there are a few trends that offer encouragement, including the increased regulation of industrial pollution in already industrialized countries, dramatic increases in public awareness, and gains in scientific knowledge.

Such progress falls short in various ways, though. Despite the alleviation of poverty for many in countries like China, India, and Brazil, they're still home to hundreds of millions in extreme poverty, and the income gap between rich and poor countries has continued to grow. The difference in average incomes between the richest and poorest countries stood at thirty-seven to one in 1960 and rose to sixty-six to one in 1990 and to ninety-five to one in 2005.[6] While millions earn incomes of a hundred thousand dollars and more each year in countries like the United States, Britain, and Germany, more than a billion people in places like Angola, Tanzania, Haiti, Nicaragua, Afghanistan, and Bangladesh, as well as China and India, live on less than one dollar a day, lacking basic necessities such as clean water, adequate food, decent housing, and access to medical care. Each day, some thirty thousand children under the age of five die in poor countries from preventable diseases rendered lethal by chronic malnutrition. Although life expectancy rose remarkably in most countries during the twentieth century, in the thirty poorest countries—including most countries of sub-Saharan Africa—life expectancy at birth in 2006 was fully thirty-two years less than in the richest countries, standing at only forty-six years. In many African countries, life expectancy was lower in 2006 than in 1976 due to the AIDS epidemic. While total public and private health expenditure per year (not limited to HIV/AIDS and malaria) averaged about fifty dollars a year for each African, Americans spent as much as one hundred dollars that year on weight loss aids alone.

Inequality within nations
Within rich countries, too, inequality has been on the rise. For example, even though the average income in the United States—calculated as total income divided by total population—has continued to rise and has reached four times its 1950 level in 2005, income and wealth inequality began an upward trend in the 1980s, a trend so sharp that the real incomes of the majority of households have failed to rise since then. People in some of the poorest US urban and rural areas had health, literacy, and crime statistics that were worse than those of many Third World countries.

The rise in American inequality is well illustrated by the housing sector. Although the average size of new houses built in the United States rose from 983 square feet in 1950 to 2,349 square feet in 2004, most houses remained well below the 2,000 square foot mark. As with income and other statistics, the average is a misleading number because it's pulled up by a few million high-end homes, with 10,000 square feet representing only the beginning of the "mega house" class.

Even the rich have their problems with inequality, the "common rich" having difficulty keeping up with the super-rich. **Wall Street Journal** reporter Robert Frank recounts the story of a man who "used to feel special cruising the world in his 100-foot yacht. ... Yet one morning ... stood on his upper deck over-shadowed by giants. ... Down the dock was the 197-foot Alfa Four, with an indoor gym, swimming pool, and helicopter pad. ... 'I used to think I had a good-sized boat,' [he] sighed. 'Now it's like a dinghy compared to those others.'" [7]

Where jealousy at the top of the economic heap borders on the comical, inequality is no laughing matter for those at the bottom, where its social impact is further exacerbated by racial disparity. In the early 2000s, African-Americans accounted for almost twenty-five percent of those below the US poverty line, twice their share of the general population. Despite encouraging signs of improving race relations and the further growth of the black middle class, some twenty-two percent of African-American males between the ages of twenty and twenty-nine are incarcerated, compared with less than two percent of the white population. Racial disparities aside, the fact that the United States has the world's highest rate of incarceration is testimony in its own right to the depth of poverty and inequality rending its social fabric.

Quality of life

Critics of industrial society often argue that its economic achievements come not only at the cost of large inequalities, but also at the expense of the quality of life and of opportunities for personal development. Their criticism should be treated with caution because the case can be made that increased prosperity, the introduction of labor-saving devices (such as the washing machine and the microwave oven), and more convenient modes of transportation and communication have increased the scope for recreational and other activities in the generations since Robert Owen's time. Still, it remains unclear how much change has occurred in the balance between competitive consumption and other values.

Evidence that modern life continues to bring with it unrelenting economic pressure, increasing social isolation, and an abundance of psychological stress is not hard to find. Economist Richard Easterlin and psychologist Robert Lane point to studies showing that even though average incomes increased five-fold in Japan and two-fold in the United States in the decades following World War II, there was no increase in how happy people reported themselves to be in these countries, on average.

Lane argues that many people are misled by what he calls "market culture" into placing too high a premium on seeking more income and goods. Their concentration on making money at the expense of doing fulfilling work and investing in emotionally satisfying relationships results, he believes, in the declines in happiness with marriage and with jobs that US survey respondents reported between the 1940s and 1990s. He goes on to argue that a rise in clinical depression in industrial countries is linked to these trends.[8] The argument that more income has not made for more happiness in industrial societies has also been made by some economists, including Easterlin and Andrew Oswald.[9]

The state of the environment

Atmospheric concentrations of carbon dioxide, the most important greenhouse gas released by human activity, have risen by twenty-five percent since the start of the industrial revolution, with fully half of the increase occurring since 1950. While the danger of global warming has become common knowledge, solutions remain elusive. The prospect of adding two and a half billion Chinese and Indians to the existing half-billion car-driving, industrialized world inhabitants—the number of households owning automobiles was doubling every ten years in India and every five years in China at the beginning of the twenty-first century—gives nightmares to scientists watching the world's glaciers and polar ice caps melt away.

The footprint of human activity on our natural environment grows larger in other ways, as well. According to the Harvard biologist Edward O. Wilson, during the tens of millions of years preceding the appearance of humans, about one in every million species became extinct every year as a result of climate and habitat changes and of competition from other species. Today's extinction rate is anywhere from one hundred to ten thousand times as high, and "the rate [is] projected to rise, and very likely sharply."[10] Wilson and others have described what is happening as a mass extinction of species rivaling the one that saw the disappearance of the dinosaurs sixty million years ago, but with the cause this time being human activity, including the conversion of vast tracts of the earth's surface into forms serving short-run human interests.

Summing up, looking ahead

Our initial look at the ills of today's world focused on a poor industrializing country, India, which we situated in the context of both the high growth, high pressure economies of east Asia and the impoverished farmers of the world who've yet to experience the dynamic of industrialization. Critics have been identifying inequality, stress, and environmental harm as byproducts of the industrialization process since the early eighteenth century, so we considered an early attempt to pioneer a better form of society and the reasons for its failure. Problems of motivating and organizing economic activity, and of the separate pursuit of individual interests, were central to New Harmony's early demise, hinting at the potential conflicts between self-interest and cooperation that will feature repeatedly in our discussion. We then took advantage of the temporal sweep from early industrial age to present and identified some of the social progress that's been achieved in those two centuries and some of the daunting challenges that remain to be addressed.

Our discussion thus far has been panoramic, but we've collected only a few clues at most as to why society's progress since the 1820s hasn't been greater. What constrains humanity, with its rapidly increasing capacity to understand and appropriate the fruits of nature, from doing better? The next chapter begins to lay out our answer.

Notes:

1. Tom Paulson, "Life in a Delhi Slum: 'We are Always in God's Hands'," *Seattle Post-Intelligencer* (December 8, 2003).

2. Hilke Brockmann et al., "The China Puzzle: Falling Happiness in a Rising Economy," *Journal of Happiness Studies* 10, no. 4 (2008): 387-405.

3. Yaacov Oved, *Two Hundred Years of American Communes* (New Brunswick: Transaction Books, 1988), 114. Much of my discussion of Owen and New Harmony depends on his account. Other sources consulted include J.F.C. Harrison, *Quest for the New Moral World: Robert Owen and the Owenites in Britain and America* (New York: Charles Scribner's Sons, 1969) and Edward Royle, *Robert Owen and the Commencement of the Millennium: A Study of the Harmony Community* (Manchester: Manchester University Press, 1998).

4. The quotations from Thomas and Sarah Pears's letters are found in Oved, *Two Hundred Years of Communes.*

5. Oved, *Two Hundred Years of American Commune*, 118.

6. In an article titled "Divergence, Big Time," published in the *Journal of Economic Perspectives* in 1997, World Bank economist Lant Pritchett reported the ratios of average incomes in the richest versus poorest country as being 8.7:1 in 1870, 38.5:1 in 1960, and 45.2:1 in 1990. My somewhat different calculations are based on the gross domestic product (GDP) per capita in purchasing power parity (PPP) terms from a slightly different data set, the Penn World Tables (Mark 6.2). According to the tables, the richest country was Switzerland in 1960 and 1990 and the United States in 2004, and the poorest country was Ethiopia in 1960, Cambodia in 1990, and the Democratic Republic of the Congo (the former Zaire) in 2004. World Bank data on GDP per capita, also in PPP terms, in constant dollars of 2000, again give somewhat different results but still show a slight increase from a 59.5:1 ratio in 1990 to a 62.8:1 ratio in 2005.

7. Robert Frank, *Richistan: A Journey Through the American Wealth Boom and the Lives of the New Rich* (New York: Crown Publishers, 2007), 121–2.

8. See Robert Lane, *The Loss of Happiness in Market Democracies* (New Haven: Yale University Press, 2000).

9. In a recent paper, "Obesity, Unhappiness, and *The Challenge of Affluence*: Theory and Evidence," 117, no. 521 (2007): 441-454, Oswald and Nattavudh Powdthavee link the lack of a happiness payoff from rising affluence to the problem of self-control and specifically of obesity.

10. E. O. Wilson, "On Bjorn Lomborg and extinction," *Grist* (December 12, 2001).

CHAPTER 2
Not in Our Stars

Economics and the social sciences provide at least two approaches to answering the question of why, despite enormous technological and scientific progress, we humans continue to struggle with problems of poverty, inequality, and environmental degradation and why—to put the issue more broadly—our quality of life is blemished by economic insecurity and by a culture that nourishes the consumer, rather than human potential as a whole. One approach follows T. R. Malthus in emphasizing physical limitations to the abundance of resources and the carrying capacity of our planet. I'll call this the *scarcity* approach. The other approach puts the emphasis on human nature and, in particular, on the complex interplay between selfish and cooperative impulses. "The fault," the second approach says, echoing Cassius in Shakespeare's *Julius Caesar*, "is not in our stars, but in ourselves." Let's take a look at each of these approaches in turn.

A miserly Mother Nature?

The problem isn't that there's anything rotten about *our* natures, the scarcity approach says; rather, it's *Mother Nature* that deals us a limited hand of cards. In other words, we live in a world in which resources are limited. There's just not enough for everyone. Under the circumstances, it's only natural, only rational, to protect ourselves and our families first before worrying about others.

With regard to inequalities, the scarcity approach indicates that those countries that have little land and capital and a big and largely unskilled population will naturally exhibit the most dire poverty, while those countries that have more land and capital and smaller and more skilled populations will naturally exhibit more prosperity. Inequalities between individuals will follow the same pattern: those with more physical and human capital will obtain higher incomes; those with less will have lower ones. We shouldn't try to tinker with this too much, the approach says, because redistributing from the rich to the poor will destroy the incentive of the rich to continue generating wealth from their physical and human assets, making everyone the worse off for the attempt.

A limited resources response to limited human progress has some merit. It's arguably what most research and teaching in economics is about. If we're living in isolation on a small island and we devote more land to grazing cattle, then there'll be less land for growing grain, so at some point we'll have to choose between more meat and more bread. In a world economy with various small and large islands, called nations, international trading can ease some constraints because England, for instance, can devote more land to raising sheep and growing barley, yet still consume more wheat grown in, say, Canada, whose people might in turn buy English woolens and whiskey. But while trade allows specialization, it doesn't prevent overall scarcities. We're stuck with them, and we respond to them in ways that come naturally.

To further argue the case that it's scarcity that's to blame for our woes, consider how the world's success at producing more goods than ever in the industrial age has been subject to the constraint of limited supplies of fossil fuels, the principal energy source supplementing and replacing human and animal muscle power under the technologies of the past hundred plus years. As we've had to look ever farther afield for more petroleum, it's only natural that there've been conflicts over limited supplies. Had we discovered in 1945 not the destructive power of the atom but the way to generate abundant and inexpensive energy by cold *fusion*, rendering fossil fuels obsolete, then we might find ourselves in a world in which we could use plentiful power to cheaply make everything that the people of every continent need. But we didn't, so we of course go on struggling over who will and who won't get the limited supplies of petroleum that we can find. Sometimes competition over scarce supplies leads to wars. Sometimes no arms are taken up, but limited supplies lead to high prices, and those less able to pay get less. A few hundred unlucky Nigerians die every now and then when an accidental explosion is set off while they're trying to tap into oil pipelines. Everyone else merely ends up a bit poorer than they might have been in a world of abundant energy. But this has everything to do with the miserliness of *nature*, not human nature. Right?

A complex human nature

The fact that resources are limited and that human ingenuity hasn't yet discovered how to feed us, clothe us, shelter us, and power our industries without facing the hard choices imposed by scarcity is a very real economics lesson to be ignored at our peril. But the economic insights that we need for explaining our world's shortcomings aren't only the familiar refrains about *material* scarcity and *technological* limits. We need to add to them the insights that economics and its sister sciences offer about *motivation*, about the forces of human nature that drive economic activity, and about the way in which the economic arrangements we've fashioned—arrangements that are *social* realities, not material and technological ones—work (and sometimes *fail* to work) to harness those forces. A few examples should begin to make clear that motivation and economic arrangements are at least as important as resources and technologies are for explaining why we dream of but, like Owen's New Harmonists, fail to attain a better world.

Let's start with the example that global expenditure on the treatment and prevention of malaria totaled less than $0.3 billion per year during 2000 to 2005, while spending on, say, treatment of and research on the prevention of male pattern baldness (almost all of it in rich countries) totals in the billions every year. The scarcity approach points out correctly that the number of trained scientists and physicians, the amount of laboratory space, and the equipment for medical research are at any given time finite, so that any more devoted to malaria would mean less devoted to baldness, heart disease, or other problems. But with another child dying of malaria every ten minutes, and not a single individual dying of baldness, wouldn't a humane and rational decision-maker choose to allocate far more of the available resources than mentioned to malaria? The failure of more resources to flow towards malaria research must be telling us something—and not about scarcity alone. What is it?

One possibility is that it's basically a matter of poor coordination and planning that leads to a misallocation of medical resources towards attempting to slow hair loss. By this view, if there were a humane and rational decision-maker determining the world's medical research expenditures, some sort of Philosopher King or benign administrator, the outcomes would be noticeably better. As it is, no one individual is empowered to play that role, and decisions are instead made by many separate actors, without any central clearing house.

So, does *lack of coordination* account for our failings?

Not likely. The managers of the world's big pharmaceutical companies, a small number of individuals with the power to allocate tens of billions of research and development dollars per year, didn't fail to allocate more resources to malaria and fewer resources to baldness because they didn't *know* that people are dying of malaria and not of baldness. That information wasn't hard to come by. It's also unlikely that their problem lies in figuring out how to *interpret* the information, in other words that they had faulty judgment or even faulty moral sensibilities that told them that the social discomfort occasioned by baldness is every bit as terrible as is the waste and sorrow of young deaths from malaria. Rather, more money was invested in baldness research and products because companies knew that there were more customers willing to pay for hair-loss remedies at the prices required for profitability, and this was the case due to the far greater purchasing power of prosperous balding men in industrialized and rapidly growing economies and the far smaller purchasing power of poor malaria sufferers in African villages and towns.

While tens of thousands of American men can afford to shell out twenty to fifty dollars every month for their supplies of Minoxidil, Propecia, and the like, millions of poor families living in mud houses in Africa have been found to be unable to afford the purchase of a mosquito net capable of lasting several years, even at the subsidized price of about three dollars. The pharmaceutical companies don't raise capital and pay their workers on goodwill, so they steer their efforts towards where the paying customers are. In the same fashion, billions of pairs of nylon stockings and pantyhose were sold to women the world round (mainly in more prosperous countries), versus far fewer mosquito nets to drape over the beds of African children, even though it was estimated that these nets could have prevented millions of cases of malaria and saved tens of thousands of lives. The stocking makers could easily have switched to making mosquito nets had that been profitable, but the market wasn't there, since most African families don't find them affordable.[1]

These facts are simple enough, yet they are ones that even intelligent people can manage to overlook and that schools, until recently at least, neglected to teach. How else can we explain that the world's richest man could say straight-faced and without embarrassment to some of America's brightest college students that he himself hadn't learned them while a student at Harvard and that he had only discovered them after becoming a billionaire and beginning to think about what to do with his money. "During our discussions on this question," Bill Gates told the Harvard class of 2007 at their commencement, "Melinda and I read an article about the millions of children who were dying every year in poor countries from diseases that we had long ago made harmless in this country. We were shocked. We had just assumed that if millions of children were dying and they could be saved, the world would make it a priority to discover and deliver the medicines to save them. But it did not. For under a dollar, there were interventions that could save lives that just weren't being delivered. ... We asked: 'How could the world let these children die?' ... The answer is simple, and harsh. The market did not reward saving the lives of these children, and governments did not subsidize it. So the children died because their mothers and their fathers had no power in the market and no voice in the system."

Or consider another example, that of hunger. At the World Food Summit held in Rome in November 1996, leaders of 180 countries pledged to fight hunger, setting an intermediate goal of halving the number of undernourished people by 2015. But as of 2006, the World Food Program (WFP), a United Nations agency, estimated that the number of people still hungry is "within the margin of error" of their previous best estimate—in other words, with half the time to the goal post passed, no progress had been made. The WFP put the number of the malnourished in the developing world, in 2001 to 2003, at 820 million, including 206 million in sub-Saharan Africa, 212 million in India, 150 million in China, and 162 million in other parts of Asia and the Pacific. Statistics of the United Nations Children's Fund (UNICEF) put the proportion of children under five suffering from malnutrition severe enough to prevent normal growth at thirty-eight percent in sub-Saharan Africa and forty-four percent in south Asia (including India), with the proportions suffering "severe stunting" put at seventeen percent and twenty-two percent, respectively.

If Malthus could be brought back from the grave and told these facts, he might at first suppose that his predictions had been vindicated: so many more mouths since his time and no more arable land left to clear. But actually, despite population growth and limited land, the facts belie the assumption that food production had been unable to keep up. The Food and Agriculture Organization (FAO) statistics show that world production of calories per capita has outpaced the hefty seventy percent increase in world population in the thirty years prior to a recent study by a full seventeen percent. And the FAO estimated that enough food was being produced, in the early 2000s, to provide every person alive with an adequate diet. The problem was not the inability to produce enough food, in any absolute sense, but rather that much of the increase in production attributable to better seeds, more fertilizer, and expanded use of irrigation took the form of feedstock to support increasing meat consumption by the well-off, including tens of millions of newly better-off consumers in countries like China. While the number of malnourished in India and Africa and in the poorest parts of China itself was holding its own, the number of people over-eating, heading for the obesity clinics, and increasing their probabilities of developing serious cases of coronary disease was steadily on the rise. Not an inability to produce enough, but maldistribution and poor utilization of what was produced, appear to be the key problems.

Agricultural land *is* relatively scarce in countries like China, but it's relatively abundant in other countries like the United States. During considerable parts of the twentieth century, the US government paid farmers to keep land out of cultivation in order to keep food prices from falling too low for them to make a decent living. Were the farmers accepting government payments to keep their land out of production only because they hadn't heard of hunger in other countries and even in poor neighborhoods and communities in their own country? Certainly not. Farming is a difficult business, requiring careful attention to the bottom line in order to achieve good financial results (or for many smaller farmers, simply to break even). Thus, with a few exceptions, farmers grew extra food for the poor in Mali, India, Appalachia, and US inner cities only when there was a paying customer, be it a consumer supplied with government food stamps, the World Food Program, a donor government, or a private aid organization like Care or Oxfam. There were simply not enough government grants to the World Food Program, not enough private donations to Care and similar organizations, to make sure that all of the world's poor were well fed. During an episode of particularly severe famine, for example, an appeal by the World Food Program for $7.4 million to aid a million at-risk individuals in Mali raised only fifteen percent of the amount requested during the first seven months of 2005. Similar appeals to aid famine victims in Somalia and elsewhere in eastern Africa were falling short as this chapter was being written.

For a final illustration that's closer to home, consider again the US housing market mentioned in the last chapter. In the lead up to the "Great Recession" of 2008–09, many thousands of houses having five, ten, or even thirty thousand square feet of living space were constructed. Yet a government count in January 2008 identified more than 650,000 homeless individuals, of whom forty-two percent were living on the street. While some of the homeless suffered from other chronic conditions, such as mental illness and drug addition, a large share were ordinary individuals and families that had simply fallen on hard economic times. The Department of Housing and Urban Development estimated that there were only thirty-seven affordable and physically adequate rental units available for every hundred households with incomes of less than a third of the median for their area. Why do hundreds of thousands lack adequate housing in a country as rich as the United States?

Again, the answer is that, with few exceptions, the construction, sale, and rental of housing in our society is a for-profit business. Most carpenters, electricians, bricklayers, backhoe operators, and everyone else involved aren't consulting their spiritual guides or roaming the shelters trying to identify where *need* exists. Rather, they're seeking to earn as much as possible with their time and resources, and the money that's invested in developing real estate is invested with the aim of earning a good return. Not "what there's a need for" in the abstract, but "what there's a market for" guides construction.

If markets tell pharmaceutical firms, farmers, and builders what to produce, and if pharmaceutical firms then fail to conquer malaria, farmers fail to conquer hunger, and builders fail to end homelessness, does this mean that markets are bad institutions? Joseph Stalin, Mao Zedong, and plenty of others around the world have said "yes." But most today believe that the twentieth century showed these market critics to be wrong—or at the very least showed that their proposed cure was worse than the disease. Markets are mechanisms that coordinate economic decisions. There might be a better way to coordinate those decisions, one that would see more resources aimed at the most important problems, such as malaria, hunger, and homelessness. But attempts to replace markets outright with anything entirely devoid of market forces have so far run up against the fact that it's human nature to seek rewards for our efforts. A market system functions smoothly, relative to alternative coordinating devices, because it's well matched to these aspects of human nature. So, conclude Bill Gates and others, rather than toss the market out, the answer is to learn to put the market to better use. "We can make market forces work better for the poor if we can develop a more creative capitalism—if we can stretch the reach of market forces so that more people can make a profit, or at least make a living, serving people who are suffering from the worst inequities," Gates said in his address to the Harvard class of 2007.

A selfless economy?

So far, my case for saying that scarcity alone doesn't explain why more mosquito nets aren't protecting the beds of African children—or more generally, what stands between us and a better world—might seem to be focusing on the way that markets work. So while you'll find the phrase "human nature" twice in the last paragraph, you might still be wondering why I'd said that the alternative to the scarcity explanation would be one that revolves around human nature itself. To make clear that human nature, motivations, and conflicts between selfish and cooperative impulses really do lie at the center of the alternative approach I'll be emphasizing, let me carry the argument a little further.

Try imagining a situation in which the main motivation in the work-a-day world is to accomplish the most possible good with our time and other resources. Drug company CEOs, farmers, and builders would get up every morning and look for needs that they could meet, not ways to stay in business and earn a good return on their investments.

A central figure in the founding of modern economics, Alfred Marshall, tried this same thought experiment a century ago. "[I]n a world in which all men were perfectly virtuous," he wrote:

> . . . [m]en would think only of their duties; and no one would desire to have a larger share of the comforts and luxuries of life than his neighbours. Strong producers could easily bear a touch of hardship; so they would wish that their weaker neighbours, while producing less, should consume more. Happy in this thought, they would work for the general good with all the energy, the inventiveness, and the eager initiative that belonged to them; and mankind would be victorious in contests with nature at every turn.

How could such a world fail to be a better one than the one we know today? Marshall urged caution:

> Such is the Golden Age to which poets and dreamers may look forward. But in the responsible conduct of affairs, it is worse than folly to ignore the imperfections which still cling to human nature.[2]

Reliance on an urge to do good, rather than to gain profits, might suffer from coordination problems because it's not clear that anything as effective as market prices and rates of financial return would emerge to signal to people *where* the most good could be done and what each person's part should be. Also, there could be differences of opinion as to *what* the most good was. With limited time and resources and with people heading off in different directions without coordination, perhaps even a world full of "do-gooders" trying day by day to "serve mankind" would fall short of our hopes.

But probably more important than problems of coordination and problems of defining the good, and clearly what Marshall had in mind with reference to "human nature," is the problem of sustaining the motivation to do good day after day, morning, noon, and night. Most Americans wanted to help their neighbors in the week or two that followed the terrorist attacks of September 11, 2001. More people helped elderly ladies across the street; more carried the grocery bags and held doors open for women with small children. Donations to help victims' families for a time outran the Red Cross's processing capacity. The army and police departments saw surges in new applicants. People left baked goods at firehouses to thank their local firemen. A pro football player, Pat Tillman, turned down a $3.6 million contract offer from the Arizona Cardinals to enlist in the army, ultimately giving his life for the cause in a friendly-fire incident in Afghanistan.

Within a few months of 9-11, however, things were more normal, vindicating Marshall's statement that "ordinary men are seldom capable of pure ideal altruism for any considerable time." Even in the first weeks, few people were spending *most* of their time on "doing good" only. Even the makers and venders of small flags and ribbon decals who revved up production and distribution to meet public demand for displays of patriotism were doing so by dint of the ordinary workings of the marketplace. Flags and decals were still sourced from China, where they were cheaper to make. Much fulfillment of army recruiting goals was explicable by an economic cost-benefit calculus on the parts of the recruits.

We can observe many other "experiments" in which the attempt was made to put the community, or social ideals, first, and selfish or family interests second. During World War II, Americans rallied around the flag when their navy was attacked at Pearl Harbor, beginning an all-out effort that put war production first and left consumer satisfactions waiting until after the victory. The war years saw countless examples of heroism and self-sacrifice. But self-interest didn't quite disappear. An investigative committee chaired by then Senator Harry Truman found many millions of dollars worth of fraud and waste by defense contractors, some of which were profiting handsomely from the war. A pledge by the Congress of Industrial Organizations not to disrupt the war effort by striking was not respected by all unions, and wildcat strikes by smaller groups of workers were numerous. Even soldiers weren't all models of self-sacrifice all the time. Out of consideration for their men's "needs," American generals were known to have arranged respite periods during which they could visit brothels. The Japanese military went further, forcing women in captive countries into sex-slavery to their soldiers.

Probably the last century's largest-scale experiment in working for the common good was the one that took place in China under Mao Zedong's Communists. In a country containing almost a fifth of the world's people, caring about profits was judged politically criminal, and young and old alike were urged to "serve the people." But when collective farming teams steered clear of political criticism by not paying more to those individuals who cultivated or harvested more crops in the field, the work pace typically slackened. Some peasants conserved their energy for after hours, when they might raise some extra chickens, ducks, or pigs for their families in their private yards or grow more vegetables in their tiny private plots. Officials who couldn't request more pay without arousing suspicion extracted favors from their subordinates as a quid pro quo for extra work points or better work assignments. China's most prominent leftist, Mao's wife Jiang Qing, while loudly criticizing any with "bourgeois" tendencies, was later found to have been hoarding libraries of Western films, while Mao himself was procuring dozens of young women to keep him company in bed as he grew old and his faculties waned. If proof were still needed that materialism was alive and well in China, the return of the country's farms to control by households able to profit from their crop sales soon after Mao's death led for a time to double-digit rates of output growth in China's rural economy.

A more benign example of a "selfless economy" is provided by the Israeli kibbutz communities mentioned in Chapter 1. These settlements of one to five hundred families helped to build a Jewish presence in Ottoman, and subsequently British Palestine, eventually providing a disproportionate share of the new Israeli state's top soldiers and political leaders. Members of a kibbutz (plural: kibbutzim) ate in communal dining halls, took turns doing all required tasks, and were allocated housing and other needs without differentiation by skill or level of responsibility. The system worked well enough during the decades of pioneering, with the kibbutzim actually exceeding private farms and factories in their agricultural and industrial productivity as late as the 1970s. But self-interest gradually resurfaced. As kibbutzim became more reliant on industry and as the principle of rotating workers from job to job became less practical, some of the more skilled technicians, engineers, and managers began comparing their compensation to that of counterparts in conventional firms, wondering why they should accept having no greater benefits than ordinary workers. Informal perks, like access to a community car with which to conduct official business in neighboring towns—and then maybe eat out or do personal shopping—slowly grew in magnitude, creating resentment by those not so advantaged. With growing exposure to the norms of the wider society, reinforced by the arrival of television sets airing the usual array of "bourgeois" TV shows, the general aspiration to emulate more middle class lifestyles by enlarging family living quarters, bringing cooking facilities and TV sets from the community recreation hall to the individual home, building swimming pools, and so on, led to a crisis of communal indebtedness. When an unsympathetic national government came into office and contractionary economic policies drove up interest rates, the ensuing financial crisis and the waning of ideological inhibitions caused most kibbutzim to adopt more conventional systems of organization. Within twenty years of that mid-1980s crisis, most kibbutzim had abandoned strict egalitarianism in favor of differentiated wages, and many had ceased to exist except in name.

We'll revisit some of these examples later. For now, the point to take away is that, for the most part, the world's societies have achieved what material successes they have by using economic arrangements that build on *the natural self-interest of individuals and their families*. The system works well, when it does, because it allows people to earn more when they work harder or smarter and lets them convert the extra earnings they obtain into ownership of land, machines, and financial assets. Resulting differences in such wealth holdings can then accumulate, for better and for worse, almost without limit. People also come to hold different amounts of wealth thanks to the different qualities of up-bringing, wealth, and connections they get from their families and to their different talents and abilities, their different levels of drive and effort, their different tolerances for risk-taking, and differences in sheer luck. How ethically defensible each of these is as a basis for differences in wealth and income varies from factor to factor. But the factors are difficult to separate in practice. So the package, with its more and its less savory bits together, has stood as a whole because attempts to found economic life on other motivations have tended to founder.

More broadly, putting self-interest and acquisitiveness at the center of social organization has contributed to what many deem unconscionable inequalities of income and wealth, to allocations of effort and resources that seem tough to square with humane and rational criteria, and even to wars to control access to markets, land, oil, and more. But realists defend the market and hope to tackle those problems in other ways, ranging from government-provided insurance and transfer payments to voluntary acts of charity.

A market/state balancing act?

If I've done my job well, you've seen how the case can be made that human nature and motivation really are at least as important as scarcity is to understanding why the world's economic arrangements and outcomes are as they are. But if you're among those committed fervently to working for a more just, peaceful, and generative world—yes, I'm still trying to keep with me, and I sincerely apologize for letting Alfred Marshall call you a poet and dreamer—you might remain more than a little skeptical on the "realist's" conclusion that market systems are the world's only option because they've arisen naturally in response to what we humans are like. Even if we concede a role to markets, you're probably thinking, we surely can't trust them to do everything.

The so-called "mixed economy" is an effort to find a judicious balance between markets and democratically-controlled political institutions. Putting the profit motive and markets to work for basic production and economic coordination, then trying to achieve desirable ends by regulating them and redistributing some of their bounty, has been the approach of liberal, industrial democracies for more than a century. Proponents credit that approach for the high quality of life enjoyed by the majority of citizens in countries like Denmark, Germany, and the Netherlands during the past fifty years. But skeptics can argue that in important respects it's come up short or shows signs of wearing thin. West European countries that have tried to build "social market economies" with generous social welfare provisions and job protections have seen slowed economic growth and high unemployment. In countries like Britain, the class divisions of past centuries have continued to reproduce themselves in a variety of forms, and serious social strains have grown as Britain and other European countries have struggled to deal with inflows of immigrants. Japan, whose version of capitalism had relied less on arms length capital markets and more on tight networks of banks and family-like firms, has seen its economy stall and come under increasing pressure to Westernize.

Looking at the relatively free-wheeling capitalism of the United States, this appeared to be more successful at generating economic growth and job creation in the late twentieth century, but as we've seen, it's suffered from yawning inequalities, stagnant real wages, and shrinking leisure. A massive financial crisis in 2008–09 was followed soon afterwards by ideological and political gridlock over government spending and taxes, suggesting that the foundations of the American economic and political system were a lot less firm than many had imagined. Also, the nation found itself going to war three times in two decades due to its dependence on Middle Eastern oil and the hostilities this produced in that region. And largely owing to economic concerns and business influences, it continually resisted international calls to reduce its consumption of oil as a means of slowing global climate change.

In industrial democracies, relying on government to tinker with market outcomes on the margins suffers from inherent limitations for at least two broad reasons. First, major decisions get made at levels where the electorate numbers in the millions or tens of millions. Feeling that they have almost no chance of making a decisive difference, John and Jane Voter might invest little time and effort into becoming experts on the issues and knowing the exact positions of each candidate. Second, although speech may be free in an abstract sense, reaching large numbers of people usually requires access to mass media, which is affordable only to large firms and wealthy individuals or to large groups of people organized around particular interests or viewpoints. So, while governments can in principle regulate and correct many of the shortcomings of markets, the fact that the government "of the people" is so imperfectly "by the people" and "for the people" means that this often fails to happen. Regulation of industry by bureaucrats in such imperfect democracies has been compared to the fox guarding the hen house, since the same individuals move from industry to regulatory body and back through a well-worn "revolving door."

Self-interest prevents better outcomes not only when acted upon by the rich or the heads of big companies. We just saw how self-interest can explain the relative lack of involvement in political matters by the average citizen. Government workers failing to provide an honest day's work, politicians padding government payrolls with unneeded employees to dispense favors to friends and relatives, taxpayers finding ways to avoid paying their fair share, and people claiming government benefits to which they're not entitled all sap faith in the ability of the public sector to deliver social improvements, thereby providing arguments for keeping government small and trusting the market, not government, with society's problems.

But market critics can see nothing worse than expanding the reach of market-like institutions. Their concerns include not only injustices in the distribution of things and lack of protection of nature, but less material dimensions of the market's impact on our lives. By stoking the desire for possessions and encouraging people to judge themselves by the money they earn, market systems seem in some ways to narrow, rather than to widen, the space for personal creativity and growth, while perhaps also weakening people's abilities to balance the value of relationships and other dimensions of life against the struggle for material security and success. Other institutions, such as the family, churches, and schools, can, and to some degree do, counter the overriding influence of "market values," but there are limits to their influence. Schools attempt to impart civic virtues, for example, but they also have to prepare students to be competitive in a market economy. One of the main preoccupations of institutions of higher learning in the United States is turning out and building links with the cadres of wealthy alumni who are their principal donor base.

Moving on

Clearly we can't resolve in a few pages the debate about market/government balance that's raged on for decades. These last pages were mainly meant to illustrate in the more realistic context of a mixed economy that how we organize our economic and political system is crucial to understanding what limits our achievement of a better world. My broader goal, though, has been to argue that the kind of economic and political systems we've ended up with are determined in large part by aspects of human nature, including the balance between selfishness and cooperation, public-mindedness, and civic virtue. There's scope for writing books about how to solve fundamental problems by attacking issues of resource scarcity and technology, but it's at least as important, I'm asserting, that we dig into that part of the roots of our problems which resides in our own natures.

Our plan of attack going forward is simple. Starting with the next chapter, we'll be launching into a sustained discussion of what human nature really is in those respects that are critical to our problem. To gauge just how right the market realists are, and to understand just what raw material it is that we have to work with in our world-improvement projects, we'll look both at the evidence that people are primarily self-interested (Chapter 3) and at the evidence that people can be altruistic or socially-minded (Chapter 4). After that, we'll draw on scientific approaches to correctly weigh the balance (Chapter 5), then apply the knowledge gained to study the behavior (Chapter 6) and evolution (Chapters 7–9) of economic, social, and political systems. Hang on, then. Here we go.

Notes:

1. In the relatively rich African country of Nigeria, for instance, a 2003 study found that only ten to twelve percent of households had a mosquito net and that almost all of the nets that were found were ones untreated with the insecticides that can greatly increase their effectiveness. See Obinna Onwujekwe, Kara Hanson, and Julia Fox-Rushby, "Inequalities in purchase of mosquito nets and willingness to pay for insecticide-treated nets in Nigeria: challenges for malaria control interventions," *Malaria Journal*, 3, no. 6 (2004).

2. Marshall, *Principles of Economics*, Eighth Edition (London: Macmillan, 1920), Book 1, Chapter 1.

CHAPTER 3
Self-Interest

In that most memorable of English language declarations to echo forth from its side of the Atlantic at the three-quarter mark of the eighteenth century, Scottish social philosopher Adam Smith famously expounded on the central role played by self-interest in a market economy:

> It is not from the benevolence of the butcher, the brewer, or the baker that we expect our dinner, but from their regard to their own interest. We address ourselves, not to their humanity but to their self-love, and never talk to them of our necessities but of their advantages.

The Wealth of Nations was revered by many as a manifesto of free markets, and it's been hailed ever since as the work that launched the science of "political economy." Conveniently enough for American students cramming dates for their social studies exams, the book was published in the same year that the thirteen English colonies destined to become the capitalist powerhouse of the future began detaching themselves from mother Britain.

The year 1776 was a year in which some eight thousand captive Africans were shipped to the western hemisphere to be sold as slaves. Of the Europeans heading across the Atlantic that year, about eighty percent were themselves indentured servants obligated to work several years before obtaining their freedom. At the time, Russia had twenty-three million serfs, practically all of whom would be dead before their great grandchildren's emancipations by the Tsar Alexander II. Britain had only recently consolidated its conquest of India, and Louis the XVI, the unlucky monarch who was to have head and body separated by the guillotine during his country's coming revolution, had recently ascended to the thrown of a still expanding French empire. The eighty-hour factory workweek, Engels, Dickens, and the smokestacks and black moths, all lay decades ahead in England's future.

Possibly the pursuit of self-interest knew less restraint in Adam Smith's day than in our own. In the years since then, we've seen the abolition of slavery and serfdom, the emergence of democracies with universal suffrage, progress towards the legal equality of women, and shifts in cultures and value systems giving more weight to the all-round development of human beings. Has Smith's view of human nature become outmoded, then?

Economists don't think so. Changes in institutions, such as abolishing slavery and reducing the absolute power of monarchs, are always in the interest of some people if not of others, so such changes could reflect changing balances of influence and power, not sudden shifts to selflessness. The vast majority of economists, in any event, still consider the Smith quotation to be as relevant as ever. To understand society's workings, they assume, it's best to start by assuming that people act out of self-interest.

Studies of economic behavior ever since Smith have taken this assumption as their bedrock. In the 1840s, the English economist Nassau W. Senior contended that economics relies on four basic postulates, the first of which is that "every person desires to maximize wealth with as little sacrifice as possible." Around the same time, the philosopher, social thinker, and economist, John Stuart Mill, wrote that "Political Economy … proceeds … under the supposition that man is a being who is determined, by the necessity of his nature, to prefer a greater portion of wealth to a smaller in all cases, without any other exception than … aversion to labor and desire of the present enjoyment of costly indulgences." In 1898, Francis Y. Edgeworth, a leading British proponent of the new, more mathematical form of economics that would triumph in the universities of the twentieth century, wrote, "The first principle of Economics is that every agent is actuated only by self-interest."

Today's economics textbooks still explain how individuals decide what goods to purchase and how many hours to work by doing whatever maximizes their satisfaction from consumption and from avoidance of effort. You're assumed routinely to encounter situations in which you have to choose between various alternatives, for example buying a US-made car versus a Japanese-made car, or putting more money into a retirement account versus spending it now, or having another child versus not having one, or voting for a politician espousing tax cuts versus one committed to keeping taxes the same. The alternative chosen is the one that maximizes your "utility," an intangible but hypothetically quantifiable construct that takes on a larger value when you have more income, goods, and leisure and a smaller one when you have less. The effects of your choices on *other* people's incomes and leisure are ordinarily assumed to be sufficiently unimportant to you as to require no consideration. The same goes for the *means* by which your goal is reached, if the choice of methods in itself doesn't affect your income and leisure.

But is there really evidence that self-interested motives govern our decisions? Well, yes, quite a bit. Here are some examples.

The business of business

The enterprise system that powers every successful economy today is founded on for-profit companies whose main goal is to make money for their owners. Successful businesses create jobs, but profit-seeking companies create only as many jobs as will improve their bottom line, cut jobs when that's good for profits, and pay their workers no more than is needed to achieve those profits. Evidence includes: (a) American companies' on-going efforts to avoid unionization of their non-unionized employees; (b) frequently fierce resistance to union wage demands; (c) outsourcing of work to locations where labor is less costly; and (d) positive response of stock prices, often accompanied by rewarding of top executives, when workforces are "downsized."

Cases in which corporate executives cheat employees out of their pensions and shareholders out of their wealth by withholding information and manipulating stock prices—for example, the Enron scandal of the early 2000s or the more recent hacking of private voice communications by Britain's *News of the World* newspaper to help sell papers—make headlines, but they may be exceptional only in the naked displays of greed entailed and the fact that the perpetrators got caught. Yet making money is what even ethical companies are about.

Consider the case of America's fastest growing enterprise of the late twentieth century, the retailer Wal-Mart. Starting with a modest five-and-ten store in Bentonville, Arkansas, company founder Sam Walton's laser-like focus on "everyday low prices" made Wal-Mart one of America's largest retailers by the time of his death in 1992. Today, it's the world's largest retailer and one of its largest companies, with well over three thousand stores in the United States alone, and 1.8 million employees. Its revenue accounts for more than two percent of the entire gross domestic product of the United States. While most of the company's cost-cutting is passed on to its consumers and is attributable to unquestionable efficiencies like finding ways to reduce unneeded packaging and to keep trucks full on both directions of long-distance hauls, its success has also depended on paying low wages and providing only the most basic employee benefits. In its original American base of operations, its business model included a built-in growth dynamic: as it caused better-paying and lower-volume competitors to shut their doors in consequence of intense price competition and pressed manufacturers to shift operations to lower-wage economies, it was helping to increase the number of Americans for whom shopping at a discount is a necessity.

Businesses design and deliver products that improve people's lives—better medicines, lower cost personal computers and cell phones—when profits can be made from it; but businesses just as often design and deliver products that harm people—fast food French fries drenched in cooking oil, carcinogenic cigarettes, gas guzzling SUVs—when the money's in that. (Some might add a mindless, caustic, and degrading culture to their list of profitable, but harmful, products.)

Businesses that start out with creative young people motivated by adventure and creativity grow, when successful, into fiercely competitive, turf-protecting monoliths. Think, for instance, of Microsoft or Google, or, if your memory's long enough, of the counter-culturally iconic Beatles grown into a business empire, suing each other right and left ("You never give me your money / You only give me your funny paper") and recycling bits of old recordings to keep stoking their "money machine." Or to quote James Taylor's 1976 song of the same name ("Money Machine"): "When I began the game / See me singing 'bout Fire and Rain / Let me just say it again / I've seen fives and I've seen tens."

The immigration debate

In recent years, the United States has seen a far-ranging debate over immigration that offers a nice window into the role of money and self-interest in both private and public life. Throughout the world, perceived economic opportunity drives migration more than any other single factor. The fact that the United States finds itself to be a desired destination for immigrants is thus explained more by its higher average income level than by any other factor. That the country restricts the number of immigrants allowed to enter it legally is also probably explained mainly by the self-interest of US citizens who fear that uncontrolled immigration will reduce their earnings or threaten their jobs. More than a million Mexicans are apprehended trying to cross into the United States illegally each year, with perhaps half a million succeeding at getting in and similar numbers attempting the same from countries to Mexico's south. (Some 215,000 Central American migrants, most of them in transit to the US, are intercepted by Mexico itself each year.)[1] These movements are mainly attributable to the fact that average US wages are about twenty-two times those in Mexico, roughly the same number of times as those in Brazil, and so on, and that even a migrant farm worker in the United States can earn roughly ten times as much per hour there as for casual labor at home. Economic interest also easily explains why organized labor and employers part ways on migration policy: US labor unions are on record favoring tougher migration controls to reduce the downward pressure on wages caused by immigrants, whereas American farmers and companies that benefit from hiring immigrants at lower wages than most Americans will work for have been strong advocates of an amnesty or guest worker program and of easier immigration rules—a case of the capitalists being the "good guys" from the would-be immigrant's standpoint.

That the temptation to hire lower wage workers is great, even when one has to break the law to do so, is illustrated tragicomically by the infamous nanny problems that plagued nominees to important posts in the Clinton administration in the 1990s. Clinton's first nominee to be chief law enforcement officer of the US government, Zoe Baird, was forced to withdraw following an initial confirmation hearing due to adverse publicity over having hired illegal immigrants from Peru to provide childcare and driving services and not paying the social security taxes due. His second nominee for the post of Attorney General, Kimba Wood, also had an illegal immigrant nanny problem, and this turned out to be the case for several other administration nominees, as well.

Lest the United States appear to be singled out unfairly, let's also note the following item from the *International Herald Tribune* of July 11, 2006: "In a sign of growing international concern about African migration to Europe, leaders from more than fifty nations gathered here yesterday to seek a coordinated approach to controlling the waves of sub-Saharan migrants who are taking increasingly desperate measures to reach the European Union. The meeting reflects a growing realization in Europe that current measures for dealing with sub-Saharan migration may soon become obsolete as the region produces more and more young workers likely to seek opportunities unavailable at home."

Competing for academic success
According to numerous accounts, millions of South Korean mothers are obsessed with the goal of helping their children to do well in school and to get a high score on the national college admissions exam in order to obtain a place in a top university and thereby secure a prosperous future. "Education manager"

mothers spend eighteen-hour days helping their children prepare for school, scheduling their after-school educational activities, and even attending classes so as to better help their kids with their homework. The children themselves frequently spend six after-school hours a day in "cram schools," known in Korean as *hagwon*. A popular saying is: "sleep five hours a night and fail; sleep four hours a night and pass!" So little time is permitted to these young Koreans for non-academic activities that the United Nations Committee on the Rights of the Child concluded in 2003 that the pressure to study violated the children's "rights to play."

The Korean Educational Development Institute calculated that private (mostly after-school) education expenditures were $6.9 billion in the country of 47 million people, or about $1200 a year per child of middle and high school age. Numerous suicides of students in their teens are viewed as a symptom of the pressures, with some forty-five percent of students reporting having contemplated suicide. All of this is so the child gets into a good school, ensuring his or her economic future (including marriage prospects). Similar scenes of intense competition for school places play out every year in Japan, China, Taiwan, and India. Some Asian parents even send their children to school in the United States, or move the whole family there, with the idea that their children can achieve equal academic success with less sacrifice in quality of life.

In the United States itself, the prospects of financial success conferred by attending the most prestigious schools has helped to drive their tuition rates up dramatically. In the thirty-year period ending in 2005–06, tuitions rose at a rate of 7.4 percent per year, while the general inflation rate averaged under 4.5 percent. This brought four years of tuition (not to mention room, board, and other expenses, which add another 22 percent or more for many) to roughly three times the average per capita income in the United States. Parents of high schoolers were parting with additional hundreds of millions a year for SAT preparation courses and private college application advisors.

The marriage market

A romantic might have hoped that at least love, reputed to be as strong as death (Song of Songs 8:6), would be immune to the influence of money and self-interest. Yet sociologists, economists, and even biologists frequently note the resemblance of mate selection to a market. In an article titled "Impact of Market Value on Human Mate Choice Decisions,"[2] Boguslaw Pawlowski and Robin Dunbar studied newspaper personals ads placed by men and women, arguing that such studies demonstrate "that advertisers adjust their bids in the light of their perceived status in the market place" and "that male advertisers are largely concerned with traits that reflect women's fecundity [capacity to produce offspring], while female advertisers emphasize wealth and commitment in prospective male partners." Based on advertised age preferences, they calculate that the "market value" of marriageable females in Britain in the 1990s peaked in their mid-twenties while that of marriageable males peaked in their mid-thirties, a finding they take to be consistent with the fact that women's fertility peaks at an earlier age than does men's earnings capacity, while male "market value" is also affected by predicted longevity (i.e., male earnings peak later than the mid-thirties, but women take into account the number of remaining years a partner is likely to remain a healthy breadwinner).

Recent studies of dating preferences carried out by economists, one using data from an online dating website and another the decisions of participants in "speed dating" events, provide parallel evidence that young women place more emphasis on those attributes of a prospective partner associated with wealth and income earning potential (e.g., intelligence and socioeconomic background) while men pay more attention to physical attractiveness, the immediate lure that researchers like Pawlowski and Dunbar associate with "fecundity."[3] While it might be slightly consoling to egalitarians that men pay little attention to prospective dates' incomes, when it comes to marriage, there's still a high correlation between the education and earnings power of men and women. If men and women married randomly or on the basis of physical attraction only, the random pairing of high-income men with low-income women, and vice versa, would tend to reduce income inequality among households. In reality, though, sorting by education level, and also by economic background and economic potential, has been the rule and shows signs of a recent upward trend. A Canadian government study found that fifty-four percent of couples in Canada and fifty-five percent in the United States, in 2001, involved a man and a woman with the same basic education level, up from forty-two percent and forty-nine percent, respectively, in 1970 and 1971. The study found, further, that "intermarriage across education levels occurs primarily between adjacent education levels, and intermarriage across more than one education level is relatively rare."[4]

The pursuit of self-interest doesn't necessarily end with marriage, either. Divorce and remarriage are susceptible to similar kinds of analysis. For example, those whose marketability rises relative to that of their current partner are more likely to initiate a divorce and return to the "marriage market." Since female attractiveness as viewed by males declines from the mid-twenties onwards, while male earning power may be rising for another quarter century, the high-earning male who dumps his now less-attractive wife in favor of a younger model can be seen to be acting on predictable self-interest, although preferences of which he's only partly conscious are likely to be his more immediate motivators. While the practice of monogamy helps human males to have more equal life-chances of reproducing than do, say, gorillas, in which harems are monopolized by a dominant male, enough high-status men have children with several women during their lifetimes—a pattern dubbed "serial monogamy"—that there's a shortage of mating opportunities on the low end of the totem pole—a problem that at least one research team has linked to the incidence of rape.[5]

It's always the other guy who's rich

As Chapter 1 noted, numerous studies suggest that in societies with incomes above those reached by the industrialized world in the 1940s, further increases in the average person's income are associated with almost no gain in the average level of happiness that people report in surveys. For example, although average income (controlling for inflation) doubled in the United States between 1946 and 1991, the average person's response when asked to rate their level of happiness remained unchanged.[6] At any given point in time, however, increases in individuals' incomes *relative to others* in their country *are* associated with greater happiness. (For instance, an individual who's just moved from being in the poorest forty percent to being in the richest forty percent of wage-earners tends to report a higher happiness level.) Some scholars see these results as implying that for the most part people are on a "hedonic treadmill": they believe that if they earn more they'll be happier, but when, on average, other people's incomes also rise, they feel as if they are running in place.

A large majority of people never think they have as much money as they would like to. In the 1960s, a social psychologist asked people in both a poor country, India, and a rich country, the United States, what it would take to make them really happy. A forty-year-old skilled worker earning thirty dollars a month in India replied:

I hope in the future I will not get any disease. Now I am coughing. I also hope I can purchase a bicycle. I hope my children will study well and that I can provide them with an education. I also would sometime like to own a fan and maybe a radio.

A twenty-eight-year-old lawyer in the United States replied:

I would like to provide my family with an income to allow them to live well—to have the proper recreation, to go camping, to have music and dancing lessons for the children, and to have family trips. I wish we could belong to a country club and do more entertaining. [7]

Almost no one surveyed in either country was *unable* to identify something that they didn't yet have and that they thought would make them really happy, were they to have it. Run the process in fast motion, as has happened in more prosperous parts of China in recent years, or in South Korea a decade or two earlier, and it's likely that you'd sometimes find the same individual who had earlier dreamed of owning a bicycle and a radio soon attaining them, then hoping for a motorcycle and a TV set, even as they raise children who'll soon be aspiring to own personal cars and home entertainment centers.

In societies in which income and wealth are distributed unequally, as is true to varying degrees of all societies, hardly anyone (excepting, maybe, some embarrassed children of the highest income parents) thinks of his own family as rich. That even most people in the top 5 percent of income earners in a country don't see themselves as rich may be explained by the way that income is distributed. Consider the figure below. The heights of the bars, and the numbers above them, show the percentage of the US population with incomes in each of ten categories that increase from left to right. The most common income bracket is $10,000 to $20,000 a year, with 13 percent of individuals, followed closely by the $20,000 to $30,000 a year bracket, with 12.6 percent. If we add these two figures to the 8.6 percent who earned less than $10,000, the 11.1 percent who earned $30,000 to $40,000, and the 9.5 percent who earned $40,000 to $50,000, we see that more than half of the population, or 54.9 percent, had incomes of $50,000 or below. So earning anything above $50,000 would put you above average. And if you were among the 5.7 percent with an income between $70,000 and $80,000 a year, say, you could consider yourself relatively rich, since more than two-thirds of the population earn less than you do.

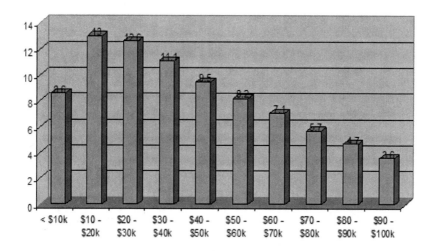

But few of those earning $80,000 and above consider themselves rich. Moving rightward from the $10,000 to $20,000 bracket bar and up, the bars keep getting shorter and shorter, but without ever falling to zero. Now, a complete version of the figure would show ever smaller bars, but still not reaching 0 percent of population even as you looked out to the $150,000 to $160,000 bracket, to the $250,000 to $260,000 bracket, to the $350,000 to $360,000 bracket, and beyond. Here's what you'd see, roughly, as you extended the figure above further to the right[8]:

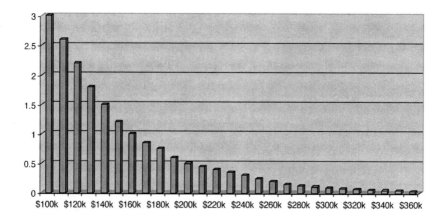

Up into the brackets earning a quarter of a million dollars, a million dollars, or several million each year, you can still look to your right and see bars reflecting people who are a lot richer than you. Now, suppose that you belonged to the percentile of the income distribution that is ahead of 94 percent of individuals but below the top 5 percent—that is, you're in the 6th percentile. Chances are good that you'd live in a community in which most other families belong to, say, the 4th, 5th, 6th, 7th and 8th percentiles. Among those with whom your family lives, you'll have no reason to feel particularly rich, since you are merely average. Your family might own two nice automobiles, but quite possibly the top luxury models are somewhat too costly for you. You might live in a house with five bedrooms and three full baths, but chances are there'll be at least a few much larger houses that you pass on your way to work or shopping, or to which you might even be invited for your child's school's PTA meeting. You may vacation for three weeks a year in the mountains or seashore, but you'll hear of others who own private vacation homes and who vacation abroad at least once a year.

Much the same applies the whole way up the scale. If your family's income exceeds that of 99.5 percent of households, with only a half a percent of the population above you, that still leaves a good many people who are richer than you, and by the shape of the curve, some of them are several times richer than you. Graphically, the pattern of shortening bars is repeated almost indefinitely, so you may belong on a fairly short bar with many far taller bars way off to your left, but unless you're in the top hundredth of one percent or so, there are always plenty of still shorter bars trailing off to the right of your own. You may live in a quite large house, own three cars, belong to a country club, have a swimming pool, hire a housekeeper, and vacation abroad, but you're not rich in your own mind. Rich people, by your understanding, are those who own yachts and limousines, employ chauffeurs and household staffs, own several homes, and earn the salaries of Fortune 500 CEOs and top-earning athletes. And even if you make it to that category, you'd still be small potatoes compared to Bill Gates.

Wall Street Journal reporter Robert Frank's review of survey responses collected by the wealth-management firm, PNC Advisors, supports this view perfectly. Clients were asked how much money they'd need to make them feel secure. Writes Frank: "They almost always answer that the amount they need to feel secure is twice their current level of net worth or income. Those worth $500,000 to $1 million said they needed $2.4 million. Those worth $1 million to $1.49 million said $3 million. And those with $10 million or more said $18 million. In other words, people's definition of 'rich' is subjective and is usually twice their current net worth." [9]

Looked at from a global standpoint, the large majority of Americans' incomes are in the top five percent of incomes in the world as a whole, so even the family at the US median is rich by world standards. Just be careful not to tell them that on a day when gasoline prices are high or their next credit card payment is due.

Notice, too, that while many people feel some envy and even resentment against the very rich, most of the same people have no desire to eliminate the possibility of becoming wealthy, since it's a possibility they enjoy imagining for themselves (consider the popularity of magazines, television programs, and websites displaying the lives of the super rich, of lotteries, and of game shows in which an occasional lucky contestant is made wealthy).

What does any of this have to do with demonstrating that self-interest is important? Perhaps very little. But a plausible conjecture is that people look up, rather than down, the income and wealth scale in part because they're innately acquisitive, and the thought of having enough is mostly foreign to them. Quite likely, they also at least partially equate wealth and consumption with status. So, the fact that it's almost always the other guy who's rich may after all serve as a telltale sign of the drive to have more.

Trust and lemons
In mid-2006, the manufacturer's suggested retail price of a new Toyota Camry LE Sedan in the northeastern United States was $23,360. Suppose that you had bought one of these cars from the dealer, but two days later, you learned that you were being laid off from your job, and you decided you should have bought a less expensive car, perhaps a used one, given the new uncertainties in your life. You could always sell your new car for close to what you bought it for and buy some-thing else more within your means, right? Wrong. Once driven off the dealer's lot, that car could be sold to a private individual for not much more than $18,600, a loss in value of $4,760 or 20 percent! Why?

University of California at Berkeley economist George Akerlof offered an explanation in 1970, developed its broader theoretical implications, and in 2001 shared the Nobel Prize in Economics for this and related ideas. The car's value takes a sharp drop when you drive it off the lot, Akerlof explained, because the information in your head and the information available to others don't coincide and because in such situations people are inclined to be distrustful and not to give strangers much benefit of the doubt. Consider first that some fraction of the cars manufactured every year have defects that will end up being time-consuming and costly to deal with. Consider second that a small fraction of new car buyers have reason to change their minds about the cars they buy. The question is: What proportion of the people wanting to sell their new car a few weeks later are selling a "lemon," a car that showed signs of trouble just after it began to be driven? The answer is: even if half of the new car sellers are people who had unrelated reasons to sell, such as job loss or winning the lottery, chances are that the proportion of "lemons" in the set of newly purchased cars that get put up for sale is substantially higher than the proportion of "lemons" among new cars still on the dealer's lot.

Suppose that three-quarters of the buyers who discover they've bought a "lemon" wish to sell it and that those individuals represent about fifty-percent of the overall set of people wanting to sell their almost brand new cars. Selling their car is more beneficial to them the more of the purchase price they can recoup, so it's in their interest to hide the fact that the car has problems and to offer some other reason why they're selling it. If potential buyers believe that most sellers of "lemons" will lie about their cars' defects, then they'll put little credence into *your* story that you're selling yours because you lost your job. Because potential buyers assume that there's a high probability that your car is defective, you would probably have had to sell it at a significant discount below the price at which you purchased it two days earlier.

Unlike the previous examples, this case provides indirect rather than direct evidence of how self-interested people are. It's evidence that people believe that *others* are so self-interested that they'll lie to or at least withhold information from a stranger to avoid losing money. Imagine a country, Halo-land, in which no one ever lies and everyone knows that to be the case. Knowing that other Halo-landers are honest and won't withhold information about the quality of their cars, almost brand new cars can sell in Halo-land for only a tiny discount below their original purchase price once the sellers vouch for their good quality.

Is there any reason to think that the belief that many will lie or withhold information for personal profit is in fact accurate? A general reason is that a lot of people's best guesses are influencing the market price of resold cars, and experience accumulates with time. If it became clear that the vast majority of those almost brand new cars being put up for sale were in fact without defect, it would also be clear that their bargain-basement prices were unwarranted, and this should drive up demand and cause their prices to rise. One reason is that if most people were wrong in their assessment of almost brand new cars, there would be money to be made by "betting against" their evaluations. Someone could go around buying up the unnecessarily underpriced almost new cars, warranty them, and sell them for closer to the original price without incurring too much cost to compensate the new owners when their cars break down—because in fact they are hardly any more likely to break down than are the average new cars on the original dealer's lot. So competition to buy up the underpriced cars would tend to drive their price up. If people's beliefs were a lot *less* pessimistic than warranted, on the other hand, almost new cars would sell at too small a discount, which would encourage more people to sell their defective new cars. Assuming that markets are efficient in this sense, then, people's beliefs about the proportion of others who are honest and the proportion of almost new cars that are "lemons" are neither much more nor much less pessimistic than warranted.

The sad demise of the "new socialist man"

We've already noted that the question of whether people will be motivated to work as hard as required without the kinds of material rewards that might breed inequality is one that's come up time and again in the context of attempts to organize more egalitarian societies. Some have proposed to substitute honors for monetary rewards, while others looked for ways to make work fun: the French utopian writer, Charles Fourier, proposed to solve the problem of who would do the dirtiest work by giving such jobs to children—who love playing with dirt! On the more "realistic" end of the spectrum were Karl Marx, who argued that unequal rewards for unequal work would be necessary during the early stages of socialism, and the leaders of most twentieth century Communist parties, including Josef Stalin, who embraced Marx's view and even labeled those opposing the use of material incentives as ideological deviants.

As hinted at in the previous chapter, China's Mao Zedong was just such a deviant from Marxist orthodoxy. Though always admiring Stalin's no-nonsense approach to the wielding of violence, he distinguished himself from more prag-matic, in some cases Soviet-trained, colleagues by asserting that a "new socialist man" was ready to be born if society, as a whole, began working together for a common purpose. He criticized the payment of bonuses to workers, peasants, and managers who completed more work, arguing that such practices perpetuated a capitalistic mentality. Only revolutionary spirit and service to "the people" should be recognized and rewarded. To Mao, the Russian society of the 1950s was another form of class society, with party officials and technocrats as the new ruling class.

Mao's China achieved some real economic progress compared to the country's preceding century of conflict and instability. During the years of Communist ascendancy under Mao (1949–76), industrial production rose at a rate of about thirteen percent a year, although little of the growth was in goods families could consume. Farm output grew more slowly, but (apart from the disastrous "Great Leap" famine of 1959–61) it nonetheless kept pace with an exploding population—the added 388 million mouths that China had to feed during that quarter century exceeded the entire population of non-Communist Europe at the time. Thanks to more equal distribution of available food, to sanitation campaigns, and to low cost preventive health measures, life expectancy rose from an estimated thirty-two years in 1949 to sixty-five years in 1978. In that same year, Pakistan, with a higher average income than China, had a life expectancy of only forty-nine years. India's was fifty-one years and Bangladesh's forty-seven.

Still, by the late 1970s, it was clear that China's "self-reliant" form of industrialization, which ignored profitability and focused on old heavy industries like steel, oil, and chemicals, had made relatively slow progress in comparison with the frenetic modernization of neighbors Japan, South Korea, Hong Kong, Taiwan, and Singapore, countries whose paths of economic growth accorded far greater roles to the profit motive and international trade and focused more on consumer goods and advanced technologies. Mao's successors, who had little sympathy with his ultra-left proclivities, wanted to put their country on a fast track to join this east Asian pack. So the new leadership under Deng Xiaoping, while also following in the path of his neighbors' outward-looking trade orientation, restored bonuses to industrial workers, gave state enterprise managers a cut of their companies' profits, let peasants sell their surplus crops for the highest price on the market, and declared that "some must get rich before others" and that "to get rich is glorious!"

Did China's people accept this ideological about-face from egalitarianism without protest, after three decades of Maoist rhetoric? China's politics were totalitarian under both Mao and Deng, so it's hard to know what people really thought. What people *did* once convinced that making money would not put them under suspicion of being class enemies is clear enough, though. Farm output, which had been rising at an average pace of about 2 percent a year since the early 1960s, rose by some 6.6 percent a year from 1979 to 1984. Tens of millions of rural and urban Chinese started small businesses, sending the retail trade, services, and construction sectors into explosive growth. The rate of growth of the economy's overall output rose from five or six percent a year to nine or ten percent, consumer spending and consumer goods production rose still more sharply, and the leadership's goal of quadrupling incomes before the end of the century, a goal that seemed ridiculously optimistic in 1979 and had never been matched by any large economy, was handily achieved.

Ironically, one of the most convincing signs that Maoist rhetoric had succeeded in inculcating idealism in some Chinese came more than a decade after Mao's death. In 1989, the perception that people with connections to Communist Party officials were profiting, while those dependent on wages from state enterprises were having trouble keeping up with rising prices, triggered mass protests in Beijing and other cities. In Beijing, in particular, student-led protests received considerable support from the general population. But within a few years after their movement had been crushed by tanks and political controls had been tightened, the incoming cohorts of college students seemed apathetic to politics and ever more focused on getting ahead materially. Fierce competition for places in top universities that put a student on track to earn a higher income in the ever more unequal society seemed to be the new ideal of young urban Chinese. Where there had been protests and banners for democracy in 1989, within the following decades, Deng's reforms seemed to have succeeded in making of urban China another South Korea full of cram schools and status competition.

Beyond polite self-interest

The examples above may be enough to make you concede that most people act, as Adam Smith asserted, out of "regard to their own interest." But it can be argued that so far I've painted only the gentlest case for the proposition that human beings are selfish. The people I've described want better bicycles, motorcycles, or cars; they want bigger houses, richer husbands, younger wives; and they want their children to get into better schools. But most for the most part obey laws and social norms, and they stop short of the using violent means to get their way.

Unfortunately, people don't always stop at merely putting themselves first. They sometimes act as if placing no value at all on the well-being of others, and some go beyond that, seeming to get satisfaction from others' suffering. Rather than bemoaning the sorts of self-interest discussed so far, an appreciation of the full range of human disregard for others might leave us feeling grateful that so many pursue their interests *within* social bounds.

Here are a few examples of the still darker side of human nature.

Producing, stealing, and guarding

Working harder and doing sharper deals in the market aren't the only ways to obtain more consumables and to accumulate more wealth. Why bother trying to convince people to give you more for your own products or services if it's easier to simply *take* things from them?

Sometimes, of course, there are sensibly selfish reasons not to steal. In organized societies, you can be locked up for doing it, and a reputation for theft won't go down well at your next job interview. (Whether such conventions would emerge if everyone were strictly self-interested is a question for later chapters.)

But, then again, crime sometimes pays, or at least appears to some to pay, better than their alternatives. One estimate suggested that as much as forty billion dollars a year was stolen and embezzled from US companies by their own employees in the late 1990s. The FBI put the value of property and money stolen from homes, businesses, plus stolen vehicles, at more than five billion dollars in 2005. To keep property theft in check, American banks, businesses, and entities like hospitals, museums, and universities employed some 295,000 security guards, paying them around six billion dollars for their services. In the same year, about $1.4 billion worth of security cameras and $6.1 billion worth of locks and alarm systems were reportedly installed in homes and business premises. If we assume that police and detectives spent about a fifth of their time dealing with property crimes and that the same proportion of the 2.2 million inmates in the local, state, and federal prisons were there for such crimes, then the cost to citizens for police protection and for the incarceration of property criminals comes out to about $29 billion a year.[10] The combined costs of private guards, police, security hardware, and prisons equals about half of a percent of the gross domestic product (GDP), with estimated theft and embezzlement causing another half of a percent of GDP to change hands. This still leaves out costs of insurance. It also neglects losses in output that accrue because some economic activities are simply too costly to insure or protect and are accordingly not carried out.

Economic theory implies that there must be an equilibrium of sorts between productive activity, theft, and property protection. Individuals and the entities into which they organize themselves would be expected to calculate and compare the anticipated returns on time, effort, and money spent producing with those that could be generated by time, effort, and money spent stealing and time, effort, and money spent protecting existing property. When there's lots of movable wealth and little protecting going on, it's more profitable on the margin to steal than to produce, but the presence of such stealing might also make it profitable to invest some resources in protecting your existing property rather than *either* producing *or* stealing. When the anticipated return from an extra day's stealing is less than the amount of your existing wealth that you can expect to prevent from being stolen by investing the same time in protective efforts, you protect more; when producing is the more remunerative activity, you produce; and so on.

Unfortunately, if people decide between producing, stealing, and guarding on the basis of financial returns only, then society will be far less productive than it could be had it been possible to equip them with moral scruples. If, for instance, only eighty percent of all time and other resources are used for production, five percent for theft, and fifteen percent for protection from theft, then total production might be twenty percent less than it could be if there were no theft and if all resources were used for production. In fact, output might rise by even more than twenty percent if there were no theft, since another alternative use of time is leisure, and with more certainty of keeping what you produce, your willingness to expend productive effort might increase. (I'll argue later that the level of theft and the cost of protecting against it are probably both lower than would be the case in a world with zero moral scruples, but the reasons are related to the more complex human nature to be introduced in later chapters.)

Slavery, human trafficking, and sexual violence

Although recognition and low-cost enforcement of property rights is seen as critical to a well-functioning modern economy, since the nineteenth century there have been concerted attempts by governments to outlaw one form of property once widely condoned: the ownership of one human being by another. Historically, people often became the saleable and acknowledged property of others as members of a conquered tribe or nation, as punishment for a crime or simply for belonging to a group viewed as inferior and suitable for enslavement. Though not as common as serfdom, a heritable status that entailed obligations of unpaid labor but left certain rights to the serf, slavery existed in Europe throughout the Middle Ages, the term "slave" actually being derived from the same root as "Slav" because Slavic-speaking areas were major sources of slaves in some periods. African slaves were common fixtures in Arabia during the same era. In earlier times, slavery was common in the ancient world, and more recently, it was found to exist among numerous pre-state peoples upon contact by Europeans in the eighteenth and nineteenth centuries.

As noted in the Preface, formal abolition of slavery during the nineteenth and twentieth centuries has not prevented its perpetuation in various forms. A US State Department report in 2005 estimated that "600,000 to 820,000 men, women, and children are trafficked across international borders each year, approximately eighty percent [being] women and girls and up to fifty percent [being] minors." The United Nations put the number trafficked at more than two million but also put the proportion of women at eighty percent. Both the State Department and the UN agreed that the majority of transnational victims are trafficked into "commercial sexual exploitation," but a wide variety of other uses are also documented. Figures on trafficking across borders leave out what might be hundreds of thousands of girls sold into prostitution by their own destitute families in countries including India, Thailand, and the Philippines. This exploitation cannot be laid exclusively at the doorstep of Japanese or Australian "sex tourists" in notorious destinations like Bangkok. In their powerful book *Half the Sky*, journalists Nicholas Kristof and Sheryl WuDunn report a conversation with an Indian border monitor in which Kristof asks whether the best way to meet the needs of young Indian men who wait until thirty to marry is "to kidnap Nepali girls and imprison them in Indian brothels." The officer agrees that "it's unfortunate" but offers a justification: "These girls are sacrificed so that we can have harmony in society. So that good girls can be safe." An estimated forty thousand prostitutes are said to have come into Germany to meet the demand from spectators at the World Cup soccer games in June and July of 2006, adding to the country's registered four hundred thousand prostitutes. Many of the "visiting" prostitutes are assumed to have been women trafficked from Eastern Europe.

Trafficking aside, the coerced and semi-coerced use of other human beings for the satisfaction of sexual "needs" is one of the most ubiquitous examples of self-interest crossing the boundaries of aggression. In recent years, the United Nations has sought with mixed success to prevent peacekeepers and aid workers from abusing their control over scarce food and medicines to barter for sex from local girls. Even in an ostensibly rich and modern nation like the United States, a 2010 telephone survey of more than nine thousand women analyzed by the Centers for Disease Control and the National Center for Injury Prevention and Control found that almost one in five had been raped at some time in their lives.[11]

Power, terror, and other horrors

Most people who live in countries with democratic political systems tend towards the hopeful view that government is at least sometimes a means of improving social welfare and curbing the evils that can be unleashed by selfishness run amuck. The seventeenth century English philosopher, Thomas Hobbes, argued that government is created by the people to protect them from one another's predations. Without it, there's chaos as each pursues his own interest in disregard not only of the possessions but also the lives and limbs of others. Life is "nasty, brutish, and short." With it, people can live in security, each pursuing his interests without fear of unpunished attack by others.

Historically, though, there are few examples of societies coming together and creating states by mutual consent. Many states of both the distant and recent past can be better understood as the creations of strongmen who imposed their will on a territory through the mastery of superior force, and governments responsive to their populations remain absent or incapable of exerting real control in some parts of the world today. Recent examples of political violence with or without the involvement of a government are not hard to find.

The Congo

The sad history of the region surrounding the Congo River, which collects the water falling on a vast expanse of central Africa and empties it into the Atlantic Ocean, provides a litany of examples of the concatenation of power and violence. In the 1480s, Portuguese merchants entered the mouth of the river and began trading with the people of the Kongo Kingdom for gold, ivory, and slaves captured up-country. While the Portuguese never attempted to rule the Congo, competition for control of the lucrative trade and an infusion of European firearms led to increasing political instability. As a result, the local people, many of whom had been ruled by the indigenous kingdoms of Kongo, Luba, and Lunda, were unable to mount a unified resistance when King Leopold of Belgium cobbled together hundreds of treaties that his hired agent, Henry M. Stanley, had secured with local chiefs.

In 1884, Leopold declared the vast river basin a personal holding, the "Congo Free State." With a few hundred European soldiers leading a force of several thousand Africans, Leopold's henchmen subdued local resistance and coerced the population into providing ivory and wild rubber through a variety of forced labor schemes. Untold numbers of people had hands or even heads lopped off to dissuade thoughts of rebellion. When the nature of Leopold's brutality was made sufficiently clear to the public in Europe and North America, the king was forced to turn the colony over to the Belgian government, which curbed its worst excesses but continued the exploitation of local resources with little investment in public welfare and next to no involvement of the population in the colony's administration.

Homegrown independence movements led by educated Congolese and the influence of nationalist agitation throughout French-speaking Africa led to Belgium's departure in 1960. There followed several years of struggle between competing political leaders. In 1965, a young army officer named Joseph Mobutu seized power over the Congo, a position he would hold for thirty-two years. Tolerated by the West as a bulwark against Communism, Mobutu exploited his country's vast reserves of copper, cobalt, and diamonds, freely pillaging the revenues generated until mining came to a virtual standstill due to the rampant corruption and the neglect of basic investment requirements. Although rumored to have stashed billions of dollars in foreign bank accounts, little of Mobutu's wealth could be accounted for upon his death, and it appeared possible that he had spent nearly all that he had stolen on lavish living, even as the annual per capita income of Congo's people fell from around one thousand dollars in 1965 to an estimated three hundred dollars in 1997.

Mobutu's ouster by a rebel army ushered in a new nightmare era in which armed conflict between competing militias and supporting external armies led to at least four million, and perhaps more than six million, deaths—about nine percent of the population. The carnage was due not only to combat, landmines, and massacres of civilians, but also to malnutrition and disease fostered by lawlessness and economic collapse, especially in eastern parts of the country. An untold number of women have been raped by soldiers and guerillas, leading a senior UN official to call the Congo "the rape capital of the world."[12] The life expectancy of Congolese, placed at about forty-six years circa 2010, was one of the lowest in the world.

Myanmar

According to the 2006 Human Rights Watch statement to the EU Development Committee, Burma, also known as Myanmar, "is the textbook example of a police state. Government informants and spies are omnipresent. ... [T]housands of student demonstrators were killed in 1988. ... [I]n 1990 [the] National League for Democracy [led by Aung San Suu Kyi, daughter of the country's independence leader] won eighty-two percent of the vote in a national election, after which the generals ... summarily threw [her] ... and thousands of others in jail." The International Labor Organization concluded that "forced labor continues to be a policy and practice of the military, with thousands forced to participate in money making schemes for the army." Human Rights Watch states further, "Torture continues to be routine in Burma. ... [R]ape has been documented as a political weapon. ... An estimated 70,000 of the country's 350,000–400,000 soldiers are children," many of them recruited by kidnapping. "Human rights abuses in the countryside are so rampant, and life is so hard ... that as many as four million of the country's fifty million people may be internally displaced. As many as two million Burmese may be living in Thailand, where they are exploited as cheap labor and live in constant fear of arrest and deportation, yet prefer a hard life in a foreign land to the abuses they left behind.

"Burma once was a leading post-colonial state, with a highly educated and literate population, excellent universities, and abundant natural resources. All of this has vanished under military rule. One in ten children does not live past his or her first birthday. HIV/AIDS is mushrooming. Malaria and tuberculosis are rampant. Demonstrating its indifference to the welfare of its people, more than fifty percent of the national budget goes to the military. ... While most Burmese live in abject poverty, the generals are wealthy. The number of Mercedes and BMWs in Rangoon is astonishing. Sumptuous meals are served to thousands in the elite at fancy hotels. The money to support this lifestyle comes from legal foreign direct investment, much of it from EU countries, and illicit businesses, such as those documented by 'Global Witness' in its most recent report about the devouring of Burma's forests."

"Human rights are bourgeois"

Some of the worst examples of the human ability to treat individuals as means and to display indifference to their suffering have been ones associated with civil wars and struggles to control illicit drug and gem trades in poor regions of Latin America, Africa, and Asia. While appropriating the classical rhetoric of leftist guerrilla war, groups like the FARC in Colombia and the Sendero Luminoso ("Shining Path") in Peru have developed the drug trafficking profiles of criminal cartels and have been guilty of atrocities as cruel or crueler than those of their pro-government and paramilitary adversaries. In its 2006 report on Colombia, for example, Human Rights Watch reported that the FARC continued to engage in kidnappings, killings, "indiscriminate bombings," use of anti-personnel land-mines, "which result in hundreds of civilian injuries and deaths every year," and the recruitment of child soldiers, including several thousand under the age of fifteen (the minimum recruitment age permitted under the Geneva Conventions).

In an article titled "The Evils of Ideology" appearing in the *New English Review* and *FrontPage Magazine*, writer Theodore Dalrymple wrote, "The worst brutality I ever saw was that committed by Sendero Luminoso ... in Peru, in the days when it seemed possible that it might come to power. If it had, I think its massacres would have dwarfed those of the Khmer Rouge. As a doctor, I am accustomed to unpleasant sights, but nothing prepared me for what I saw in Ayacuccho, where Sendero first developed under the sway of a professor of philosophy, Abimael Guzman. I took photographs of what I saw, but the newspapers deemed them too disturbing to be printed." Sendero leaders had no difficulty justifying their behaviors with ideology. One of their documents stated: 'Our position is very clear. We reject and condemn human rights because they are bourgeois, reactionary, counterrevolutionary rights, and are today a weapon of revisionists and imperialists, principally Yankee imperialists.'[13]

I killed him for nothing

In post-Cold War Africa, diamonds and other resources have financed guerrilla movements that have controlled large areas through terrifying brutality. In Liberia, Sierra Leone, and Angola in the 1990s, and in Uganda since the late 1980s, armed groups have inflicted unspeakable suffering by pressing children into their ranks, hacking off the limbs and breasts of victims, raping women, and committing wanton killings. In a 1997 Human Rights Watch report, *The Scars of Death*, Ugandan children who had escaped rebel captivity recorded their experiences:

> One boy tried to escape, but he was caught. . . . His hands were tied, and then they made us, the other new captives, kill him with a stick. I felt sick . . . I refused to kill him [but] they pointed a gun at me, so I had to do it. The boy was asking me, "Why are you doing this?" I said I had no choice. After we killed him, they made us smear his blood on our arms. . . . They said we had to do this so we would not fear death and so we would not try to escape. I still dream about the boy I killed. I see him in my dreams, and he is talking to me and saying I killed him for nothing, and I am crying.

We see a spark of humanity in this child's description of self-torment over his participation in a senseless killing. But there are situations in which the remnants of humanity and sympathy, too, seem stretched beyond their limits. In *The Devil's Gardens: A History of Landmines*, Lydia Monin and Andrew Gallimore describe cases in which family members themselves are unable to muster sympathy for innocent victims of conflict. "Victims in developing countries who can't shake off their depression don't find much sympathy because they are surrounded by people who face a daily battle to survive anyway." They quote Canadian-born journalist Michael Ignatieff, after extensive reporting from mine-affected regions, as saying that "[amputation] is...a very different thing in a poor and destitute [country] than it is in a Western one....A woman without a leg is human refuse in patriarchal societies...and that's a differential that prosthetic limb fitting can only partially compensate for." [14]

Conclusion

The examples of aggression and cruelty just reviewed make you yearn for the polite self-interest of the marketplace, where the seller's only sin is seeking a price more to his own advantage than to the buyer's, and *visa versa*. Added to our accounts of the normal operation of business, of competition for mates and school places, of immigration, lemons, and "the new socialist man," these less constrained examples of malice seem to clinch the argument that human benevolence is an illusion and that unalloyed selfishness lies at the core of human nature.

But the fact that we needed to look to cases of extreme lawlessness and social stress to find so many acting so badly might be a clue that human nature is not so one-sided. The very extremeness of these examples suggests that selfishness is commonly kept within more circumscribed bounds by various social norms and countervailing inclinations. Even in the most hellish stories, there were some glimmers of humanity, for instance public opinion forcing Leopold to relax his personal hold on the Congo and the child's sense of wrong over the killing he was forced engage in.

In Chapter 5, I'll attempt to set out a more balanced view of human nature that allows for a clear-eyed, but not entirely pessimistic, appraisal of the difficulty of building a better world. To be fair, though, let's first give human goodness the same chance to shine as selfishness and malevolence were given to dim the pages of this chapter. Come with me, now, to see whether we can spot what Lincoln may have had in mind when he closed his first inaugural address with the phrase "the better angels of our nature."

Notes:

1. Estimates by the International Organization for Migration (IOM), an intergovernmental organization that works with most UN member states. The information appeared on the IOM's website in mid-2007.

2. *Proceedings of the Royal Society, Biological Sciences* 266 (1999): 281–5.

3. See Raymond Fisman et al., "Gender Differences in Mate Selection: Evidence form a Speed Dating Experiment," *Quarterly Journal of Economics* 121, no. 2 (May 2006) 673-697 and Gunter Hitsch, Ali Hortacsu, and Dan Ariely, "What Makes You Click?—Mate Preferences in Online Dating," *Quantitative Marketing and Economics* 8, no. 4 (2010): 393-427.

4. Feng Hou and John Myles, "The Changing Role of Education in the Marriage Market: Assortative Marriage in Canada and the United States since the 1970s," Analytical Studies Branch Research Paper Series, *Statistics Canada* (May 2007).

5. Philip Starks and Caroline Blackie, "The Relationship between Serial Monogamy and Rape in the United States (1960–1995)," *Proceedings of the Royal Society, Biological Sciences* 267 (1999): 1259–63. Note that the explanatory rubric of evolutionary psychology *doesn't* imply that the perpetrators aren't culpable for their actions. For a valuable discussion of the relationship between genetic predisposition and moral responsibility, see Steven Pinker, *The Blank Slate: The Modern Denial of Human Nature* (London: Penguin Books, 2002).

6. This and related evidence is reported in Richard Easterlin, "Will raising the incomes of all increase the happiness of all?" *Journal of Economic Behavior and Organization* 27 (1995): 5–47.

7. From a study by Cantril, 1965, cited in Chapter 10 of Richard Easterlin, *Growth Triumphant: The Twenty-first Century in Historical Perspective* (Ann Arbor: University of Michigan Press, 1996).

8. While the first figure is based on census data (U.S. Census Bureau, *2007 Statistical Abstract*, Table 674, Money Income of Households: 2004), the second is an approximation that should hold well enough for our purposes. Precise data for bands of their width are harder to come by in this range.

9. Frank, *Richistan: A Journey Through the American Wealth Boom and the Lives of the New Rich* (New York: Crown Publishers, 2007), 50.

10. In this case, the estimate is for 2003.

11. M. C. Black et al., *The National Intimate Partner and Sexual Violence Survey: 2010 Summary Report* (Atlanta: Center for Injury Prevention and Control, Centers for Disease Control and Prevention, 2011).

12. Margot Wallstrom, UN special representative on sexual violence in conflict, quoted by BBC News, April 28, 2010.

13. Communist Party of Peru, "Sobre las Dos Colinas" Part 5. http://en.wikipedia.org/wiki/Shining_Path.

14. Both quotes are from Lydia Monin and Andrew Gallimore, *The Devil's Gardens: A History of Landmines* (North Pomfret, VT: Pimlico, distributed by Trafalgar Square, 2002) 107.

CHAPTER 4
"The Better Angels of Our Nature"

We opened the last chapter with Adam Smith's famous remark about the self-interest of the butcher, baker, and brewer. It's fitting to open this one, then, by noting that Smith stopped well short of contending that selfishness is the *only* element in people's nature. Quite the contrary, in *The Theory of Moral Sentiments* (1759) he wrote: "How selfish soever man may be supposed, there are evidently some principles in his nature, which interest him in the fortune of others, and render their happiness necessary to him, though he derives nothing from it except the pleasure of seeing it. Of this kind is pity or compassion, the emotion which we feel for the misery of others, when we either see it, or are made to conceive it in a very lively manner. That we often derive sorrow from the sorrow of others, is a matter of fact too obvious to require any instances to prove it; for this sentiment, like all the other original passions of human nature, is by no means confined to the virtuous and humane, though they perhaps may feel it with the most exquisite sensibility. The greatest ruffian, the most hardened violator of the laws of society, is not altogether without it."

Rising to the occasion
On the morning of March 2, 2005, a forty-five-year-old sales manager named Anthony Blaskoski left his home in a suburban subdivision in Elburn, Illinois, to drive to work. Not far from home, he realized that he'd forgotten his cell phone and turned his car around. When he left his house for the second time, he noticed dark smoke coming from another part of his development and drove out of his way to investigate. Arriving on the scene, he found a woman whom he'd never met standing outside of her burning house. When she told him that her husband and daughter were still in the house, he phoned 911 on his cell phone, handed the phone to the woman, and entered the house to look for them. Unable to see anything and choking for air from the thick black smoke, he came out to catch his breath, then reentered the house from a different door. After a short time, he came upon the foot of an adult man and began trying to pull him to safety, but the man

could not be moved easily, and Blaskoski needed to catch his breath again. "The smoke was so black, you could not see your hand in front of your face," he later said. "You really, really couldn't breathe." After stepping out for another breath of air, Blaskoski plunged back into the house, going directly to the spot where he'd found the leg, which turned out to be that of one William Gunderson. He was able to pull Gunderson out and administer CPR, but since no rescue workers had yet arrived, he went back into the house again to look for the Gundersons' five-year-old daughter. Unfortunately, he couldn't reach her. When firefighters arrived, they found the little girl in a closet on the second floor. She died a day later. Blaskoski himself was taken to the hospital to be treated for smoke inhalation and an injured shoulder.

The Gundersons lived a mile and a half from Blaskoski, and he had never met them. What made him risk his life to try to save two people whom he'd never met? "It's just acting on instinct," he explained when a reporter asked him. "You find out someone is in danger or hurt and you think, 'What can I go do?'" How many people would do what Blaskoski did? Probably not many. The Carnegie Hero Fund Commission of Pittsburgh awarded Blaskoski one of about one hundred hero awards it gives out every year to "civilian[s] who voluntarily" risk their lives "knowingly, to an extraordinary degree while saving or attempting to save the life of another person."

The fact that such an award was conferred implies that Blaskoski's behavior wasn't commonplace, though it is neither unique nor necessarily the most impressive example of its kind. While this chapter was being written, a twenty year old from the ex-urban community of Harvard, Massachusetts (not far from where I live), suffered an apparent seizure and fell onto the subway tracks at the 137th Street Station in New York City as a train approached and as horrified people looked on. In the wink of an eye, a fifty-year-old construction worker named Wesley Autrey leapt to the tracks, placed his body on top of the younger man's, and pressed him into the trough between the tracks, with perhaps two inches of clearance as the train passed over them. The action seems unbelievable enough without commenting that Autrey, a black American living in Harlem, had left his own four- and six-year-old daughters on the platform to perform this feat and that he risked his life for a perfect stranger who was white and affluent. When deluged with offers of rewards and invitations to appear on television interview programs, Autrey kept things in perspective, remarking in a low-key manner, "I'm going to take these fifteen minutes of fame and run with it."

Even when mankind's dark side is most ascendant, isolated acts of compassion and moral bravery sometimes break out. In the spring of 1994, the plane carrying the president of Rwanda back from Hutu-Tutsi peace negotiations in neighboring Tanzania was shot down as it returned to the country's capital, and extremist Hutu leaders signaled their militias to begin attacking and killing members of the country's Tutsi minority. The modest UN peacekeeping force stationed in the country was overwhelmed and ordered by UN headquarters to withdraw, leaving only a small number of observers. As the violence that would end up taking the lives of at least eight hundred thousand Rwandans escalated, a Senegalese member of the UN observation team, Mbaye Diagne, ignored orders to avoid intervening. Carrying out a series of independent rescue missions, he managed to save the lives of hundreds of Rwandans. Nothing could deter him from his efforts until one day, as he drove back from one of his outings towards UN headquarters in Kigali, his jeep was hit by a mortar shell, taking his life.

Some Rwandan Hutus also undertook to save Tutsis, as well as moderate Hutus whom the militias were targeting for being "too weak." The most famous Rwandan rescuer is the hotel manager Paul Rusesabagina, whose bravery in saving more than 1200 Tutsis and moderate Hutus within the walls of his hotel by bribing Hutu soldiers, petitioning local officials, and repeatedly risking his safety is depicted in the 2004 movie *Hotel Rwanda*. But others also did what they could to save people.

Damas Gisimba was the director of an orphanage in Kigali that housed sixty orphans at the time the genocide began. He turned it into a shelter for roughly four hundred people, risking his life repeatedly by refusing to allow militias to enter. When he realized he could no longer keep the militias away, he risked his safety by attempting to win protection of the orphanage by government officials, despite their own complicity in the genocide. With the help of an American aid worker who had himself refused to evacuate when almost all other foreigners left Rwanda, Gisimba succeeded in getting those sheltered at the orphanage evacuated to a more secure location, where they waited out the remaining months of violence safe from harm. On a smaller scale, a sixty-seven-year-old widowed Rwandan midwife named Therese Nyirabayovu prevailed upon her children to help her hide eighteen people who were being sought by the militias. Together, Nyirabayovu and her family stood up to repeated searches, questioning, and the throwing of a grenade at their house.

When the Israeli memorial to the Holocaust, Yad Vashem, asked survivors to provide documentation of individuals who had incurred significant personal risk to help prospective victims of Hitler's extermination camps to escape their fates, it received verifiable reports not only about a few now well-known heroes, such as Oskar Schindler and Raoul Wallenberg, but about more than twenty-three *thousand* other named individuals, including more than 6,000 Polish, 5,000 Dutch, 3,000 French, 2,000 Ukrainian, and 1,500 Belgian citizens.

Common helpfulness is often the norm

Finding thousands of righteous souls in the midst of an evil of such magnitude is encouraging. But people don't have to risk their lives to cast doubt on the assumption that we humans are selfish from head to toe. The fact of the matter is that the inclination to help rather than harm isn't difficult to document on average days in everyday lives. A motorist arriving from a side street hoping to enter a line of traffic that continues without break is offered a way in with a wave from a sympathetic driver he's never met. A man holds a door open for a mother accompanied by small children, an individual carrying packages, or an elderly person.

A traveler who'll never return to a restaurant tips a waitress. A cashier smiles in a more-than-perfunctory way, wishing you a nice day far out of earshot of her supervisor. A customer offers a cheerful or sympathetic expression to a cashier, who looks beat from her long, boring day.

In fact, the notion that people always and exclusively pursue their own interests can be countered by almost any example of strangers helping or simply desisting from doing harm to other strangers. When we ask someone if they can tell us the time or point us towards a particular destination, we routinely assume that whatever time or direction they respond with will reflect their best knowledge of the matter. But what incentive do they have to be truthful? Citing such examples, the economist Amartya Sen argued that traditional economics takes the notion of self-interest to absurd lengths. Sen challenged readers to ask themselves whether the following interaction seems to be a good depiction of ordinary life:

> Two strangers encounter one another on a city street. One is looking for a train station where he has a train to catch. The other is walking the few blocks he needs to go in order to mail a letter. "Where is the railway station?" the first asks. "There," responds the second, pointing at the post office, "and would you please post this letter for me on the

way?" "Yes," the second says agreeably, but determined to open the envelope and check whether it contains something valuable as soon as he is out of the first one's sight.[1]

To be sure, just how confident people feel of their ability to trust strangers varies from one society to another. A survey carried out among thousands of respondents in dozens of countries asks the question: "Generally speaking, would you say that most people can be trusted or that you need to be very careful in dealing with people?" The respondent is asked to choose between two answers only: either "Most people can be trusted" or "You can never be too careful when dealing with others." In a recent administration of this survey in the United States, almost seventy-nine percent of respondents chose "Most people can be trusted." When the same question was asked in Mexico, only forty-two percent chose the trusting response.[2] We'll want to look, later, at what might account for the very different levels of trust exhibited in these different countries. For now, the point is that in a large number of societies, considerable numbers of people feel that the default inclination of others whom they encounter is to share an honest set of directions, tell the right time, and perhaps even watch your package for a minute if they promise to do so. It's quite reasonable to assume that these perceptions reflect everyday experiences that run counter to the most extreme form of a doctrine of strictly self-serving behavior.

That warm feeling in your chest

One afternoon in 1996, a woman and her daughter were enjoying watching a football game in which the girl's older brother was playing when the girl suddenly complained of feeling ill. By the time the mother had driven the girl, who had until that moment seemed to be a healthy eight years old, to the local emergency room, she had gone into acute liver failure.

Hours later, with the girl unconscious and kept alive on life support, the parents, who hadn't even imagined the crisis the previous evening, realized that her situation was hopeless and thought to ask themselves what good could come from their tragedy. They asked their pediatrician whether some of her still healthy organs could help other children. Within days, half a dozen others had been given new leases on life thanks to the girl's heart, lungs, and kidneys and "new eyes to see" thanks to her corneas.

Even more significant for our quest to understand human nature than the parents' altruistic thoughts in the midst of their tragedy may be the way that others reacted to it. Years later, after more than twenty-four years in his practice, the young girl's pediatrician was asked by his own daughter what had been the most memorable moments in his career. He then told her of the incident, his eyes welling up with tears. It wasn't so much his patient's death that had stuck him, he said, as it was the parents' wish to give the "gift of life" to others in their own moment of tragedy. The story's power to touch an emotional chord struck radio producers, who broadcast the daughter-father interview on public radio, touching the emotions of tens of thousands of listeners as they prepared their dinners or drove home from work.[3]

How are we to reconcile the human capacity for kindness and the human tendency to be moved by stories of unusually kind deeds with the conception of human beings as strictly self-interested calculators of their own advantage? Don't even try, Adam Smith would have said; the purely selfish depiction is a hopeless caricature. "How selfish soever man may be supposed, there are evidently some principles in his nature, which interest him in the fortune of others."

A University of Virginia psychologist, Jonathan Haidt, showed a short film about Mother Teresa to one group of experiment subjects and short comedies or documentaries about less emotionally engrossing topics to other subjects. He found that many of the subjects shown the Mother Teresa film expressed a sense of awe and inspiration and a desire to help others and that significantly more of the subjects in "the Mother Teresa treatment" subsequently volunteered to work at a humanitarian charity organization.

Haidt argues from this and other evidence that there's a universal human emotion, which he calls "elevation," that's a response to "inspiring beauty of human action or character" and that manifests itself in every culture. Just as there are universal physiological signs of anger, sadness, and other emotions identified by scientists who study the association of such emotions with specific facial muscles, posture, and heart rate, so, Haidt says, there are distinct signs associated with "elevation," including a warm feeling in one's chest.

Haidt situates his work in a field called "positive psychology," which has among its goals "to bring about a balanced reappraisal of human nature and human potential." He writes, "We can grant that people are capable of perpetrating great cruelty upon one another, but we must also grant, and study, the ways in which people are good, kind, and compassionate towards one another."[4] In a book entitled *Born to be Good*, a University of California at Berkeley psychologist, Dacher Keltner, argues similarly that positive emotional engagement with others, including empathetic and helping behaviors, measurably enhances the individual's health and emotional well-being, a sign that evolution favored such social tendencies due to their survival value in ancestral times.

In another study, Haidt asked his subjects to write about the bodily changes, thoughts, and action tendencies or motivations produced by any of five possible situations, of which one was "a specific time when you saw a manifestation of humanity's 'higher' or 'better' nature."

Most often, respondents who chose this situation wrote of a time when they saw someone give help to an individual who was poor, sick, or stuck in a difficult situation. One story involved seeing a young man ask to be let out of a group car ride without explaining why and then help an elderly woman he had just noticed by the roadside shoveling snow from her driveway.

Another individual described being moved by seeing many people come to visit and support his family while his grandfather was dying. He remembered these feelings after more than five years and cited them as having influenced his decision to become a doctor.

Nice work if you can get it

The example of the young man deciding to become a doctor after being inspired by others' caring suggests that we may want to take a look at occupational choice as one way of investigating the impact of principles besides "self-love" on the way in which people conduct themselves. Earning a living may be a necessity, and that's undoubtedly the principal motivator of work for most people, but many who get satisfaction or pleasure from interacting with others or helping others find ways to blend making a living with meeting those other needs. Probably, you yourself can think of at least one person in your extended family or circle of acquaintances who chose their occupation, or who gave up one line of work for another, with such aims in mind. A computer programmer who becomes a pediatric nurse, an investment analyst who switches to studying social psychology, a stockbroker who becomes an elementary school teacher—one knows of such stories, but just how exceptional are such instances of social motivation influencing work choices?

One way to make a start on answering this question is to look at the World Values Survey, an international study of social attitudes from which comes the measure of trust attitudes in the US and Mexico that we mentioned above. Begun by University of Michigan Sociologist Ronald Inglehart in 1981, by 2005 the World Values Survey team conducted interviews with 92,000 respondents in sixty-two countries representing every major region of the world. Answers to one of the questions included in the year 2000 surveys conducted shed light on what people care about most in their choice of occupation. The interviewers asked: "Now I would like to ask you something about the things which would seem to you, personally, most important if you were looking for a job. Here are some of the things many people take into account in relation to their work. Regardless of whether you're actually looking for a job, which one would you, personally, place first if you were looking for a job?" They also asked "Which would you place second?" The main alternatives offered were: (a) a good income, (b) a safe job with no risk, (c) working with people you like, and (d) doing important work. Although the answers have large subjective components and don't tell us, for instance, just how much pay or job security a person would sacrifice for more of the alternative attribute in question, the way the answers vary from country to country, between women and men, by income, and by education level, are suggestive.

In the US and Canada, forty-four percent of women and forty-one percent of men listed doing important work (option d) as the factor most important to them, while in a group of Latin American countries (Argentina, Chile, Mexico, Peru, Venezuela, and the US-linked commonwealth of Puerto Rico), the corresponding shares choosing (d) were twenty-three percent and twenty-four percent, and in a set of African countries (Niger, Tanzania, Uganda, and Zimbabwe), they were ten percent and eleven percent. Together, choices (c) and (d) (working with people you like and doing important work) accounted for about fifty-eight percent of first answers for women and fifty-four percent of first answers for men in the United States and Canada versus thirty percent and thirty-two percent in the Latin American countries and thirteen percent and fourteen percent in the African ones. Since the US and Canada have high incomes (averaging about $42,000 per person in 2010), the listed Latin American countries have middle incomes (averaging a little under $13,000 in that year), and the African countries have very low incomes (averaging less than $1,000), a conjecture that springs to mind is that as more of a country's people live safely above the threshold of economic survival, a larger proportion of them can indulge, or at least think of indulging, tastes for work that they find satisfying or meaningful, not simply remunerative and secure.

The responses also suggest that in countries in which people are least hard-pressed by economic necessity, women tend to value the social (and societal) dimensions of work more than men do. This follows not only from the US and Canadian numbers, but also from European responses: in a set of five high income European countries (Germany, Finland, Norway, Sweden, and the UK), forty-six percent of women listed either option (c) or option (d) first, whereas only thirty-nine percent of men did so.[5] But in sub-Saharan Africa, where women are often principal breadwinners and are more likely to be economically subordinated to their husbands, it was the men who in larger numbers chose the non-economic responses, though the difference is small.

The idea that "liberation from economic necessity" might increase the weight given to factors other than financial compensation is also supported by grouping respondents by income class. Among the American and Canadian respondents, those in the bottom fifth of the population by income had only about a thirty-three percent chance of listing "doing important work" as their principal consideration, while those in the top fifth listed it about fifty percent of the time. Similarly, for the Latin American respondents, around eighteen percent of those in the bottom fifth by income prioritized "doing important work," while as many as forty-three percent of people in the top ten percent of income earners did so.

The effect of education resembles that of income, probably in part because it helps to determine income but possibly also for other reasons. Looking only at those with university degrees, we find that fifty-seven percent in the United States and Canada, fifty percent in the high-income European countries, and forty percent in the Latin American countries listed "doing important work" as their first concern. In contrast, among those who began but didn't complete secondary school, forty-seven percent in the US, twenty-seven percent in the European countries, and twenty-three percent in the Latin American ones listed this factor first. In Latin America, just fifteen percent of those with a primary school education only and just thirteen percent of those with no formal education reported "doing important work" to be a priority.

We can't be certain that these responses reflect what those surveyed really believe or would act upon as opposed to what they thought would make a favorable impression on the interviewer. But if there's enough truth in the responses, and if the differences among countries are indeed due more to income and education than to culture, then the answers given to the interviewers can be seen as strongly suggesting that a substantial proportion of people, possibly the majority, consider socially meaningful and socially connected work to be highly desirable when not in conflict with basic economic survival. Some people may always be attracted to whatever activity they can earn the most in, but increasing numbers may be looking for ways to contribute to society, to express or develop their interests, and to interact with others in the course of their workdays, even if it means earning less.

The wages of virtue

Some jobs appeal more than others do to those seeking to help people or to find work meaningful to them in other ways. A study conducted at Harvard's Graduate School of Education found a large gap in earnings between teachers and those with the same level of education working in non-teaching jobs. In 1998, twenty-two- to twenty-eight-year-old teachers in their sample holding bachelor's degrees earned an average of $21,792, which was twenty-seven percent less than peers in non-teaching fields. Asked to explain why they chose teaching over other professions, none of the teachers interviewed for the study mentioned salary or financial rewards; instead "they talked about the value of meaningful work, the appeal of working with children, and the enjoyment of pedagogy and subject matter." A twenty-three-year-old elementary school teacher stated, "I feel like I'm really giving something. I feel like what I do is important, which is important to me." A thirty-three-year-old elementary school teacher, who'd left her previous job as an accountant, explained her choice by saying, "I need to enjoy what I'm doing. I need to feel useful. It seems to fulfill all of my needs, and I hope I'm doing the same for the kids." A male teacher who left a career as an industrial chemist said teaching gave him "the personal reward of doing something good." A high school teacher said, "I need to be doing something that involves working with people. I wouldn't be happy doing anything that didn't."[6]

Pure research is another field in which motivations other than the financial can play a part in occupational choice. The enjoyment of learning, teaching, and, in the some cases, the hope of contributing something more to society draws tens of thousands to study for advanced degrees so as to enter teaching and research in universities and research institutes instead of more lucrative careers. In his paper titled *Do Scientists Pay to be Scientists?*, the economist and management professor, Scott Stern, identified a large set of research scientists who'd chosen lower-wage jobs in research organizations that permit employees to pursue and publish their own research on topics of their choice, even though they'd been offered higher-paying jobs in more commercially oriented research organizations that dictate research topics and control the output. On average, the pure research jobs paid twenty-five percent less, leading Stern to conclude that scientists are indeed willing to pay for the privilege of doing pure science.

Even the decision to enter the academic field of economics, which analyzes most decision-making from the standpoint of self-interest, reflects a voluntary surrender of potentially higher earnings for the sake of the autonomy and perhaps a social contribution from research and teaching. Although market competition has driven the salaries of those teaching in university economics departments above the salaries of counterparts in other social science and humanities disciplines, many teaching economists seem to reveal, by way of their job choice, a preference for earning forty or fifty percent less for the privilege of training Ph.D. students in an academic economics department, instead of earning higher pay for teaching MBA students in a business school or working for an investment bank. Students of economics professors entering successful careers in banking and finance, where Ph.D.s are not required, frequently end up earning many times more than what their former teachers are paid.

Economists who study labor markets recognize that job compensation may consist not only of wages and of benefits like health insurance, but also of desired job characteristics, such as work that's more challenging, that allows more autonomy, and so on. According to the theory of "compensating wage differentials," we should expect that, comparing two workers with similar education and other characteristics, the one who accepts a more dangerous, boring, or otherwise undesirable job receives higher monetary compensation, while the one who takes a more pleasant or satisfying job receives lower pay since some of her compensation takes the form of safety, interest, pleasantness, or job satisfaction. In one early study of the issue, economist Alan Matthios wrote: "Nonmonetary factors are likely to be an important part of total compensation for many jobs. Nurses, for example, often explain how the rewards from helping others help to compensate them for their hard work."

Matthios studied data on 652 less-educated and 785 more-educated individuals who were asked to state whether any of eighteen nonmonetary factors helped to explain why they took their current job and which of these factors was the most important. The factors included "represented a challenge," "liked that kind of work," "status," "chance to help others," and "convenient hours." Consistent with compensating differentials theory, Matthios found that pay was better explained by considering *both* standard factors like education and gender *and* non-pecuniary factors like "challenge" and "chance to help others." Specifically, to explain what determines how high or low a given worker's money earnings are, he used the statistical method of multivariate regression analysis and found that less than a quarter of the variation of wages in his sample could be explained by factors like education and gender, whereas about a third of that variation, or an additional nine percent, could be explained when the nonmonetary factors ("challenge," "chance to help," etc.) are also accounted for. Although explaining only a third of the differences in earnings might seem unimpressive, it is in fact quite respectable in studies of this kind, since many factors that might be important, including intensity of effort and realized skill as opposed to educational credentials, are missing from the available data.

In discussing the World Values Survey data of various countries, I noted that more-educated individuals seem to attach more importance to intangible aspects of work. Matthios also found support for this proposition from the data in his study. Moreover, he found that the item "chance to help others" was statistically one of the most significant nonmonetary factors at work. By his estimate, workers who reported "chance to help others" to be an important factor in their choice of jobs were earning an average of three percent, or in dollar terms $641, less than otherwise comparable workers.[7] A critic of markets might point to this as proof that "capitalism punishes those with good intentions." Maybe so, but the point for present purposes is that the study's findings indicate that many are willing to sacrifice money for the opportunity to help others, a fact clearly at odds with the assumption that self-interest is the one and only real human motive.

Parents, beware!

America's colleges and universities, while well supplied with students laying the groundwork for careers in business, finance, and high tech, are also full of young people hoping to play their part in saving the planet, alleviating Third World poverty, eliminating discrimination, and other noble causes. Many of those who chose to study law or medicine or to enter into scientific research also cite a desire to help people or society as important motivators. The danger that children sent off to college for forty thousand dollars a year might forsake more remunerative paths for alternatives that appeal to their idealism is a real one, and before paying their first tuition bills, parents should perhaps be warned that many of the best universities will actually *help* their kids to find their way into careers in social entrepreneurship, social service, and social change. Harvard has a Center for Public Interest Careers, Brown has a similar center, and its career services office, like those of Columbia, University of Pennsylvania, Cornell, Dartmouth, and other schools, offers information about "Careers for the Common Good," including access to websites like www.idealist.org.

It's not true that idealists fail to find employment, but it does seem that they pay a price.

For example, the University of Pennsylvania's career services office reported that 2006 graduates who had found employment reported an average salary of a little more than $46,000, varying from an average of less than $32,000 for those choosing jobs in the not-for-profit, social service, and health sectors to more than $55,000 for those finding work in the financial services sector. While fully fifty percent of employed graduates had taken jobs in the high-paying financial services or consulting sectors—average salary $54,797—twelve percent went into nonprofit, social service, and health; twelve percent went into teaching (average salary $35,292); and four percent went into government (average salary $33,750). Twenty-eight percent of the school's graduates took jobs that earned them more than a third, or about $20,000, less than their fellow students. Similar numbers—spun less controversially, of course—were reported on the career service websites of Princeton, Cornell, and other elite schools.

Even students who choose more traditional and lucrative career paths aren't necessarily devoid of social concerns. A May 2006 article in *The Lawyer* stated: "Many study law because they have a strong interest in justice, including social justice. Many also have a strong sense of community and want to be able to give something back." Accordingly, involving young attorneys in *pro bono* work is considered a good way for law firms to attract and keep good attorneys! A 1985 survey of motivations for choosing a career in law, conducted for the American Bar Association, concluded: "A concern for social justice and a long-standing desire to be a lawyer were the dominant motivations, followed by financial considerations and job security." There are Legal Aid Societies in numerous US cities and states in which lawyers donate their services to provide legal help to the indigent.

That's not to say that most practicing lawyers find it easy to maintain and exercise their earlier idealism. An article in the *Boston Globe* in January 2004 discussed "the progressive law movement" which, the article said, "posits human and spiritual values as an essential but ignored part of law practice." The article quoted a discouraged lawyer who said, "I chose this profession because I wanted to be of service to people and to our greater society. But I didn't feel the system I found myself in encouraged that. The whole environment was very toxic." Numerous organizations for lawyers have sprung up in response to such concerns, the article said.

A similar mix of "helping inclinations" with desires for financial and job security influences decisions to enter medicine. The website of the American Association of Medical Colleges advises students who are considering going to medical school to ask themselves four questions before making this career choice. The first two are: "Do I care deeply about other people, their problems, and their pain?" and "Do I enjoy helping people with my skills and knowledge?" A survey asking doctors why they choose medicine as a career included among its top eight reasons "the joy of helping and taking care of others." As with law, medical students and doctors with social justice concerns form numerous programs and organizations focusing on bringing care to underserved populations within both rich and poor nations, raising public awareness of the health consequences of war and pollution, and so on. Of course, many doctors, like lawyers, find it difficult to sustain their idealism once the financial and managerial problems of maintaining a busy practice in a complex environment set in.

Volunteering

In addition to their choice of paid work, many demonstrate concern for others by performing volunteer work. One of the most dramatic, as well as best-known, examples of professionals putting social values into practice is the organization Doctors Without Borders. At any given time in recent years, the organization has had more than four thousand volunteers and staff members from developed countries working in some seventy developing countries, including such dangerous and inhospitable environments as those of Somalia, western Sudan, and Chad. About a thousand of these volunteers are physicians who, instead of earning a six figure salary and working in a comfortable, sterile environment in a country with an average of one doctor per two to three *hundred* people, have signed on for six-month stints sleeping in adobe huts or tents, going without a hot shower or bath for weeks at a time, living amidst the unpredictability and danger of civil wars, and receiving a stipend no bigger than the salary of a supermarket check-out worker—all this to help out in places with a hundred times as many patients per doctor. Benefits include a guarantee to be airlifted out in a medical emergency, or, if necessary, to have one's remains repatriated. For this, some doctors, nurses, and other volunteers sign on again and again.

Doctors Without Borders isn't the only organization of its kind. In 1987, American doctors based in Boston, Massachusetts, established Partners in Health with initial projects to help the poor in Haiti. Within two decades, the group was carrying out health care work, also training and involving hundreds of local health care workers, in Haiti, Rwanda, Lesotho, Russia, and other countries. It played a leading role in bringing medical care to the million and a half Haitians displaced by the massive earthquake of January 2010. Over and above work with such high-profile organizations, thousands of doctors from the United States, Canada, and other wealthy countries volunteer weeks, months, or years of their careers to work in poor country settings under a wide variety of arrangements, including ones sponsored by religious organizations.

Right now, more than seven thousand American volunteers are serving in the Peace Corps in more than a hundred countries. They include recent graduates of the best US colleges and universities, but also mature adults (the average age of Peace Corps volunteers being twenty-eight). Some seventy thousand others are participating in various forms of service within the United States, in AmeriCorps. Both organizations pay living allowances and provide only a few modest benefits after service.

Much larger numbers of people volunteer their services regularly on a part-time basis. Recent surveys in the United States suggest that about twenty-eight percent of adults do some volunteer work in a typical year, helping to tutor or mentor children, collecting or distributing food, providing transportation, and engaging in fund-raising activities. Many do volunteer work in organizations that provide activities, values training, and mentoring to youth, including 4-H clubs, Boy Scouts, Girl Scouts, YMCA, YWCA, Big Brothers/Big Sisters, and youth sports leagues. Others are volunteer firemen or participate in the charitable and service activities of groups like the Elks, Kiwanis, Knights of Columbus, Rotary, Masons, and Shriners. While the median time volunteered was only fifty hours, about twenty-eight percent of those reporting some volunteer time contributed between one hundred and five hundred hours in the year in which they were surveyed. The organization Independent Sector estimated their combined work hours as being equivalent to about nine million full-time jobs.

Donating time to political campaigns and participating in elections provides still another example. True, individuals stand to benefit, at times, from the policies favored by the candidates for whom they work. But some people support candidates whose policy positions they believe are right, even though they aren't in their own private interest (for instance, some wealthy individuals who favor higher taxes on the rich). More important to gauging how selfishly people behave is the fact that according to traditional economic theory, rational and self-interested individuals would judge working for a political cause or candidate to be a waste of time because in a large country, state, or city with millions of voters, any one person's efforts have a negligible chance of changing the outcome. The individual will enjoy the benefit (or sting) of her candidate's victory (or loss) regardless of whether she involves herself in the campaign, so enjoying (or suffering) it while saving more time for other things is the only rational choice. The same analysis implies that no one will ever bother to vote, a fact we'll want to return to later on.

The point, for now, is that the people concerned would not be acting rationally if they were perfectly selfish yet went out and devoted hundreds of thousands of afternoons and weekends to making calls, knocking on doors, and handing out leaflets on behalf of the candidates and causes they support. The same applies to the millions who incur the cost to go to the polls and vote, including many in poor and politically unstable countries who devote hours, and sometimes even risk their lives, to participate in elections. The existence of genuine concern for causes and the presence of true public-spiritedness among significant numbers of people can make sense of these otherwise mysterious behaviors.

Far more unpaid time, of course, is devoted by parents to the care of their young children, and to other types of care among family members. Since altruism within the family is so much a part of the fabric of nature (as discussed further in the next chapter), such unpaid service, at least among genetically related individuals, might be set aside as not worth noting in an inventory of exceptions to the rule of self-interest. But the millions who care—sometimes for years—for a disabled spouse aren't as easily dismissed using this kind of logic. There probably isn't much of a genetic payoff to caring for elderly parents, either, as millions do today.

Also puzzling, from the standpoint of the self-interested "economic man" assumption, is the fact that millions of people in countries around the world actually raise as their own children who are not their biological offspring. In recent years, between one and two percent of children added to American families each year are genetically unrelated adoptees, with between a fifth and a half of these being adopted from other countries and substantial numbers being of different race (as defined in government statistics) from that of the parents. Similar levels of foreign adoption and interracial adoption occur in other high-income countries. In poor countries, where social and private insurance systems are weak to nonexistent, children are still viewed as a means of ensuring some care to a parent in old age. But why would strictly selfish people in much richer countries bring unrelated strangers—including helpless infants who need to be fed, bathed, clothed, and have diapers changed—into their homes?

Donating money

Apart from time, people contribute money to help others in need. Even after paying more than a quarter of their earnings in taxes, a non-negligible part of which go to fund assistance to the indigent, elderly, and disabled, some eighty-five to ninety percent of American households are estimated to make charitable donations in a typical year. In 2005, for example, the Giving USA Foundation estimated that a total of $199 billion was donated by private individuals, including a little under six billion donated to help the victims of the December 2004 Indian Ocean tsunami, the October 2005 Pakistan earthquake, and Hurricanes Rita and Katrina. The $199 billion figure works out to some $663 per person, or about two percent of total personal income, with some giving much larger and others smaller proportions.

Experts note that the impulse to give behaves in a maddeningly irrational fashion. Sympathy can be easily aroused by the image of a single needy child, while reports of millions of needy can fail to stir the emotions. Thus, psychologists found that people donated more money when told it was to help a very poor child in Mali named Rokia, whose photo was shown to them, than when told it would help some of the several million victims of famine in need of immediate relief in her country. This may remind Americans with longer memories of the saga of a child, "baby Jessica," who fell into a well near her home in Texas in 1987. Seven hundred thousand dollars was donated in short order by people riveted to their TV sets as rescuers worked for more than two days to free her.[8] But, however frustrating to those trying to raise funds for pressing needs, the fact that this widespread kernel of human empathy behaves so irrationally is clear evidence that the urge to help isn't just a matter of grandstanding or of calculated self-interest; rather, it's part of an empathetic quality that's hardwired into human nature.

For another example, consider again the hefty proportion of college students who, as noted a few pages back, were busy laying the groundwork for careers in business, finance, and the like. Oddly enough, quite a few of them attempt to "give back" once they've acquired some wealth. An immediate example is the billions of dollars that alumni donate to their old colleges and universities. Of course, a cynic can argue that such donations are exercises in ego gratification; they purchase prestige for the donor while perpetuating elitist institutions that can give out only so many entry tickets into an upper class lifestyle. But an objective appraisal would have to take into account the billions that go to providing financial aid to students from low-income families, to supporting medical education and research, and to making possible some of the world's best research in the sciences, social sciences, and humanities. Many billions are also donated annually to other nonprofit institutions, including hospitals, museums, cultural institutions, and community welfare organizations.

For a selfish world, "doing good" has a curious cachet sometimes. Consider the Livestrong yellow rubber wristbands Nike sells as a fundraising tool for the Lance Armstrong Foundation. Providing support to people with cancer, the bands acquired immense popularity among young people in many countries after their launch in 2004. So did the "(Red)" products, sold by companies like Apple Computer (red iPod) and The Gap in 2006, with proceeds going to the Global Fund to Fight AIDS, Tuberculosis, and Malaria. Obviously, companies like Nike and The Gap find participation in such campaigns both profitable in the short run and good for their images and thus profitable in the long run, as well. And most of those who purchase and sport the products are simply jumping on a bandwagon that allows them to project rectitude and hipness with a modest outlay of money.

It may in fact be impossible to prove that the vast majority of acts of kindness, generosity, and magnanimity are done for anything more than to win other people's approval or to gain a relatively inexpensive image boost in one's own eyes. But even if that relatively downbeat view is correct, the facts in question still can't be dismissed or used to prove that human nature is self-serving through and through. After all, if there were nothing but selfishness in our nature, wouldn't people simply laugh at generous acts and see them as a sign of feeble-mindedness? Instead, most people seem to admire, respect, or feel inspired by virtue, as nothing demonstrates more clearly than the fact that most of us wish to believe that we ourselves have some virtue, that we're worthy of others' admiration. As Adam Smith wrote in *Theory of the Moral Sentiments*: "Man naturally desires not only praise, but praiseworthiness; or to be that thing which is the natural and proper object of praise." This is easier to explain if we adopt the more complex view of human nature discussed in detail in the next chapter than if we adhere to the one-dimensional assumption of pure selfishness.

Cooperation around the world

The tendency to cooperate, work together, and help others is exhibited to a greater or lesser degree in virtually every society. Evidence gathered by anthropologists suggests that it's not only old but nearly universal, and thus it is likely to be a part of the human genetic make-up.

In one example, anthropologists studied a tiny group, called the Ache, who roamed an area of broadleaf forest in eastern Paraguay before being peacefully contacted by members of the outside society and beginning to live in permanent settlements in the 1970s. The Ache (not to be confused with the people of the similarly pronounced Aceh region in northern Sumatra, Indonesia) typically lived in groups consisting of fifteen to sixty individuals (the average being in the upper thirties) and moved camp frequently, sometimes every day, sometimes every few days or every week. When some of the remaining forager groups among the Ache were studied in the 1980s and '90s, wild game made up almost eighty percent of their daily caloric intake. A typical hunter was found to acquire about four kilograms (a little under nine pounds) of meat on an average day, but he also had about a forty percent chance of acquiring nothing on any particular day, so that, in the absence of food storage possibilities, his family depended on the practice of food sharing among members of the band.

According to anthropologist Kim Hill of the University of New Mexico, upon returning from the hunt, the male Ache hunter often left any game he had procured at the edge of the camp. There, it was collected by his wife or other women to be cooked. Once ready, the cooked meat was divided by an older male, not the hunter, who handed out pieces to each family that was due a share according to Ache practice. If anyone was passed over, the divider was reminded of this by other band members, but never by the passed over individual or family themselves. All adult members receive equal shares, except that the hunter himself usually does not eat from his own kill. Similar kinds of food-sharing have been documented in forager societies in Australia, Africa, and elsewhere. Interestingly, it's more common when the food in question is more difficult to procure, more prized, and when cooperation is involved in obtaining it, whereas easily foraged plant foods are usually retained by the gatherer or the nuclear family.

That such behaviors go back a long way in our pedigree is also suggested by observations of food sharing among non-human primates. Accordingly to a description of hunting parties of chimpanzees in Taï National Park in the Ivory Coast, the animals "arrive at a task division in which individual hunters perform different but complementary actions. Some of them drive the prey; others encircle them or block their escape to a distant tree. If meat is the incentive for working together, Taï chimpanzees should also share readily. Such indeed proved to be the case, particularly with regard to adult males. Rather than taking meat into the trees, where beggars can be avoided, Taï chimpanzees typically form feeding clusters on the ground, where there is room for everyone."[9]

There's little indication that these animals share out of pure altruism. Primatologist Frans de Waal, who argues that the origins of human moral nature can be traced back to prehuman ancestors, describes instead a complex balance of competition for rank within the band, shifting alliances, and exchange of favors, including access to food and sex. Yet social harmony is also a goal that chimp and ape "power-brokers" seem, however selfishly, to seek. So amidst the complicated picture of scorekeeping and give-and-take in the societies of our closest living relatives, there are indications that concepts of fairness and emotions like empathy are making themselves felt.

What's indisputably unique about human beings, however, is our capacity to sacrifice, and to fight, for people whom we've never met. We alone expend effort for causes, for abstractions. Although many who enlist in armies do so under coercion, social pressures, or economic duress, and although actions in the midst of war are said to be almost entirely driven by small-group dynamics, there's at least sometimes an element of real voluntarism in the decision to enlist. This is strikingly illustrated by the case of the Spanish civil war of 1936–39, during which thousands of volunteer fighters from other countries, including almost three thousand Americans, ten thousand French, and ten thousand Scandinavians, came to Spain of their own volition to fight for the abstraction of democracy or anti-fascism. Almost ten thousand of them fell in battle. Whereas those fallen may have seen themselves as "merely" *risking* their lives for their case, human beings sometime even sacrifice themselves with certainty, as was the case with Japanese Kamikaze fighter pilots in World War II and suicide bombers in recent years.

Turning back to more garden-variety sacrifices, estimates suggest that at least some three percent of Americans, or about nine million people, donate blood with some frequency. While that process is quite safe, it typically requires up to forty-five minutes of the donor's time on site, at least one good needle prick, and the possibility of slight light-headedness in the immediate aftermath. Worldwide, enormous amounts of blood are donated to be on hand for the medical emergencies of unknown strangers. Less numerous than blood donors are those who volunteer to have whole quarts of bone marrow drawn from their hips, a process that takes hours, has been described as being excruciatingly painful when not done under general anesthesia, and that commonly leads to headaches, nausea, and light-headedness lasting a day or more, with local pain and discomfort often lasting up to three weeks. More than two thousand people a year made such donations in the United States during the late 1990s through 2001, many of them to unrelated individuals.[10]

Still more remarkably, at least a few thousand worldwide don hospital gowns each year and are wheeled into operating rooms to have part of a healthy liver, or one of their two kidneys, removed in order to keep an individual with a failing liver or kidneys alive. In 2006, for instance, 864 Belgians, Dutch, Germans, and Austrians donated a kidney, 365 of these being to biologically unrelated individuals (including 269 spouses).

Not by bread alone

We needn't look towards the most extreme cases to recognize that enormous numbers of people devote appreciable amounts of their time and resources to ends other than their own physical well-being or accumulation of wealth. Vast amounts of labor have been expended throughout history on projects bearing no obvious relationship to the material welfare of those concerned: the construction of temples, cathedrals, and mosques. This work was undertaken not for anyone's shelter or physical sustenance, and not—or at least not always—for the aggrandizement of a ruling or priestly class, but often to a significant degree for pure aesthetic expression and for the glorification of transcendent beings or spiritual guides. The better part of the world's great architecture has had a religious purpose, a sizeable chunk of the world's wealth is in the hands of religious institutions, and considerable numbers of adults are employed in religious occupations, serving as priests, nuns, ministers, imams, Catholic and Buddhist monks, and full-time religious scholars. US Bureau of Labor Statistics and Census numbers suggest that one in every four hundred employed Americans are in the clergy—implying that others are contributing to support their religious work.

Of course, some of these investments of effort into causes seemingly unrelated to self-interest can be traced back to self-interest thanks to the peculiarly human ability to form beliefs that push the calculation of costs and benefits to a realm beyond the one present to the senses. Large numbers of people, that is, believe that their self-interest isn't limited to their fortunes on this earth. People's investments in raising their probability of religious salvation and of a propitious rebirth or afterlife are arguably every bit as self-interested as is their planting of a drought-resistant crop as a hedge against famine or their offering of service or gifts to a powerful patron in the expectation of protection. It's also perfectly consistent with self-interest to spend time petitioning invisible powers for wealth, health, and happiness if you think those powers exist. Polls have repeatedly shown that large majorities of Americans believe in life after death, with more than seventy percent replying affirmatively to the question "Do you think there is a heaven where people who have led good lives are eternally rewarded?" And political elites have exploited, for their own ends, people's confidence in their ability to intercede with the gods at least since the first temples were established in the ancient Near East some four thousand years ago. Not only the accumulation of fortunes by religious hierarchies, but the use of their alliance with these hierarchies by rapacious emperors and monarchs, are perfect examples of human selfishness.

As in the case of charitable donations, though, these signs of self-interest are clearly not the whole story. In particular, cynical rulers and clerics may have used religion to induce passivity and wealth transfers to religious and state institutions, but what aspect of human nature allowed the elites of the last two millennia to induce reverence in the faithful using images of mild and saintly figures like Buddha, Jesus, and Francis of Assisi? Shouldn't a world of selfish brutes have been receptive only to archetypes of physical strength (say, Zeus or Thor)? To make sense of what we observe, it helps to posit that something along the lines of Haidt's "elevation" is part of our natures, after all.

There are also aspects of the religious impulse that seem to satisfy needs of other kinds: for affiliation, for meaning, and to be part of something greater than oneself. In this respect, devotion to religion shows little difference from devotion to other causes, for example to social, political, or even aesthetic ideals. The individual who devotes his life to achieving equality for women, justice for an oppressed group, the protection of civil liberties, the preservation of cultural treasures, the perfection of technique on the piano or violin or in his own voice, or the arrangement of a garden according to the principles of Zen is finding meaning in seeking a goal that has no direct bearing on his physical comfort or safety, state of nutrition, or number of offspring. With all of the time, energy, and resources that human beings devote to causes and activities that do them no earthly good, there's ample basis for questioning the assertion that each of us cares at bottom only about our own material wealth and gain.

To your health

Perhaps the most definitive evidence that human beings are not meant to be disconnected islands are findings by medical researchers suggesting that people require social connections for their very survival. The facts that married men live longer than their unmarried counterparts, for instance, and that people with strong family and/or friendship networks are healthier than those without, are by now widely familiar to anyone who picks up a newspaper or magazine. Studies of such matters are almost always possible for scientists to question on methodological grounds: How can one be sure that it's marriage that causes longevity, rather than relative health making it more likely that a person is married? But thorough analysis of dozens of independent findings have lent support to the conclusion that being well situated within a social support network is beneficial to cardiovascular health, to the functioning of the endocrine system, and to immune system function.[11] Indications that the companionship of a pet is associated with better health outcomes are also of this kind, as are favorable health outcomes associated with the petting of specially trained dogs by psychiatric patients, elderly nursing home residents, and others. These and related findings support the notion that human beings have an innate need for relationships with other warm-blooded and sympathetic living things.

Such observations also might be linked to results from the new body of happiness studies that was were mentioned in Chapter 1. In theory, economics is more concerned with human well-being than with income, per se, and treatises by economists often claim to use income as a proxy for well-being, happiness, or satisfaction only because those concepts are more difficult to measure. In recent years, though, some economists have decided to take self-reported, subjective measures of happiness and to investigate their correlations with economic outcomes, such as earnings and employment, as well as with things like health and the status of marital and other relationships. A consistent finding is that people's perceptions of their own happiness are much better predicted by their satisfaction with their relationships than by their income and that income seems to matter mainly for its impact on one's position *relative to* others—that is, earning more than ninety percent of people in your society makes you neither more nor less happy at one hundred thousand dollars a year than at fifty thousand dollars a year. These findings seem to align well with the above and other indications that we're at least as much social as we are economic animals. Indeed, perhaps more often than not, economic success is mainly sought as a means towards achieving social ends (influence, attractiveness to potential mates, leisure to enjoy activities with others).

Conclusion

It was easy enough to fill Chapter 3 with evidence that people act in their own self-interest in lots of settings. This was found to be true not only in the polite sense that people try to get good deals in business by not paying their workers more than the market forces them to pay, for instance. We also found it to be true in ways that cross the line into physical brutality and worse.

Despite that, it wasn't difficult to fill the present chapter with similar indications that many people display concern for others or act for the sake of abstract principles and causes. Even for as narrow a purpose as describing our economy, we'd be overlooking quite a bit, we found, if we ignored the roles that concern other than the chooser's material wealth play in choice of occupation, volunteer work, charitable donations, religious activity, and more. Most people seem to admire those who are helpful to others, and their desire to think well of themselves propels them in a similar direction. People constrain their self-interest often enough that Amartya Sen's depiction of a meeting of hyper-opportunists was immediately recognized as satire. And the fact that in well-functioning societies most people stick to the polite side of self-interest, rather than crossing the line into darker acts, also suggests that forces beyond pure self-interest are often at work.

But just what is the balance between the aspects of human motivation and human nature that these two quite different chapters have explored? Is there even a human nature that can be known? And if so, what investigative strategy might reveal it to us? We'll confront these questions squarely in the next chapter and with that begin to get to the heart of our exploration of what stands between us and the better world of which people have for so long dreamed.

Notes:

1. Adapted from Amartya Sen, "Rational Fools: A Critique of the Behavioural Foundations of Economic Theory," *Philosophy and Public Affairs* 6, no. 4 (1977): 317-344.
2. From the World Values Survey, which is discussed further, below.
3. "A Girl's Gift of Life, Recalled by Her Doctor," *Morning Edition,* NPR (July 8, 2006). Available at http://www.npr.org/templates/story/story.php?storyId=5587031.
4. Jonathan Haidt, "Elevation and the Positive Psychology of Morality," in *Flourishing: Positive Psychology and the Life Well-Lived* (Washington: American Psychological Association, 2003): 275-289.
5. The responses reported here for European countries are for the 1995 wave of the World Values Survey, whereas the rest of those mentioned are for the year 2000.
6. Edward Liu et al., "Barely Breaking Even: Incentives, Rewards, and the High Costs of Choosing to Teach," (Harvard Graduate School of Education, 2000).
7. Alan Matthios, "Education, Variation in Earnings, and Nonmonetary Compensation," *Journal of Human Resources* 24, no. 3 (1989), 456-468.
8. Deborah Small, George Loewenstein, and Paul Slovic, "Sympathy and Callousness: The Impact of Deliberative Thought on Donations to Identifiable and Statistical Victims," *Organizational Behavior and Human Decision Processes* 102, no. 2 (2007): 143-153.
9. From Frans de Waal, *Good Natured: The Origins of Right and Wrong in Humans and Other Animals* (Cambridge, MA: Harvard University Press, 1996).
10. National Marrow Donor Program, 2001 Biennial Report of the National Bone Marrow Donor Registry.
11. Bert N. Uchino, John T. Cacioppo, and Janice K. Kiecolt-Glaser, "The Relationship between Social Support and Physiological Processes: A Review with Emphasis on Underlying Mechanisms and Implications for Health," *Psychological Bulletin* 119 no. 3 (1996): 488-531 and Bert N. Uchino, *Understanding the Health Consequences of Relationship* (New Haven: Yale University Press, 2004).

CHAPTER 5
Evolution and Human Complexity

Selfish creatures who can never trust one another or kind creatures who respond empathetically to one another's distress and are capable of feeling inspiration from the example of unselfish role models? It would be helpful to know which depiction is more accurate, or what balance between them is realistic, if both hold some truth.

In the history of economic science, thinking took a turn towards the selfish creature answer in the 1840s when the English-speaking intellectual heirs of Adam Smith decided it would be more convenient to set aside Smith's qualifications about human sympathy and to focus on the self-interested motives that he'd ascribed to his immortalized butcher, brewer, and baker. John Stuart Mill, though in his broader writings a quite forward-looking social thinker who wrote a seminal tract on the emancipation of women and anticipated a day when all factories would be owned by their workers, agreed with his contemporaries that a self-interest centered approach made sense for economics as a science. It was Mill who codified the assumption in the leading political economy text of the day, declaring that the protagonist in the drama studied by economic analysis is the "rational economic man," *Homo economicus*. With this move, the very subject matter of economics began to be defined not by its substantive concerns, such as markets and trade, but by its methodology, that of positing a rational, self-interested actor and working out the implications of that assumption using deductive logic and mathematics.

The assumption of the rational economic man became ever more entrenched in economics during the decades following Mill. By the end of the nineteenth century, a leading economist of the English school, Francis Edgeworth, declared in his singularly titled *Essay on the Application of Mathematics to the Moral Sciences* that "The first principle of Economics is that every agent is actuated only by self-interest." The same assumption remained the dominant approach of the leading economics textbook of the early twentieth century, by Alfred Marshall, and of the textbooks of the mid- and late-twentieth century, by Paul Samuelson,

William Baumol, Gregory Mankiw, and others—books studied by tens of millions of college students.

There were always dissenters. The late nineteenth and early twentieth century American economist, Thorstein Veblen, advocated an economics based on empirical observation of human behavior instead of abstract theory built on simplifying assumptions. Veblen ridiculed the English school's depiction of the individual as a perfectly selfish and perfectly rational maximizer of his own satisfaction. In one article published in 1898 under the title "Why is Economics Not an Evolutionary Science?" he wrote:

> The hedonistic conception of man is that of a lightning calculator of pleasures and pains, who oscillates like a homogeneous globule of desire of happiness under the impulse of stimuli that shift him about the area but leave him intact. ... He is an isolated, definitive human datum, in stable equilibrium except for the buffets of impinging forces that displace him in one direction or another. Self-imposed in elemental space, he spins symmetrically about his own spiritual axis.

We saw in Chapter 4 how Amartya Sen, a Cambridge-trained economist who won the Nobel Prize in Economic Science in 1998, criticized the assumption of absolute self-interest as an absurd caricature of actual human beings. Dozens of others could be pointed to. Yet the definitional stricture embraced by Mill and Edgeworth appeared safely on top until at least the late 1970s.

But thereafter, signs of changing opinion began to grow. When Sen's article appeared in print in 1977, he was battling a still overwhelming practice of assuming a selfish "economic man." It seems noteworthy, for instance, that Sen's article appeared not in one of the prestigious journals of the economics profession, but in *Philosophy and Public Affairs*, a specialized publication for philosophically-minded readers, mostly non-economists. Today, by contrast, dozens of papers exploring the evidence for and the implications of altruism, fairness, and other so-called "social preferences" (including more negative ones like spite) appear in the top scholarly journals of economics each year.

Arguably the most important cause for this change is the growth of the research technique called experimental economics, in which volunteer subjects are asked to make choices having monetary costs and benefits, sometimes in interaction with others, and with consequences for the amount of money they'll be paid for their participation. Repeated violations of the predictions of the "economic man" assumption, including ones suggesting a puzzling willingness to punish unfairness even though it drives down one's own earnings, gradually increased interest in reopening the discussion. Some of those experiments are discussed in Chapter 6.

Another cause may simply be that basic theorizing about hypothetical firms and consumers had already been done by the late 1970s. Members of the now much larger cohort of academic economists, a group whose number had swelled many times over since the days of Edgeworth and Veblen and whose careers depended on publishing novel research, found themselves looking at more specific and complex decisions, such as how families in a poor country decide whether to send a daughter to school or keep her at home to help run household and farm, how individuals choose between two different retirement savings plans, or why some people have difficulty controlling their caloric intake or quitting smoking. In attacking such questions, they noticed failures of their traditional assumptions similar to the failures or anomalies seen in the experiment labs, and many found themselves searching for explanations in the literatures of psychology and biology, including ideas informed by evolutionary theory. As economists trying to understand human behavior looked at the scientific literature on human behavior, they found the species under discussion to be not their theoretical construction, *Homo economicus*, but the actual evolved creature *Homo sapiens*. And increasingly they were finding that while the *Homo economicus* simplification could help them to understand things like movements in the prices of potatoes or wheat, it might better play a more partial or complementary role when studying other topics—for example, explaining employee effort choice, charitable giving, or voting in elections.

So who is *Homo sapiens*, and what can he or she tell us about the extent to which we're selfish maximizers of our own interests alone versus social beings capable of concern for each other and of working together towards common interests?

Levels of complexity

Understanding *Homo economicus* requires us to understand only a few simple postulates. He—probably the preferred pronoun here since no women were in the room at the founding of economics—is relatively easy to understand because he's the product of the minds of a few economists at work for three or four generations with a fairly clear goal in mind, that of deducing what will happen when a set of rational selfish actors interact in a market. All that we need to know is that *Homo economicus* places a positive value on wealth and consumption and a negative value on work. If we want to delve more deeply, we have to decide what sorts of mathematical functions better capture the actor's willingness to trade disliked work for valued wealth, to take risks, and to make trade-offs between present and future consumption. Will an additive function suffice to capture his objectives, or should the form be multiplicative, exponential, or something else again?[1] Much analysis has been done to work out the implications of various alternatives. The empirically minded can go on to obtain data on labor supply, investment, and other decisions and to see which functions fit the data better. The analysis can become extraordinarily complex, which is why physics and math majors make good economics students and are well represented in economics Ph.D. programs. But the assumptions about human nature are at base quite simple.

In contrast, understanding *Homo sapiens* poses a very different challenge, since *Homo sapiens* is not a theoretical construct devised by a few individuals in a few generations with a definite purpose in mind. Rather, it's a living species whose evolution was influenced by an array of biological, climatic, and other forces acting over hundreds of thousands of generations with no explicit goal in mind. It won't do to write down two or three equations. What's required, rather, is to bring together thoughtfully at least three kinds of elements. First, we need a set of observations of what actual human beings are like across the whole spectrum of societies, from hunter-gatherers in the Amazon and Kalahari whose lifestyles probably resemble those of our remote ancestors, to pastoralists and peasant farmers in places like Afghanistan and Bolivia, and to urban dwellers and suburbanites in places like Mumbai and Los Angeles. Second, we need an adequate appreciation of the evolutionary process as it has come to be understood by thinkers from Darwin to William Hamilton, Stephen Gould, E. O. Wilson, Richard Dawkins, and others. And third, to have a sense of the selection pressures that shaped the emergence of our species, we need knowledge of the time line and environmental conditions under which human evolution occurred. To meet all of these requirements requires that we draw on many fields of knowledge, including anthropology, sociology, history, biology, paleontology, and archeology.

Becoming human

During life's first billion and a half to two billions years—up to roughly the half-way point in the earth's career to date—bacteria and other simple organisms constituted the earth's entire biosphere. Had extraterrestrials dropped in on our planet to check for life at the halftime, their probes could have discovered plenty of bacteria in soil and water samples, but there wouldn't have been a chipmunk, alligator, or bird—not even a dinosaur—that they could invite to join their Federation of Planets or other club of sentient life forms. It took hundreds of millions of years for single-celled organisms having nuclei and cell membranes, things like the paramecium or amoeba you may have seen under a microscope in your sixth grade science class, to appear.

Only relatively recently in geological time did some of these organisms give rise to still more complex lineages of multi-cellular plants and animals. Trilobites, creatures a few inches long with rudimentary brains lying beneath glassy calcite eyes, appeared about 540 million years ago and dominated the oceans for more than a hundred million years, longer than the career of our primate order from its appearance to the present. Fish arrived about 450 million years ago, the first amphibians about 380 million years ago, reptiles about 280 million years ago, and mammals about 220 million years ago. Within the class of mammals, the order of the primates arose about 65 million years ago, with the founders of this mammalian order from which we're descended being comparable to today's tree squirrels in size, lifestyle, and intelligence. The family of the great apes, or *Hominidae*, to which we belong, emerged only 20 million years ago. When the line that gave birth to modern humans diverged from the line of today's chimpanzees around seven million years ago, about 99 percent of the history of multi-cellular life on earth had already unfolded. It would take another six million years of change in pelvic, spine, and hand structure, size and organization of brain, positioning of the larynx, and more before recognizable humans would emerge.

Why bother recapping stages that most are glad to have left behind after high school biology class? Because evolution itself rarely leaves anything fully behind; so remembering one's ancestors can come in handy. Evolution is all about natural selection acting on chance variation, and since an accidental change of many features at once is almost certain to produce an organism that isn't viable, the mutations on which evolution selects nearly always involve rearranging what has already proven workable, not inventing from scratch.

Signs of our evolution are ever-present in our bodies, minds, and even culture. Sitting in front of our computer screens or holding a smaller digital device in front of our faces in our twenty-first century world, we're enjoying the benefits of highly developed vision and dexterous hands and fingers that exist only because our primate ancestors lived for tens of millions of years high up in the trees, where such visual and manual equipment was useful for navigating the forest canopy and spotting small prey. We're able to unscramble all those letters on page or screen and to think big thoughts today because our brains became larger as part of an accidental, but ultimately successful, strategy for dealing with the harsher and more dangerous environment that forced more recent ancestors to get back on the ground as their wooded east African habitat turned into a grassy savannah a few million years ago. And if the majority of those reading this book today are in temperate places like North America, Europe, and northeast Asia, rather than in the more equatorial climates in which we evolved, it's only possible because, after more than two million years of walking on two legs and letting nature tinker with their posture and gray matter, our ancestors' brains had become sophisticated enough to control fire and to sew skins into clothing, allowing them to survive in harsher climates. The fact that the creature living in those climates was "designed" to live in more tropical ones arguably propelled our ancestors to devote more energy to devising technological responses to environmental challenges, leading from the increasing mastery of fire and tools like the needle to the harnessing of coal, petroleum, and nuclear energy.

Evolved body; evolved mind?

The evolution of our bodies from vertebrate, mammalian, and primate ancestors is on display for all to see at collections like the one at the Harvard Museum of Natural History, which I enjoyed touring with my daughter's elementary school class a dozen years ago. Seeing so many different animal skeletons side by side, it's hard not to notice that the basic body plan of four limbs, a spine, a rib cage protecting heart and lungs, and a skull housing a brain connected to organs of sight, hearing, and smell has been present in everything from fish to alligators and frogs to beavers, lions, armadillos, and, of course, ourselves. But whether evolutionary origins hold sway over *behaviors*, as well, seems a bit less obvious. No less an authority than Alfred Russell Wallace, co-discoverer with Darwin of the theory of evolution by natural selection, believed that there was a qualitative break between man and the lower animals. To Wallace, animal behavior seemed governed by instinct, whereas humans, and only humans, engage in rational thought and deliberation, have refined aesthetic sensibilities, and base their actions on moral considerations.

Humans certainly do have more sophisticated minds than the members of other species, so far as we can tell, but there's no indication of a clean break "below" which all behavior is instinctual and "above" which all behavior is deliberative. Bonobos (sometimes called pygmy chimpanzees[2]) in captivity, like the now famous Kanzi, have proven capable of learning to understand and use hundreds of human words, both by sign language and on a symbol board. Kanzi not only understands and implements the commands of his trainers; he can also express likes and dislikes, combine words he's learned in ways he hasn't heard before, and can use words to articulate feelings and desires (including requesting to be hugged). Jealousy, status competition, anger, and other elements of complex social interaction have been documented in populations of chimps, gorillas, and other primates, which also exhibit varying degrees of reasoning ability. Even the dog, an animal domesticated from a wolf species not especially close to the primates, is able to make emotional connections with humans and to learn to understand some human speech. Hunter-gatherers who attributed minds much like the human to the animals that surrounded them weren't necessarily further from the mark than were their counterparts in hierarchical civilizations who insisted on a sharp break between human and animal.

The fact that humans share some emotions and aspects of basic social interaction with primate cousins, and even with less closely related animals like dogs and elephants, suggests that many of the hallmark emotional and behavioral predispositions of the human animal, the ones that fill the tragedies of ancient Greece, the dramas of Shakespeare, and the contemporary fare of television and movies, have been evolving over millions of years in a gradual fashion. There's been no sudden jump up to a plane on which behavior is uninfluenced by genes. And, as the neuroscientist, Antonio Damasio, has argued, it's an error to think that the mind *governs* the body as a general might be imagined to direct an army. Rather, the brain is intimately bound up with the body. Emotions and the associated physiological and chemical machinery are a requirement for efficient decision-making. Indeed, representations of bodily states and sensations by clusters of neurons are probably central to the formation of memories, to the building up of abstract images and concepts, and to consciousness itself.

Culture-gene coevolution

Resistance to an evolutionary view of human behavior has also come from secular humanists who consider cultural, social, and other environmental influences to be "far more important than genes." This objection might have been worth considering if it made sense to think that genes and environment were in competition. But decades of research show that human beings are products of both genes and environments. The complex social and cultural environments in which human genes work out their expression are, like the corresponding physical environments and ecologies, environmental factors against which the fitness of each further genetic modification has been tested across time and space. Because humans evolved not just in particular niches of natural ecology, such as the African savanna, but also in niches of social ecology (e.g., societies of foraging bands), culture and genes have always evolved in tandem.

Students of the evolution of human behavior such as Robert Boyd and Peter Richerson use the term "coevolution" to summarize this interdependence and mutual influence of genetic and socio-environmental influences in the historical process of human development. No cultural influence on behavior can have had much effect if it was entirely incompatible with natural predispositions—including those governing the balance of concern between individual, close kin, and other members of the band or society—but by the same token, the human-made social environment has had the capacity to alter genes by affecting, for instance, who got more chances to procreate. So neither genes nor environment are fully in the driver's seat.

Consider the use of language, essentially a cultural phenomenon and one that constantly changes in the course of ongoing social interactions—so that those who spoke a given language a thousand years ago and their descendants speaking one of its offshoots today would be quite unlikely to understand one another, were a time machine able to bring them together. Language would have been impossible without relevant physiological changes in the vocal tract, which is why those chimps and bonobos that have mastered substantial numbers of words still can't reproduce human speech. But the appearance of primitive language capabilities may itself have been a major promoter of further brain growth and more sophisticated brain "wiring." Once a rudimentary language ability appeared, its utility in coordinating group hunts and improving outcomes of intergroup warfare would have encouraged selection for both better vocal equipment and a strengthened mental capacity for language. Thus primitive language *use*, a social phenomenon, promoted the selection of genetic changes involving physiological adaptation of the vocal chords and speech-related areas of the brain. But as the capacity to articulate sounds improved and the brain grew larger, language may have begun to be used in more subtle and social ways, for instance for gossiping about people in the attempt to punish uncooperative behaviors. The increasing complexity of language driven by such social interactions, mastery of which could have been critical to an individual's life-course, might have put a further premium on mental acuity, pushing selection of brains towards those with more neurons and interconnectivity. In this way, it's been theorized, advantages of mental sophistication conferred mainly by the complexity of human social life itself may help to account for our surprising ability to do differential calculus, build models of climate change, and perform other intellectual feats that would seem unnecessary for our ancestors' physical survival as hunter-gatherers.

No room for "warm fuzzies"?

One last source of resistance to viewing human nature as evolved is the fear that evolution implies amorality or the applicability of but one law, the "law of the jungle." "Nature red in tooth and claw," goes a famous line in Tennyson. The struggle for survival may appear to leave no room for altruism or sentiment. It's the strongest and most ruthless who beat the competition, get the mate, grab the resources, survive, and reproduce, so any that display kindness towards weaker individuals among their kind must fall by the wayside and end up among evolution's innumerable failed experiments.

But the very fact that you and I are holding a passionate conversation on the issue shows this concern to be completely unfounded. Although struggle and competition are found throughout nature, so, too, at least among social species, are dispositions towards bonding and caring behaviors. The fact that the products of evolution compete to fill limited niches doesn't mean that evolution always selects competitive inclinations over cooperative ones.

Consider maternal instinct, a symphony of hormonal secretions and responses to visual, tactile, aural, and olfactory cues that together get mother to nurse and rear junior and to often even feel good about doing it along the way. So strongly has this instinct been built into our relatives and ourselves that primatologists report numerous cases of macaques and other female primates that, upon the death of an infant, have adopted the newborn of another female to nurse and raise as its own, sometimes even kidnapping the infant to make it possible. The same behaviors are reported in northern elephant seals and other species. Indications of apparent grief or depression upon loss or separation are also reported in other species, including elephants.

Maternal instinct has its counterpart in the offspring, as well. In a famous series of experiments, psychologist Harry Harlow offered young rhesus monkeys a choice between two surrogate "mothers," one made of wire and one of ter-rycloth. Even when the "wire mother" had attached to it a baby bottle containing milk, while the cloth one did not, the monkeys preferred to spend as much time as possible with the cloth "mother," taking only brief breaks to drink from the bottle when needed. When a frightening stimulus was brought into their cage or when they were put in unfamiliar surroundings, they clung to the cloth surrogate mother and ignored the wire one, bottle or no bottle. The psychological comfort of a soft, warm object seemed a more important need to the baby monkeys than the physical nourishment offered by the milk. Of course, the reason soft, warm objects confer such comfort clearly stems from the fact that both milk, protection, and a soft, warm mother came as a package for millions of years before the first scientist in a lab coat appeared on the stage.

Not all of the examples of "warm fuzzy" relationships found in nature involve highly related individuals. Dolphins have been reported to help injured members of their group by remaining at their side, actively bringing them to the surface to allow them to breathe or traveling more slowly to allow them to keep up. Many mammals, not least of all primates, spend considerable amounts of time removing parasites from the fur of other group members—what scientists call "grooming." While who grooms whom is in part an indication of social hierarchy, in higher primates, at least, the activity appears to be a tension reliever and a major component of social bonding.

One reason why survival of the fittest doesn't imply survival of the meanest is that the unit on which nature's selective pressures work is not the individual organism or person, but the set of genes that serve as the blueprint for the assem-bly of that person—for whom, in a sense, the person is a means of propelling itself into future generations. This implies that it's not always the interest of the individual who bears the gene that dominates. Sometimes the genes do better for themselves by getting the cells they build to act as a harmonized coalition, that is, a multi-cellular organism. And similarly, the genes sometimes do better when they incline two or more such organisms to cohere as a family, pack, or hunting group. But before we go further, it's worthwhile to review some basic principles.

Inclusive fitness and kin altruism

Disappointed to find that Adam Smith wasn't the unalloyed exponent of self-interest that he'd been expecting, a believer in the view that people are at base selfish might have hoped, at least, to find a strong ally in Darwin. After all, the Darwinian man is a product of purely physical forces and must survive in a material world at the top of a long food chain. It's "eat or be eaten," so there's no room for any altruism or sentimentality, which might get in the way of the quest for resources to ensure your survival. This sort of presumption helps explain the traditional distrust of evolutionary thinking by some egalitarians.

But their distrust would be misplaced. The egoist's hope for support from Darwin proves as disappointing as were his expectations about Adam Smith. Darwin was fascinated by the evident presence of emotions and social instincts in both humans and other animals, and he wrote many prescient pages on the topic. Subsequent evolutionary theorists have begun to show why sociality and evolutionary fitness are not, in fact, at odds. At the core of the matter is the fact that it isn't what's best for the *individual*'s chances of survival that's favored by evolution, but rather what's best for the *gene*. As Richard Dawkins has colorfully argued, from an evolutionary standpoint, individuals are merely vessels, carriers and potential transmitters of the more central characters in the evolutionary story, which are the genes themselves. The "goal" of a gene—speaking metaphorically, of course, since a gene is a thoroughly mindless cluster of molecules with neither goals nor ability to reason—is to project more copies of itself into future generations. The preponderance of the genes that we observe must have acted as if having such a goal because it's those that happen to have acted as if hell-bent on proliferating that were the winners of the evolutionary race up until now and are, therefore, the ones that we see around us. Organisms bearing genes with a knack for going extinct are sure to be hard to find.

The core principle of the gene-centered view of natural selection is known as *inclusive fitness*. It says that what inclinations your genes assign to you, a single gene-bearer, depends on how you can best be used to advance *their* interest. If keeping you safe and healthy until you've procreated and have helped to raise children and grandchildren who'll procreate in their turn is best for your genes, then clever and effective genes will steer you in that direction. They'll make you fearful and thus primed to take precautions when a saber-tooth tiger or a ten-ton truck crosses your path. They'll make you feel attraction towards members of the opposite sex and help you to think up good lines to use when you approach them.

But this doesn't mean that your genes *always* steer you towards putting yourself first. Since your genes "want" you to propagate those copies of themselves they've gotten you to put in your offspring, they'll make tenderness well up in your breast when you see your baby smile or hear it gurgle and coo, to the point of sacrificing your night's sleep when necessary to make sure baby is fed and comfortable. They might even predispose you towards risking injury or death so that more of your brothers, sisters, nieces, and nephews survive and procreate. So, while it's not in your personal interest, your genes may have given you the emotional inclination to shout out a warning about the saber-tooth tiger approaching your close relatives, even though that could attract the beast directly towards *you*, whereas slinking off inconspicuously would have preserved your skin with substantially higher probability. I'll come back to this example in a moment.

Reproduction and the family

First, a bit more about the mother of all caring relationships—of course, that's mothering. The human reproductive strategy, which relies heavily on family bonds, is no doubt responsible for a large measure of our altruism. At a certain point, or perhaps at a series of junctures over the past few million years, a larger brain became desirable for our ancestors. A four-foot-tall ape having fewer trees to scamper up as its environment became dryer, already on a path towards losing its arboreal skills, would be at a disadvantage among the animals of the savannah unless it had unusually quick wits and a capacity for teamwork in hunting and defending against predators. But nature couldn't expand our brain size willy-nilly. The size of our foremothers' birth canals limited how large our heads could be at birth without threatening both mother and baby, and the shift towards walking on two legs had been narrowing, not widening, the passageway for the newborn.

The solution to this problem, as with most others in evolution, didn't involve radical reengineering of human reproductive anatomy as much as it did tinkering with elements already at hand. Nature improvised by having us give birth to less mature offspring with less fully grown heads, making up for the immaturity by adjusting our social instincts to ensure appropriate caregiving during a more prolonged childhood.[3] Probably less change was needed in the strength of the mother/child bond than in the commitment of males to the females with whom they fathered children, since the females required more material support while caring for helpless offspring. Some anthropologists argue that cohesion of the band as a whole, including additional adults, was also important to successfully bringing the young through their long period of dependency. In either case, aspects of primate sociality that had already been evolving for many millions of years were core elements of nature's solution.

When we see the gene rather than the person as what nature "cares" about, it's easy to see how tendencies towards altruism within the family could have evolved. Suppose that at a certain point in time a woman was equally likely to be born with a genetic predisposition to be a little more protective of and nurturing towards her children, or a little less so—that is, let there be two variants of the gene controlling the relevant tendency, just as there can be an allele (gene variant) for blue eyes and an alternative allele for brown ones. Then if the more nurturing women brought more children to maturity, and if they in turn succeeded in bringing up more offspring themselves, the proportion of women with the more nurturing tendency would increase; the proportion with the less nurturing tendency would shrink.

But the forces in question are subtle. Mothers who lavished too much love and attention on one child, waiting until that child was fully self-sufficient before having another, would lose the evolutionary race to ones who had a few more children a bit more closely spaced, weaning each from the breast a little sooner to push their genetic productivity a bit higher. Going too far in the opposite direction would also be punished in the evolutionary competition, as too many offspring would die before maturity. The best mother, from a gene's point of view, might even differentially invest in her children, relatively neglecting the less promising (sicklier, scrawnier) ones in favor of those more likely to make it to maturity and produce offspring of their own.

Doing the math

Let's have a closer look, now, at other family relationships, such as those within the little group that that tiger was threatening a few paragraphs back. Recall that I mentioned that genes that predisposed you towards self-sacrifice might have had evolutionary value. Suppose you and your three brothers are out foraging when you spot a tiger that they don't yet see. The tiger also hasn't seen you yet, so you can silently slip away. But you realize that this predator is likely to kill your brothers if they aren't warned. Why would genes inclining you towards shouting a warning have proliferated, even though doing that would be risking your own neck?

We need to do a bit of quick math here (which those already familiar with the basic kin selection model are welcome to skip). You share the same parents, so the likelihood that you and any given brother share the same version of any particular gene (whether it be one governing height or eye color or one helping to determine instead a behavioral predisposition like taking a risk to help a brother) is one half. Suppose that the alternative candidate for this seat on the relevant chromosome is a gene predisposing one towards indifference to siblings. If those carrying the gene for sibling solicitude occasionally helped out their siblings in ways that increased the number of offspring the siblings had, then on average they will have increased the number of people bearing it, so the gene for solicitude will become more common. Doing the math, we see that a gene for the predisposition to help more than two full siblings, more than four first cousins (each having a one-in-four chance of sharing a given gene with the helper), or at least one sibling and two cousins should do well over the generations, while a gene for either a predisposition to always put yourself first or one to take greater risks to help just one brother or sister (or only three first cousins) will tend to become less common. You may have ended up with genes predisposing you towards risking your neck for your family because even if things turn out badly for *you*, your genes are quite willing to accept your loss as a cost of preserving enough other copies of themselves.

Of course, there's no guarantee that a particular gene will ever appear by way of accidental mutation. If there are only a few hundred thousand years or perhaps even only tens of thousands of years for fine-tuning, natural selection on random variation alone may get within the neighborhood of the best solution, but remain some distance from it. It's also important to remember that the tendencies in question are likely to be governed by large numbers of genes the activity of which is triggered by many different environmental influences, and they work by setting predispositions towards emotional responses of given strengths, not by wiring arithmetic formulas into the brain. With thousands upon thousands of generations during which to experiment, nature could well have hit upon something roughly approximating a genetically ideal solution. Provided that it wasn't linked to a particularly *deleterious* change in other traits, whatever mutation closest to the ideal solution happened by chance to arise would gradually have spread. What's important for our purposes is that a purely selfish being along the lines of Mill's and Edgeworth's *Homo economicus* would not have done well under the conditions our evolution was favoring. In other words, mutants a bit more like *Homo economicus* and a bit less like *Homo sapiens* could have cropped up randomly tens of thousands of times since our now famous great-great-aunt Lucy walked the savannah near Olduvai Gorge; but each time they did so, their line would have died out since before long it would have been without surviving descendents.

Cooperation among non-kin

At this point, our naïve proponent of self-interest has hopefully become at least somewhat less naïve and more ready to concede that altruism among close relatives makes sense from an evolutionary standpoint. But how are the pressures towards kin altruism that we've discussed so far going to explain anyone's giving money to help the homeless, volunteering to work in the local soup kitchen, or sacrificing himself for comrades on the battlefield? With genetic relatedness in large groups usually far smaller than the one-fourth relatedness of first cousins, it would rarely make sense to sacrifice even your morning latte or your afternoon nap to help a nonrelative. A few sentimental types may do such things, we can imagine our skeptic saying, but they're the sorts of evolutionary mistakes whose bearers those saber-tooth tigers and mastodons used to feast on back when selection pressures were still high. If a protective society lets such dreamers hang around at little procreative disadvantage, these days, that doesn't mean that generalized altruism makes any sense or that it exists in any but a small number of people. It may exist, the skeptic might argue, but so do other fairly common genetic disorders, including those that predispose people towards schizophrenia, diabetes, and autism.

So, *could* tendencies to cooperate with unrelated individuals ever have been affirmatively selected for by the evolutionary process, not just slip by as an occasional error? The answer to this question remains controversial among evolutionary theorists, among whom kin altruism is taken as fact.

Before going further, it may be helpful to first consider a much more sanguine point of view than that of our hypothetical skeptic. If you're a novice in these matters and come at the question of altruism from a relatively upbeat standpoint, you may have found yourself wondering why evolution should not, after all, have wanted us to help even our nonrelatives. "As members of the same species," you might reason, "we probably share the better part of our genes with one another by virtue of being descended from a common ancestor who lived about a hundred thousand years ago. Wouldn't a species whose members help each other out tend to grow in number relative to a species whose members act indifferently or with antagonism? Might we not be the version of *Homo* that survived precisely because of our solidarity with one another?"

Unfortunately, this argument doesn't work. The problem is that it's not the genes we all share, for instance those that give us ten fingers and ten toes, that we need to focus on. Rather, we have to think in terms of a narrower set of genes having variants that can account for fine differences in behavioral predispositions, ones having alternative alleles that have changed in relative frequency during the past million or so years. (That genetic change can occur within relatively short time spans is illustrated by numerous examples, such as the genetically-conferred ability to digest lactose in adulthood that appeared and spread in northern Europe between five and six thousand years ago.) Like the genes governing your potential height or the shape of your earlobes, the genes that predispose you to be more or less risk-taking, nervous, energetic, or nurturing probably come in a great many variants and thus have only a small chance of being present in any given stranger.[4] One can say with certainty that your identical twin (or one day, your clone) shares all such genes with you, which means, from a statistical standpoint, there's a one-in-two chance that you share each gene with each of your parents and siblings, and a one-in-four chance that you share it with each grandparent and first cousin, and so forth. But the chance that you share a specific gene for earlobe length, anxiety, or altruism with your FedEx deliveryman, the woman at the drycleaning store, or your coworker, may be vanishingly small. Average genetic proximity among members of forager bands when world population was small was presumably far greater than in today's urban societies; but even in that context, the tendency to mate outside of the immediate kin group would have kept the degree of relatedness with non-kin, and more importantly the likelihood of sharing any particular newly evolving gene variant, fairly small.

Thus, consider the prospects for a gene inclining you towards general altruism. Suppose, for instance, that there's a site on some chromosome where one or another variant of a certain gene governs receptivity to the sort of socialization that produces willingness to sacrifice for a collective abstraction like "country." Suppose, as before, that there are two variants of the gene, one that predisposes a person towards becoming quite patriotic if exposed to stirring music, a memorable flag, and the right messages in the home, school, and church and another version that leaves the person unmoved by such things. If those having the trait more often sacrifice themselves for their country than do those not having the trait, then, unlike the previously imagined gene for fraternal altruism, the gene for broader altruism will become less, not more, common in the population. Because benefits of altruism may be widely shared while only the altruists shoulder the costs, biologists find cooperation among nonrelatives much harder to explain than that among close kin. Though they agree that humans are an unusually social animal—"ultra-sociality" is one term used to describe the only animal that frequently sacrifices itself to help unrelated members of its species—there's no agreement yet on how to explain it.

A partial solution to this riddle of cooperation among non-kin was suggested by biologist Robert Trivers in an influential paper published in 1971. Trivers argued that there are many examples of "reciprocal altruism," situations in which two individuals, whether of the same or of different species, help each other out for mutual benefit. For example, there are species of fish and shrimp that have evolved to serve as "cleaners," eating and thus removing parasites from the mouths of larger fish like groupers. The smaller animals swim into the larger ones' mouths and gill chambers, eat off the troublesome parasites, and the favor they confer is returned by not being swallowed, a fate befalling other small fish reckless enough to swim in. The explanation is that for the cleaner fish and their hosts, a mutually beneficial relationship of reciprocity, and the expectations that support it, has been established over many thousands of generations, so the host fish have developed good ways to identify their cleaners. Some of the large fish involved in these relationships are believed to spend about the same fraction of their time on cleaning sessions as they do on seeking and eating food, and populations of cleaners, evidently evolved specifically for that purpose, spend their entire lives at well-established "stations" where they are frequently visited by particular hosts. Even your dental hygienist is probably not this dedicated.

Another example of reciprocity often cited in biology textbooks, this one occurring between members of the same species, is the sharing of blood among vampire bats. These small flying mammals' only food source is blood sucked from larger animals by inflicting more-or-less painless bites. (The less skillful bat that inflicts pain is usually shaken from its prey without a meal.) Scientists who study them have determined that a vampire bat will die if it fails to obtain fresh blood for two nights in succession, and an average healthy bat has a seven percent chance of obtaining no blood on a given night. With these odds, the chance of failing to return with blood for two nights in a row some time during any given year is more than seventy-five percent, so one can calculate that, absent alternative arrangements, only a quarter of the bats would survive through a typical year. Instead, scientists studying bat colonies find that roughly three-quarters of their members survive the average year. The explanation is food sharing, a considerable part of it between unrelated adults.[5] The bats aren't pure altruists, though. Studies show that they form relationships with specific roostmates. The chance that bat A will help bat B in B's time of need is a function of whether B did the same when the tables were turned, which suggests that a bat's longevity depends on knowing who to go to bat for. Since the bat with better buddy relationships stands the better chance of surviving and passing on its genes, nature has evidently been selecting the bats for a tendency to build successful ties of reciprocity.

For an example in the human realm, consider a band of hunter-gatherers like our ancestors of twenty thousand years ago, or like the Ache of today who were described in the last chapter. Each day, the males in the band go off looking for animals to kill and bring back as food. Each day, an individual Ache hunter has about a forty percent chance of coming back empty handed. Suppose, then, that among the sixty percent who catch something, twenty percent catch only a squirrel or two, a bit short of what's needed to satisfy their families; twenty percent have a just-adequate catch; and twenty percent have caught a quite large animal, enough to feed their family for a week or more, were there the means to preserve it. But without refrigeration and salting techniques, what isn't eaten will soon be worthless. If the successful hunter alone (or he and his immediate family) feed on the large carcass, they can gorge themselves, but they'll end up suffering indigestion and will still waste some of the meat. Other members of the band will try to get by on nuts and berries, which might not always be abundant, so some of them will go to sleep hungry. To the lucky family, the last pounds of meat on their big catch are worth almost nothing because they're already quite satiated, but other members of the band, being hungry and not having eaten meat for some time, might value that meat very highly. This is a perfect opportunity to trade. The hunter with the meat would be better off exchanging some of it now for a similar amount of meat at a future time when another hunter is lucky and he's not. In economic terms, we'd say that the "marginal utility" of an ounce of meat tomorrow is much greater, for the hunter, than is the "marginal utility" of another ounce today.

Now, suppose it's 18,000 BCE, or perhaps even today or in the recent past in an essentially stateless region of Paraguay or Borneo.[6] So there are no courts, writing, or government, and thus no ways to enforce a formal contract or even to write one down. How can the trade happen if those involved are perfectly self-interested and know full well that none of them will honor an agreement when provided with any excuse or opportunity to ignore it? The answer is that the trade can take place if hunters are not quite perfectly selfish and can therefore trust one another to abide by the norm of sharing. The lucky hunter who shares his bounty now gets even more benefit because he can count on receiving reciprocal favors from those he shares with when the tables are turned later on. Abiding by a norm may make sense even for a selfish opportunist, if he's sufficiently sure that it will pay off in the long run (i.e., if he's in a band in which those with a reputation for upholding it are favored as exchange partners and those with bad reputations are shunned). There's only one problem: it would be pretty hard to get such a norm going in a group in which everyone's ready to lie, cheat, and jump on any excuse to back out of a promise.

Enter evolution, and suppose that the tendencies to share and to reciprocate are partly governed by genes. Perhaps the remote ancestors of the Ache and us, ones who lived, say, a hundred thousand years ago in what's now Ethiopia or Kenya, were capable of sharing and reciprocating only with their immediate relatives, and accordingly families went hungry, sometimes for a few weeks at a time, and occasionally they ended up either losing members to diseases that they might otherwise have survived, losing them in unsuccessful attacks on families who had food, or even killing one of their own members to eat his or her flesh rather than starve. Then along comes a mutation that facilitates the development of and adherence to a norm of sharing and reciprocity. If individuals with this mutation are successful enough to be numerous in some groups, then members of those groups would have done better on average than those in other groups: less hunger, less death from disease, less internal warfare, less cannibalism. Under such circumstances, it looks like the predisposition towards sharing and reciprocating can reproduce itself more rapidly than the alternative.

To be sure, there's still a classic free rider problem here:[7] among all conceivable hunters, one who reciprocates and belongs to a tribe with lots of reciprocators would be relatively well off, but one who belongs to such a tribe, yet who gets away with not reciprocating every now and then, would be better off still. If members of cooperative groups clever enough to get away with cheating sometimes were on average better nourished and produced a few more offspring, then over time the proportion of true cooperators within the relatively cooperative groups would be falling, not rising—so a stable equilibrium in which everyone is born a cooperator is by no means assured.

A way around the problem can start with the punishment or ostracism of those caught failing to share, reciprocate, or abide by the norm. If such individuals suffered a severe enough punishment, on average, then they would not be advantaged after all, so the proliferation of reciprocating types is free to sail ahead. Unfortunately, the problem pops up again at the new higher level: punishing non-reciprocators may itself require resources or energy or put you at risk of retaliation, so the tendency to punish has the same problem of surviving and proliferating as did the tendency to reciprocate. Groups with punishers do better, that is, but individuals within those groups who spare themselves the trouble of punishing and let others do the dirty work instead are better off still. The tendency to punish might accordingly die out over time.

Some solutions have nonetheless been suggested. Perhaps the most promising one involves what's called "group selection." If we hone in on the disparity between what's good for the group and what's good for the individual member of the group, and if we do some careful math, we can demonstrate that it's possible for group advantage to win out over individual advantage if the following three conditions hold: (1) the relative advantage of being in a group having mostly reciprocator/cooperators or norm-abiders in it is large; (2) the relative *dis*advantage of being one of the reciprocators or norm-abiders in that group who takes upon herself the cost of punishing violators of the norm is small; and (3) there's sorting among groups, in the sense that reciprocators or norm-abiders tend to be found disproportionately in groups with other reciprocators and norm-abiders. One way that (2) may hold is that a group has so many norm-abiders that there is rarely any need to expend resources punishing a violator, and when such a need arises, more or less everyone backs up the punishers. One way that (3) may hold is that groups tend to stay together over time but to expel individuals who aren't like the majority of their members. If there's a small personal disadvantage to being a reciprocator, norm-abider, or punisher of norm-violators, and if groups with these types do better and one is much more likely to be in such a group if one is oneself of this type, then the trait can proliferate.[8]

Whatever the exact explanation, reciprocity and other forms of cooperation do appear sometimes in nature, and they are found in every human society. Since genetic and other evidence indicates that some of those societies lacked either direct or third party contacts with one another for some fifty thousand years, these traits could hardly be so universal unless they were supported by innate dispositions. In the example of the Ache, a group cut off from behaviorally similar groups in southern Africa and Australia for tens of millennia, sharing and cooperation were carried to great lengths according to the recent anthropological observations of Hill. In modern society, reciprocity is still heavily relied upon to complete all kinds of transactions in which the parties take turns doing their parts, rather than acting simultaneously. For example, you might pay a house painter up front for half of the job to be performed, but you'd have trouble enforcing the agreement were he to abscond without doing it. But in practice, you trust—to some degree—that he'll proceed with it. Of course, repeat interactions and reputation are part of the story (the painter would lose his livelihood if word got around that he had a tendency to take the money and run), but those factors aren't always enough to explain why people reciprocate expectations and why others believe they're likely to do so. Even bribery, ironically, depends heavily on reciprocity: the payer of the bribe has to expect the corrupt official to follow through on his promise out of "reciprocity" or "because he gave his word," since there's no going to the courts for satisfaction if he reneges.

To flesh out the story sketched above, we need to recognize also that the roots of human reciprocity go back a lot further than a hundred thousand years, so that the adjustments in the late stages of the evolution of *Homo sapiens* are just that, adjustments or tweaks of preexisting foundations. Reciprocity in grooming and other behaviors are clearly observable in our primate relatives. So, just like maternal instinct, human reciprocity is hardly a new invention. For instance, Frans de Waal talks of a "chimpanzee politics" in which members of that closely related species keep track of who's recently helped them and who has sided with an adversary, then draw on that information when deciding who to help in the future. Such predispositions towards social accounting and reciprocity must have been modified by small differences in the frequencies of various genes, modest mutation of a gene here and a gene there, consonant changes in relevant brain structures as brain volume grew, and supportive changes in culture to bring us to be the species that we are today—a species in which, as we'll see, there remains some diversity of social predisposition from one individual to the next but a great deal of innate empathy and openness to being socialized towards helping and sharing behaviors, where a culture calls for them.

One issue that we haven't addressed is whether all acts of cooperation and helpfulness depend on reciprocity that's so fine-tuned that those involved would never engage in it without the expectation of an equal return. While it's impressive for nature to have endowed people with an ability to overcome the temptation to cheat on their reciprocal obligations, that is, if people *only* help others when they expect it to be reciprocated, then it could be argued that there's nothing altruistic about it, after all. Yet some people do apparently engage in altruistic acts and extend what was previously their side of a reciprocal relationship beyond the point at which the other party can ever be expected to repay. Examples occur, for instance, when a friend or spouse becomes incapacitated or terminally ill. In what's been termed "strong reciprocity," an individual will repay the kindness of another even when there'll be no future interaction between them and no effect on the individual's reputation—think again of a traveler leaving a tip for good service though she'll never return to the same restaurant or hotel. Strong reciprocity is also said to occur when someone takes upon herself the cost of punishing an unfair action, though she'll never benefit personally if the recipient reforms his behavior. The explanations of how reciprocity could have evolved with the help of group selection, which were discussed in this section, have been shown to have the potential of working for strong reciprocity as well as for the weaker form in which a return is expected. But the evidence that people vary in their inclinations to reciprocate is even greater where strong reciprocity is concerned, as we'll see in the next chapter.

The desire for approval

One of the most powerful motivators of human behavior is the desire to be thought of well by others. Adam Smith ranked it alongside the desire for wealth, leaving as an open question which is the more important to the average person. "To deserve, to acquire, and to enjoy the respect and admiration of mankind, are the great objects of ambition and emulation," he wrote in his *Theory of Moral Sentiments*. In many societies, of course, people admire those who are financially successful—Smith tells us this was true in his own time—so the desires for wealth and for approval are often in harmony. Yet they sometimes conflict, and it's not difficult to think of instances in which people forego some pleasure or material advantage in order to "look good" or gain importance in the eyes of others.

To the extent that modern humans descend from creatures who banded together to improve their chances of finding food, to defend themselves from predators, and to protect their vulnerable young, it's easy to see how the desire to maintain others' approval and goodwill could have evolved. In recent years, researchers in the fields of psychology and neuroscience have been accumulating evidence that the normal individual has an innate drive to understand what's going on in the minds of others with an eye towards anticipating their actions and reactions. This is noteworthy since the proposition that others even *have* minds can't be proven scientifically. Clearly the *presumption* that other people are real, that there's "someone home" in their heads and guts as we feel there to be in our own, is an inborn "working hypothesis" or default position. In recent years, behavioral scientists have come to call that inborn supposition, and the self-projecting guesses about what goes on in the other's head, a "theory of mind."

Our projection or extrapolation of our own "internality" onto others contributes to our need for approval because we observe our dispositions towards others shifting as their actions towards us are kind or unkind, and we suppose that the same must be going on as *they* process impressions of *us*. Since we want others to be helpful to us when we need them to be, taking actions likely to make their disposition towards us more positive naturally strikes us as a good idea. Indeed, for a great many the desire seems to transcend any practical calculation: they want to be well thought of and to *deserve* to be well thought of, the opposite being quite intolerable. Still, others would emphasize the practical origins and reinforcements of the desire to be on others' good side, pointing out that during the course of our evolution, it would never have been very difficult for one or two healthy human beings to kill a third one, and that this would have provided a strong reason to want to cultivate a modicum of sympathy in our companions. Our ancestors didn't sleep at night in solidly built houses equipped with electronic alarm systems.

The presence of a desire to be well thought of by others deserves mention even in the briefest discussion of human nature because it's a central pillar on which so many other manifestations of sociability appear to rest. For example, while a predisposition towards reciprocating kind action with kind action may have foundations in the bias towards cooperation discussed above, it may also be the case that specific norms of reciprocity in specific societies are strengthened by the perception that relevant expectations exist, and that one will incur the ire and dislike of others if the norms in question are violated. The same applies to any behavior that's not otherwise to one's selfish advantage but where a supposition of "expectedness" can be established. If you live in a society in which there's reason to believe that people will think less of you if you spit on the sidewalk, neglect to mow your lawn, or venture down the street with no clothes on, then you're likely to be strongly motivated to abide by the rules in question.

UCLA law professor Lynn Stout, a leading scholar in the field called "law and economics," points out that when person after person walks past a sleeping homeless man, each failing to add coins to the cup positioned near him, it's easy to look at their behaviors as evidence of selfishness. But she turns the conclusion on its head by pointing out that *not taking the coins already in the cup* is in fact a violation of self-interest! That failure to seize the opportunity to benefit oneself might be attributed to the desire to adhere to a social norm. Few would want to be known to have taken money from a helpless beggar, even if the chances of being observed are miniscule.

A striking example of the operation of concern about how others view us was provided by an experiment that psychologists conducted in a university coffee room a few years ago. The department in question had long followed the custom of using an honor system to request payments for coffee, tea, and milk, posting a price list above a payment box. Unknown to the room's users, researchers printed versions of the price list at the bottom of which they included a decorative strip containing either a photograph of flowers or a photograph of open eyes seeming to look at the viewer. One week they would post a price list with flowers, the next, a price list with eyes. Upon studying the rates of payment and nonpayment week by week, they found that the payment rate for items consumed was roughly three times higher when a price list with eyes was in place than when one with flowers was used. Yet when asked about it, none of the room's users recalled having noticed the photos at the bottoms of the lists![9] Although this study raises the discouraging possibility that only a minority tended to "do the right thing" as an expression of their moral values alone, the study certainly underscores sensitivity to how we're seen.

Wanting to think well of oneself

Not far removed from the desire to be well regarded by others, but a powerful help in filling in gaps left by that wish, is the desire to think well of oneself. Very few people, it would seem, judge themselves on entirely different grounds than those that they think others would use. Quite the contrary, typically we want "to be the kind of person whom others think well of." Our self-image is an image of ourselves as we imagine ourselves to be viewed by others. We internalize others' standards and judge ourselves accordingly.

Let's continue with the example of people passing a homeless person lying asleep on the sidewalk beside a cup of coins. Some of those passing this individual do so within seeing distance of others, and some of those who pass seemingly alone may worry that there might be someone watching from beyond their line of sight. Still, many undoubtedly would not take the change from the cup even if sure no one was watching, just as at least some paid for their coffee in the psychology study even on the weeks with flower cues. Why? Because they don't want to think of *themselves* as the kind of person who would do that. The small amount of money to be gained isn't worth the cost to their self-esteem. The importance to norm-adherence of "not wanting to be the kind of person who ___" (you can fill in the blank) is even the basis of a new behaviorally-oriented economic theory, "economics of identity." [10]

A few years ago, a thirty-five-year-old website designer named Paul Kinsella conducted an experiment to learn more about obedience to the norm of respecting others' property. He purchased a hundred inexpensive wallets and spent a month dropping them around the community of Belleville, Illinois (population: forty-one thousand). In each wallet, he placed $2.10 in cash, a fake fifty dollar gift certificate, and his own contact information. Of the hundred dropped wallets, seventy-four were returned to him. [11] Similarly, a team of economists left sixty-four unsealed envelopes each containing ten one dollar bills and the apparent addresses of their owners in various empty classrooms at George Washington University in Washington, D.C., to see how many of the students who came upon them when a class was preparing to meet would go to the trouble of returning them and in what proportion of cases they would be returned with their contents intact. They found that twenty-eight of the sixty-four wallets were returned, slightly less than forty-four percent. Surprisingly, the proportion returned by a student when the next class to meet was a class in economics was actually higher than the proportion returned when the next class was one in psychology, political science, or history. (Other experiments have shown economics students to act more self-interestedly than others.)

It should be kept in mind that a variety of factors can affect whether a generically described act, such as failing to return a dropped wallet or envelope or taking money from a sleeping stranger, actually belongs in your "I'm not the kind of person who would do that" category. I may not be the kind of person who would take money from the cup of a sleeping homeless man, but if I noticed a hundred dollar bill on the seat of my intercity express train beside a middle-aged professional in suit and coat soundly snoring, and if our section of the train were absolutely deserted, I might feel that the rule of not stealing didn't apply, since I believe that I need the money more than he does. I might also display a degree of creativity in rationalizing my taking the money; for instance, if the bill blew off the seat as I passed by and there was a shade of a doubt as to whether it was really the sleeping man's, I might more easily convince myself that it was a case of "finders keepers" and be able to retain my favorable self-image as the kind of person who doesn't steal. The "self-serving bias" of which this is an example might considerably narrow the set of actions barred by my "I'm not that kind of person" constraint. But that doesn't mean that the constraint has no bite at all.

Why might humans have evolved a tendency to judge themselves by the way they're seen by others? We've already noted that wanting to be liked by others and thus being able to imagine how others see you had an obvious evolutionary advantage given that mutual assistance was a life-and-death requirement throughout eons of human prehistory. But why care about how things that others aren't going to find out about you would have looked to them? Perhaps the development of conscience is a sort of ninety-nine percent solution, a way of addressing the problem of getting the gene-bearer to be on the good side of its fellows without taking risks that could backfire due to a mistaken belief that an action won't be noticed. More generally, remember that evolution doesn't necessarily address every issue as an intelligent designer would, but rather works with the materials at hand, amended serendipitously by chance mutations. Self-consciousness, in the full human sense of that term, appears to be a rather recent innovation on nature's part, one that's been forged to a large degree in the kiln of social interaction. Since the self is so much a product of the human social environment, it shouldn't be all that surprising that a model of the social world one dwells in becomes internalized within the self or at least in the self's "first draft" form. The very expression "self-conscious," as used in ordinary speech, has the connotation of "feeling awareness and concern about how one appears in *others'* eyes."

Genes, culture, and socialization

Earlier in this chapter, we encountered the supposed dichotomy between heredity and environment, noting that the two are never really separable and that to be asked to select one or the other as most important is to be asked to make a false choice. Some important environmental influences are physiological in nature: the quality of nutrition, both in the uterus and after birth, affects brain development, which may influence behavior both by directly influencing the expression of the genes and by affecting the way in which social influences are assimilated. Social influences, including language, are picked up in the course of one's development and become embedded in one's vocabulary and manner of thinking. What is or isn't acceptable, desirable, frightening, attractive, hip, etc., is conveyed by nuances of expression, tone of voice, and body language in dealings with peers, relatives, and authority figures. They're learned mainly in the family, but in complex societies they're also imparted by other institutions charged with influencing the development of character and values. And these days, influential cues are also delivered from many directions by a bewildering array of media.

The genetic and societal determinants of behavior aren't independent influences that simply add or subtract from each other. Their interactions are complex and flow in both directions. The social environment has influenced genetic evolution, as in the example of the development of language and speech capability given above, even as biology imposes various constraints on culture. For example, it's difficult to make most people care as much for other people's children as for their own (outside of cases of adoption), to prevent them from having sexual feelings, to impart a wish to cuddle live snakes rather than furry kittens, and to condition them to feel no grief at the death of a loved one.[12] But by the same token, genes don't constrain culture to take one and only one form. There's a degree of leeway, a zone of variability in which social influences can make a difference. Athens and Sparta seem to have succeeded in raising different types of men despite their geographic and genetic proximity to each other.

Socialization into norms, for instance teaching a child to play "nicely" with other children and to offer to share his toys, seems constrained by capabilities and predispositions that "come online" as the individual matures. One of the best pieces of evidence for the existence of an innate capacity for moral reasoning is that children between the ages of three and five so hungrily appropriate the idea of fairness and learn to manipulate it to their advantage, for instance in their relationships with parents or teachers. What parent of siblings hasn't heard the cry "That's not fair!" repeated again and again by their preschoolers and kindergarteners? Children seem to go through natural progressions, processing moral socialization in more sophisticated ways as they approach adulthood, moving through a period of assessing their values more independently, and then internalizing them further when they take on the role of moral socializer themselves.

In every society, keeping mental accounts of what you owe others, what others owe you, and how you've been treated in the past by them seems to be second nature to people. In a well-known experiment, the evolutionary psychologist/anthropologist team of Lena Cosmides and John Tooby provided evidence that people are naturally better at reasoning about when a violation of a social norm or obligation has occurred than at solving logical problems of equal complexity that lack a social cheating dimension.[13] Just what's considered fair, what one's obligations are, and what rights one has vary from society to society, epoch to epoch, and family to family.

It's helpful to think of an adult human being as displaying what biologists call a "phenotype," that is a "realized nature" that reflects not only the genes but also the environmental influences that have acted upon him or her. There are species of ants in which individuals of identical genetic make-up can become workers or guards, with quite different body type and behavior, depending on the way in which the queen and/or workers of the colony treat the egg. "Phenotype" thus refers to *gene expression*, which is not unambiguously dictated by the genes but also by factors acting upon them, as is obvious from the fact that a brain cell and a liver cell of the same individual develop from the same fertilized egg with the same set of genes but take on radically different forms as different parts of the genome are switched on or activated. In human beings, whether we're short or tall, slim or heavy, are aspects of the phenotype that are influenced by the genes but not fully determined by them—witness the fact that average heights in many countries rose considerably with improvements in diet in the twentieth century.

What applies to physiology applies to behavior, as well. Genetically identical twins aren't necessarily identical in personality—for instance, the probability of developing schizophrenia if one's identical twin has it is high, at forty-six percent, but that both of two identical twins will develop the disease is *not* inevitable.[14] Two individuals with the same genetic receptivity to moral socialization might turn into adults with different degrees of moral sensitivity and restraint because they're influenced by different cultures or grow up in households or extended family groupings with different moral climates or due to even more subtle influences and experiences. Yet there are remarkable examples of identical twins reared far apart, without contact and in very different households, who show considerable similarity of traits, which makes clear that a person is not just a blank slate that social forces can mold in any which way. The role of genes is also evident when non-identical siblings, raised in the same household by the same parents and even at the same time, can have quite different personalities.

Your society or mine?

Some of the most powerful environmental influences in today's world are those of language, culture, nationality, and ethnicity, which play a large part in determining who we imagine ourselves to be, who we perceive as "us," and who we perceive as "them." The sense of "we"-ness that must originally have developed in small bands of twenty or thirty individuals has proven remarkably durable as it's stretched itself to fit modern nations with populations of many millions. Psychologists find it relatively easy to prompt their research subjects to act differently towards members of "their own group" than they do towards non-members or "others." Simple manipulations, such as randomly telling some that they're "in the red group" and others that they're "in the blue group" are sufficient to establish such identities.

Unfortunately, suspicion, hostility, and dehumanizing the out-group seem to be the natural extensions of in-group solidarity and cohesion. "The profound irony is that our noblest achievement—morality—has evolutionary ties to our basest behavior—warfare. ... The sense of community required by the former was provided by the latter," writes primatologist de Waal.[15] The economists Samuel Bowles and Herbert Gintis, who use game theory to study the evolution of human goals, norms, and institutions, likewise view "parochialism" as the flip side of "community." An evolved human tendency to "conform" to the patterns of the group helps to distinguish one group from another at the same time as it permits norms of cooperation to emerge, according to the anthropologists and evolutionary theorists Robert Boyd and Joseph Henrich.

To say that the individual is to her society what a cell is to an organism is to put the matter a bit too strongly. But on certain emotional, psychological, and conceptual levels, there's some value in this analogy. The self is formed in a social crucible, and the individual would have little in the way of a recognizable mental life but for the ways of parsing experience that the collectively invented vocabulary of her culture gives her. Rare individuals who are raised past a certain age in isolation—in a few documented cases by animals, in others in orphanages practicing extremes of isolation like those of Ceaușescu's Romania—fail to develop normal capacities for language and emotional connection. Presumably, their experiences of self are correspondingly affected. "We belong to a category of animals known among zoologists as 'obligatorily gregarious,'" writes de Waal. "We are social to our core. . . . Being expelled is the worst thing that can befall us. Our lineage's state of nature is one of bonding and support." It's sad that the connections that bind us to those in our group have often served as disconnections from outsiders, but facing the tendency squarely might help us to moderate its effects.

Varieties of the human social animal

People *do* differ from each other. But there's more difference among the members of any one group than between the average member of one and the average member of another group. In other words, it's easy to find two Hungarians or two Japanese or two Mexicans who differ more from each other than the average Hungarian differs from the average Japanese or Mexican. Any ethnic or national group includes among its members about the same *variety* of genetic dispositions for height, intelligence, and temperament as does any other group. Each includes some people predisposed to anxiety and others to thrill seeking, some disposed towards sociability and others towards introversion, some towards caring and others to indifference.

The same probably applies to differences in individuals' receptiveness to social *norms* that balance self-interest against the interests of others. Some people deeply internalize norms of reciprocity, fairness, and cooperation, making these their inner compasses, while others take note of such norms but conform to them only when it's clearly advantageous to do so. Circumstances that make cooperation especially beneficial move some to play the role of leader or "moral entrepreneur," the group member who tries to rouse others to join him or her in criticizing non-cooperators. Others hold back to "see how the wind blows," conforming to the norm and joining in the group activity when it seems unwise not to, but free riding on the efforts of the few if enough others behave that way. A few individuals will even actively work to sabotage cooperation, stirring up jealousy of leaders and daring others to join them in resisting demands couched in moral terms. Groups containing diverse moral types thus exhibit familiar patterns of "moral ecology," with some individuals probably capable of playing more than one role and deciding where to fit in only after seeing which niches remain to be filled.

Why is it that moral exhortation—along with the accompanying push back—are such universal features of human societies? The psychologist Donald T. Campbell talked of human predispositions as lying along a continuum from complete selfishness to complete altruism or social-mindedness. He suggested that genes predispose individuals to end up at one point or another along that continuum. Although the precise points differ from person to person, Campbell suggested that the in-built disposition of almost all is towards a point fairly close to, but not entirely at, the pole of full selfishness. Cultures then try to nudge people from their natural dispositions towards points a bit farther from selfishness and closer to full social-mindedness. Noting that every world religion appears to share messages about altruism, truthfulness, and so on, and that almost no religion takes pains to remind people to be selfish, Campbell argued that civilized societies preach altruism because there's not much danger that people will end up giving too little weight to their own interests. Perhaps evolution left this job to culture because people have always lived in groups that naturally generate pressures towards a degree of other-orientation. The balance of selfishness dictated by the genes is optimal only in view of the anticipated counterweight from society.

If people end up at different points along Campbell's spectrum, it's partly due to differences in culture but more importantly due to differences in specific environmental conditions (birth order within the family, personalities, and life experiences of people influential in the individual's development) and to differences in genetic disposition. Within the same family, just as one child may be born predisposed to sensation-seeking and another to seeking security and regularity, so one child may have a natural inclination to develop a strong sense of right and wrong under the appropriate stimuli, another not. And for two individuals having *genetic* predispositions that lie at more or less the *same* point on Campbell's spectrum, differences in socialization and life experiences can still make a big difference to the kinds of people they become.

Some conclusions

What can we say, in the end, about what makes the human animal tick? Clearly the desires for physical survival and comfort are important. And the vast majority of people care about their immediate family members and will make sacrifices to safeguard or enhance the well-being of—if no one else—their children. Finally, people want to look good in others' eyes, and to some extent in their own, and that may motivate them to behave in cooperative and sometimes altruistic ways towards others, especially when likely to be observed.

Normal people have capacities for empathy, but the inclination to be concerned about others shows considerable variability, including a great deal of sensitivity to the encouragement it does or doesn't receive from their social environments. Some people merely attempt to avoid the open appearance of malevolence, others put the good of unrelated individuals near the top of their concerns, and most people fall in between. Variation in the degree of cooperativeness or social-mindedness is possibly one of the most important facts underlying the complexity of social interaction, as the next chapter will argue.

We'll see in more detail there that when people are put in situations involving conflict between the pursuit of their own personal interest and a good outcome for a larger group, there are substantial differences in their responses, with some acting almost entirely out of self-interest and others trying to signal a willingness to cooperate. The implications of this variation in human selfishness and cooperativeness for the types of economic and social institutions that have emerged in human history and for the types that may be workable in the future will begin to come out in that chapter and will be explored more thoroughly in Chapter 7.

Another take-home message of this chapter is that the human capacity for moral socialization continues to show signs of having evolved in small, rather than large, group settings, with "in group"/"out group" distinctions being a ubiquitous feature. This is illustrated, for instance, by the readiness with which people distinguish between "us" and "them" in deciding what's appropriate. The ease with which people can take to exploiting, victimizing, and simply ignoring others, even while adopting a "humane" face in their dealings with their own group members, will be of considerable use for understanding how the world became so extraordinarily differentiated into have- and have-not societies, the topic of Chapters 8 and 9.

Notes:

1. I've made sure that there's no mathematics in the text that might scare away my intended readers, but for the curious, we could say that the actor tries to select his consumption C and work W so that some function $f(C,W)$ has as large as possible a value. An example of an additive function would be $f(C,W) = \alpha C - \beta W$, where α and β are positive constants. A multiplicative form in which the constants α and β become exponents is $f(C,W) = C^{\alpha}W^{-\beta}$. And so on.

2. Along with (ordinary) chimpanzees, considered the closest living cousins of humans; see Frans de Waal, *Bonobo: The Forgotten Ape* (Berkeley, CA: University of California Press, 1997).

3. Head size at birth was still pushed to the point at which deaths of mothers and children in childbirth were considerably more common in humans than in our closest animal relatives before the development of modern medical techniques including the C-section. Rates of maternal death in childbirth remain shockingly high in poor countries. See Nicholas Kristof and Sheryl WuDunn *Half the Sky: Turning Oppression into Opportunity for Women Worldwide* (New York: Alfred A. Knopf, 2009).

4. While specific genes responsible for specific behavioral traits are still largely unidentified, scientists are fairly sure that there will be a number of different genes that work in concert to produce any given trait, so the discussion here should more properly be in terms of the marginal impact of any one gene when working in concert with others.

5. The details may be too stomach churning for the squeamish reader; the female bats share by regurgitating the blood from their own mouths into those of other females, doing the same for adult buddies as they routinely do for their juvenile offspring.

6. The abbreviations CE, (for Common Era), and BCE (for Before the Common Era), are secular substitutes for AD (Anno Domini) and BC (Before Christ), and have identical chronological significance.

7. A free rider is someone who sneaks onto the train without paying the fare, making it necessary that the fare be higher for the honest people who pay their share.

8. Such arguments are advanced, among others, by Sober and Wilson, *Unto Others* (Cambridge, MA: Harvard University Press, 1998) and in a form similar to that of this paragraph in Joseph Henrich and Robert Boyd, "Why People Punish Defectors: Weak Conformist Transmission can Stabilize Costly Enforcement of Norms in Cooperative Dilemmas," *Journal of Theoretical Biology* 208 (2001): 78-89. Other treatments include those in the 2001 book *Altruistically Inclined* by Alexander Field, in the 2005 book *Moral Sentiments and Material Interests* edited by Herbert Gintis, Samuel Bowles, Robert Boyd and Ernst Fehr, and in Bowles and Gintis's *A Cooperative Species: Human Reciprocity and its Evolution* published in 2011.

9. The research is reported in Melissa Bateson, Daniel Nettle and Gilbert Roberts, "Cues of Being Watched Enhance Cooperation in a Real-World Setting," *Biological Letters* 2, no. 3 (2006), 412-414.

10. See George Akerlof and Rachel Kranton, *Identity Economics: How Our Identities Shape our Work, Wages and Well-Being* (Princeton, NJ: Princeton University Press, 2010).

11. Brian Ojanpa, "Lost wallet experiment delves into Ethics 101" *Mankato Free Press.*

12. In his book *Nature via Nature: Genes, Experience, and What Makes us Human* (Harper Collins, 2003), science writer Matt Ridley recounts the story of a research team that attempted to determine whether monkeys learn to fear snakes because they see other monkeys show such fear or whether fear of snakes is innate. The researchers initially determined that monkeys' fear of snakes is transmitted from one monkey to another and, moreover, that the fear could be imparted simply by showing them a movie of other monkeys reacting with fear to the sight of a snake. They then prepared an expertly doctored version of the movie, replacing the snakes with flowers, so that the monkeys in the movie appeared to be reacting with fear to the sight of flowers. Although the researchers found that a fear of snakes could be reliably induced by showing the film, the fear of flowers could not be induced by the same method. Rather, the message the monkeys seemed to take from the flower film was, in Ridley's words, that "some monkeys are crazy." The lesson: there's an innate predisposition to *learn* to fear snakes, but it must be activated socially. To ask whether the disposition is innate or is learned, then, is simply asking the wrong question. Another Ridley book, *The Origins of Virtue: Human Instincts and the Evolution of Cooperation* (Viking Penguin, 1996), covers in depth ideas closely related to those of this chapter.

13. For a wonderful introduction to evolutionary psychology also closely related to this chapter's themes, see Robert Wright, *The Moral Animal: Why We are The Way We Are* (New York: Pantheon Books, 1994).

14. "Mental Health: A Report by the Surgeon General," Surgeon General of the United States of America, 1999.

15. Nicholas Wade, "Scientist Finds the Beginnings of Morality in Primate Behavior." *New York Times*, March 20, 2007.

16. Frans de Waal, *Our Inner Ape: A Leading Primatologist Explains Why We Are Who We Are* (New York: Riverhead Books, 2005).

CHAPTER 6
How Heterogeneous People Interact

If we're going to use our understanding of human nature to draw conclusions about something as critical as the improvability of society, we'll want to do our best to see that that understanding is accurate. One way to test and to improve our understanding of people and of how they interact with each other is to ask people to make decisions in the controlled environments of experimental laboratories—in most cases, simply rooms filled with desks, chairs, and computers at which participants can sit, type in decisions, and view feedback about others' decisions. The process is structured to involve a specific relationship between decisions and money earnings, so participants have tangible incentives to understand the environment and to act with deliberation. Putting it more concretely, the participants volunteer with the main goal of earning some money, so when we observe choices between their own interest and competing considerations like being "nice," adhering to norms, and so on, we're seeing decisions that carry real costs rather than simply observing what people say or do in order to look good.

As mentioned, in the last chapter, these kinds of experiments have been used increasingly during the last few years and have played a part in encouraging the reconsideration of the *Homo economicus* assumption. In this chapter, I'll give somewhat detailed descriptions of a few of them and draw on them for evidence about how people of different types interact and how their interactions determine the performance of societies and institutions.

Selfishness and cooperation: The voluntary contribution game
A much-repeated experiment that investigates the interplay between selfishness and cooperation has the following structure. Sixteen or more subjects are seated at computer terminals, each at least a small distance from the next or separated by sight barriers. They're prohibited from communicating with each other. Each is given the following instructions: You and three others, who will not be identified to you either during or after this experiment, have each been given ten dollars. Each of you can keep any of the dollars you wish to and put the remaining dollars

into a group fund. Any money that's put into the fund will have sixty percent added to it by the experimenter. The total amount in the fund will then be divided equally among the four group members. Your take-home earnings will be the amount that you keep plus your equal per capita share of the group fund (one-fourth of it).

Suppose that you're a participant in this experiment. On the face of it, your problem is relatively simple. If you and your fellow subjects each place all ten of your dollars into the fund, you'll each earn sixteen dollars. If you all place nothing in the fund, you'll each earn ten dollars. So putting money into the fund is a good thing. But there's a catch. If the other three put their ten dollars into the fund, then without any contribution from you, there will be forty-eight dollars in the fund, which means twelve dollars for each of you. If you also put in your ten dollars, you'll earn sixteen dollars, but if you hold onto your ten dollars, you'll have that ten dollars plus your twelve dollar share from the fund, so you'll earn twenty-two dollars. Putting any smaller amount into the fund also earns you less than the fully selfish alternative. For example if you put five dollars in, you'll have the five dollars you keep plus fourteen dollars from the fund, or nineteen dollars. Clearly, the less you put in, the more money you earn, so putting nothing in the fund looks like your best course of action, from a self-interested standpoint.

To make sure the problem is clear, consider your decision one dollar at a time. Every dollar you put in the fund becomes $1.60 for the group, but then it's divided four ways, yielding only 40 cents to you. So each dollar you put in is losing you 60 cents compared to holding onto it, though it's also yielding 40 cents for each other group member, or a total of $1.20 in addition to your 40 cents. Of course, it's good for you that others put in dollars, since each of the dollars they contribute gives you 40 cents at no personal cost to you. So, from a self-interested point of view, the best thing to do is to keep your money and (if you can) encourage others to put *theirs* in. If you like, you can check the table below to further test your understanding.

	0	1	2	3	4	5	6	7	8	9	10
0	10	9.4	8.8	8.2	7.6	7	6.4	5.8	5.2	4.6	4
1	10.4	9.8	9.2	8.6	8	7.4	6.8	6.2	5.6	5	4.4
2	10.8	10.2	9.6	9	8.4	7.8	7.2	6.6	6	5.4	4.8
3	11.2	10.6	10	9.4	8.8	8.2	7.6	7	6.4	5.8	5.2
4	11.6	11	10.4	9.8	9.2	8.6	8	7.4	6.8	6.2	5.6
5	12	11.4	10.8	10.2	9.6	9	8.4	7.8	7.2	6.6	6
6	12.4	11.8	11.2	10.6	10	9.4	8.8	8.2	7.6	7	6.4
7	12.8	12.2	11.6	11	10.4	9.8	9.2	8.6	8	7.4	6.8
8	13.2	12.6	12	11.4	10.8	10.2	9.6	9	8.4	7.8	7.2
9	13.6	13	12.4	11.8	11.2	10.6	10	9.4	8.8	8.2	7.6
10	14	13.4	12.8	12.2	11.6	11	10.4	9.8	9.2	8.6	8
11	14.4	13.8	13.2	12.6	12	11.4	10.8	10.2	9.6	9	8.4
12	14.8	14.2	13.6	13	12.4	11.8	11.2	10.6	10	9.4	8.8
13	15.2	14.6	14	13.4	12.8	12.2	11.6	11	10.4	9.8	9.2
14	15.6	15	14.4	13.8	13.2	12.6	12	11.4	10.8	10.2	9.6
15	16	15.4	14.8	14.2	13.6	13	12.4	11.8	11.2	10.6	10
16	16.4	15.8	15.2	14.6	14	13.4	12.8	12.2	11.6	11	10.4
17	16.8	16.2	15.6	15	14.4	13.8	13.2	12.6	12	11.4	10.8
18	17.2	16.6	16	15.4	14.8	14.2	13.6	13	12.4	11.8	11.2
19	17.6	17	16.4	15.8	15.2	14.6	14	13.4	12.8	12.2	11.6
20	18	17.4	16.8	16.2	15.6	15	14.4	13.8	13.2	12.6	12
21	18.4	17.8	17.2	16.6	16	15.4	14.8	14.2	13.6	13	12.4
22	18.8	18.2	17.6	17	16.4	15.8	15.2	14.6	14	13.4	12.8
23	19.2	18.6	18	17.4	16.8	16.2	15.6	15	14.4	13.8	13.2
24	19.6	19	18.4	17.8	17.2	16.6	16	15.4	14.8	14.2	13.6
25	20	19.4	18.8	18.2	17.6	17	16.4	15.8	15.2	14.6	14
26	20.4	19.8	19.2	18.6	18	17.4	16.8	16.2	15.6	15	14.4
27	20.8	20.2	19.6	19	18.4	17.8	17.2	16.6	16	15.4	14.8
28	21.2	20.6	20	19.4	18.8	18.2	17.6	17	16.4	15.8	15.2
29	21.6	21	20.4	19.8	19.2	18.6	18	17.4	16.8	16.2	15.6
30	22	21.4	20.8	20.2	19.6	19	18.4	17.8	17.2	16.6	16

Earnings Table of Voluntary Contributions problem. Column headings *(top row)*: *your contributions*; row headings *(left column)*: *combined contributions of others*; cell entries: *your earnings*. Each entry displays what you would earn if you put the amount shown in the column heading into the group fund while the combined contribution of the other three is the amount shown in the row heading. As you move from left to right in any given row, in other words toward higher contributions by yourself assuming any given contributions by the others, your own earnings are always going down.

Unfortunately, the incentives are perfectly symmetrical. Just as you have an incentive to keep your money, so do the others. If everyone follows the self-interested logic, you each end up with ten dollars (the upper left cell of the table), but if you'd somehow been guided by cooperative impulses, you could each have earned sixteen dollars (the lower right cell). That's why this situation is a good example of what's known to scholars of collective action as a "social dilemma." It looks as if the rationality of *each* of you is working against the real interest of *all* of you. Isn't there some way to override your "nasty" rationality and take a leap of trust?

For a long time, economists and game theorists made a simple prediction about decision tasks of this sort.[1] Working from the previously-discussed assumption that people are both self-interested and rational, they predicted that no money would be contributed to the group fund, or at least that once the subjects learned to understand the problem, they would not put money in. Behavioral scientists in such fields as psychology and sociology, working from observation and intuition, made a different forecast. The behaviorists predicted that many subjects would attempt to cooperate with fellow group members. This would follow, in part, from the conscious realization that if everyone acted selfishly, all would end up losing and, in part, from a deep-seated impulse to try cooperating. The newly emerging group of researchers calling themselves "evolutionary psychologists" argued on grounds similar to those discussed in the last chapter that this impulse to cooperate was an evolved adaptation of human nature, one that responds to tens of thousands, if not millions, of years of experience with similar social dilemmas.

Theorists can debate forever. What happened in the actual experiments?

The answer is that it depended on a number of factors, ones that should not matter according to versions of game theory that assume actors to be rational and selfish.[2] Did subjects play the game one time only, several times, or many times? If the game was repeated, did the subjects continue to play in the same group, or were groups reshuffled?

To begin with, when the subjects were asked to allocate ten dollars one and only one time, on average about five dollars was put into the group fund, so individuals earned about thirteen dollars on average. But the amounts contributed by different individuals differed, so their earnings also differed. One person might put in ten dollars, another seven dollars, a third three dollars and the last zero dollars. So their earnings would be eight dollars, eleven dollars, fifteen dollars and eighteen dollars, respectively; by the nature of the interaction, the highest contributor of course earned the least. The executive summary: a prediction of zero contributions finds no support, but individuals differ.

What if the subjects were given several opportunities to play the game? In these cases, the average amount put in the group fund tended to decline with repetition. If the average was five dollars the first time around (which continued to be typical), and if the subjects were told in advance that the decision would be repeated a total of ten times, the average typically fell to, say, three dollars by the third or fourth round, and to one dollar or less by the last round. So it seemed that while the behaviorists were more "on the money" than the economists, initially, the subjects' decisions were coming ever closer to the economists' predictions (that no one contributes anything) as the game was repeated. An attractive interpretation to the traditional economists was that the subjects were learning, coming to understand that it's not in their interest to put money into the fund.

But further experimentation raised questions. When subjects repeatedly played the game, their contributions tended to be higher if they kept a constant set of group-mates than if they repeatedly played but in randomly reshuffled groups drawn from a larger subject pool. In addition, subjects were more cooperative when the game was changed so that a dollar put in the group fund generated $2 rather than $1.60 for the group as a whole, and they were less cooperative when the dollar generated $1.20 rather than $1.60, even though logic dictates that an individual should withhold contributions regardless of what they generate, so long as it's less than $4.

In one especially suggestive set of experiments, the subjects were told that they would play the game ten times, and they did so with the usual decline towards about one out of the ten dollars per person being contributed. But after the tenth repetition, the experimenter announced ten more periods of play that the subjects hadn't anticipated. If the tendency of contributions to decline over time had simply been a matter of learning, as the traditional economists argued, then we'd expect contributions to continue their downward slide in rounds eleven to twenty, from one dollar to seventy cents and on towards zero. Instead, the unanticipated "restart" of the experiment brought a recovery of contributions towards roughly the original five dollars. Could it be that the subjects thought that they'd learned something from the decaying trend other than the idea that free riding is the only logical thing to do? For instance, might they have learned that no one individual can free ride without the others following? Could they have decided to fully cooperate, given a fresh start? That was very likely the conclusion that some had reached. But with further repetition, contributions began their decline all over again. Roughly the same pattern was observed by different teams of researchers in different countries. What could explain it?

Tapping into heterogeneous types and the idea of reciprocity

In the late 1990s, after two decades of voluntary contributions research had generated the well-replicated findings but also the puzzles just described, economists Ernst Fehr and Simon Gächter were working together at the University of Zurich, which was becoming a major center of experimental economics research under Fehr's leadership. The two proposed a new explanation of the declining contribution and restart results, one based on the assumption that the motivation of experiment participants differed from individual to individual. In their view, subject pools include both individuals having strong inclinations towards reciprocity and cooperation and other individuals lacking such inclinations. When an individual of the former type encounters the voluntary contribution game, she thinks something like, "We can all make out better here if we just cooperate with each other. I'll put my money in the group fund and see if others do the same. As long as I find that others also cooperate, I'll continue to put my money in. If the others are like me, we'll all do well." If four people of this type happen to be grouped together and if they all begin with optimistic expectations of one another's behaviors and thus contribute their full ten dollars the first time around, their hopes are fulfilled, and they can go on contributing ten dollars and earning sixteen dollars each time they play.

But if the population is diverse, say half cooperative and half uncooperative, the chance of four cooperators meeting by accident is small (one in sixteen). Most likely there's at least one uncooperative type in any randomly formed group. Suppose, then, that there are, say, two cooperative and two uncooperative types who by chance are grouped together. Suppose that the cooperative types begin by putting in ten dollars and the uncooperative types zero dollars (putting the average at the usual 50% of endowment). The cooperators each earn five dollars and the uncooperative types each earn fifteen dollars this first time around. What do they do next?

Here, we need to be clear about what's meant by a predisposition towards cooperation. In the last chapter, we saw that a key factor that could have been helpful in causing a disposition to cooperate to evolve is that some people were disposed not only towards positively cooperating in the sense of doing their part or observing the group norm; they were also disposed towards a more negative manifestation of cooperating, namely taking on the task of penalizing any free riders. If placed in the experiment, such a cooperatively disposed individual is likely to make a large contribution to the group fund at the beginning and to continue to contribute most or all of her endowment if she finds that others do the same. But if she finds some others to be contributing little or nothing while profiting from her own contributions, she'll feel a desire to punish them. What kind of punishment is possible? In the experiments discussed, the only way to punish others for free riding is by contributing less yourself. With selfish or opportunistic types already contributing little and with reciprocators lowering their contributions so as to punish them, we'd see the decline in contributions as described above.

But why would cooperation rebound after an unanticipated restart? First, suppose that play is restarted after forming new groups. For each subject, the regrouping represents a new random draw of people from a general subject pool, with no one knowing in advance just what mix of cooperators and opportunists she's been grouped with. An optimistic cooperative type can still hope that this time she's in a group with other cooperative people and reason that the only way to see if that's so is to try cooperating and see how the others respond. Even an opportunist may have learned from the prior rounds that there will be more contributions on which to free ride if he sometimes contributes something. Hence the cycle starts again. A few cooperators are pleasantly surprised to see that the others they're placed with are indeed pretty cooperative, but most groups follow the typical pattern, as before.

Restarting also triggers higher contributions when the same subjects stay grouped together. This might be explained by cooperators trying to signal a willingness to forgive and forget and opportunists calculating that pretending that they're "turning over a new leaf" will help them to better free ride on their partners in later periods. (There's no free ride unless someone is paying the fare.) But as free riders begin to show their true colors, cooperation unravels again, since the cooperators have no way to retaliate (or to defend themselves from being exploited) other than by reducing their own contributions.

Fehr and Gächter's hypothesis can thus help to explain both why cooperation declines with repetition and also why it rises after a restart. A further strength is that it's more consistent with the fact that initial contributions vary considerably from person to person. But they wanted to conduct a more definitive test of their hypothesis, and with that in mind they came up with a new experimental design. They modified the voluntary contribution game by letting subjects punish or impose costs on one another after learning of each others' contributions, but doing it in a more discriminating way than simply by reducing their contributions, which hurts high and low contributors alike. The experiment Fehr and Gächter designed startled many with its dramatically different result, ultimately earning them a publication in the *American Economic Review*, another one in the scientific journal *Nature*, numerous follow-ups with other collaborators, write-ups in the *New York Times* and *The Economist*, and a multitude of scholarly citations. It was also retested and expanded upon by other experimental economists. Before discussing it, it's useful to say something more about the idea of punishment and its appearance in earlier experiments.

Giving up money to hurt the other guy

In 1982, three German economists, Werner Güth, Rolf Schmittberger, and Bernd Schwarze, published a paper reporting observations from a simple experimental interaction they called the Ultimatum Game. Subject A and Subject B, anonymous to one another and seated in different rooms, were tasked with dividing between them an amount of money—it might again be ten dollars. Subject A, called the Proposer, moved first, proposing a way of dividing the ten dollars between the two. B, called the Responder, moved second, deciding either to accept the proposal, in which case both receive the amounts that A proposed, or to reject it, in which case both A and B receive no money. The interaction ended with the Responder's choice, so rejecting the offer couldn't be used to get the Proposer to make a more favorable one.

In the simple *Homo economicus* version of game theory (everyone selfish, everyone rational, everyone knows that everyone knows that they're all this way), there's a straightforward prediction regarding A's and B's choices. A will propose to give B the smallest divisible part of the ten dollars. For example, if A is given the money in dollar bills and can only give zero, one, or some other whole number of bills to B, then A will offer B one dollar, leaving himself nine dollars. He'll do this because he wants to keep as much money as possible and because so long as he offers something to B, B's choice is clear. For B, keeping one dollar is better than ending up with zero dollars, so she'll accept the offer. So A offers one dollar, B accepts, and A ends up with nine dollars, the largest amount he can ensure himself. End of theoretical story.

This game has now been played experimentally by thousands of subjects, ranging from university students in Germany, Japan, the United States, and Israel to slum dwellers in South Africa and fishermen in Colombia. In the vast majority of cases, A offered four or five dollars of the ten dollars to B, B accepted the offer, and they walked away with similar amounts of money (six dollars and four dollars, or five dollars and five dollars). A smaller number of As offered three dollars, and some of those offers were rejected, leaving both A and B with nothing. A still smaller number of As offered one dollar or two dollars, and in those instances, the majority of offers were rejected.[3]

There are two anomalies that call for explanation. First, why do most As offer more than one dollar, when the theory says that that should be enough and should guarantee A the most possible earnings? Second, why do most Bs who are offered one dollar or two dollars reject it, preferring to end up with nothing?

That second anomaly is the real surprise; after all, if Bs are known to reject low offers with substantial likelihoods, then it makes good sense for rational and self-interested As to offer more. It's the Bs' behaviors that are harder to make sense of.

One way to rationalize the B players' actions and square them with self-interest is to argue that in ordinary life, people expect to play similar games with other partners in the future, and they calculate that a reputation for toughness will bring them better offers, causing them to earn more in the long run than if they were known to accept anything they're given. The experiments are set up in such a way that what B does is *not* revealed to others, so investing in a reputation is in reality ruled out. But it's possible that B subjects aren't entirely convinced that their action will stay unknown, or that Bs simply act in a way that's normal for most real world situations, not working out carefully enough what makes sense for the unusual set-up implemented in the lab. Usually, investing in a reputation for tough bargaining makes sense, and that spills over into an action that happens to be irrational for an unusual environment, goes the argument.

But not all economists accept the explanation that rejecting small offers in Güth and colleagues' Ultimatum Game is due to a habitual but misplaced concern for reputation. A substantial number think that understanding the behavior requires a willingness to question the version of economic theory in which decision makers' only concerns are that they earn as much as possible. Most players, these economists argue, might feel that there's something *unfair* about a very small offer, since the power to be Proposer rather than Responder came A's way entirely by chance. Being treated unfairly, they go on to argue, triggers a desire to retaliate or punish. Having been offered only one dollar out of ten dollars, the game's set-up puts B in a position to punish A with the loss of nine dollars at a cost to herself of only one dollar. If B is angry enough, this could look like a pretty good deal. In other words, if B values the chance to deprive her unfair counterpart of nine dollars more than B values having one extra dollar in her own pocket, then it makes sense for B to reject the offer.

Notice that rejecting the offer does not have to be *irrational* if we suppose that B has a *taste* for something besides money—in this case, for punishing an unfair act. If we don't view it as irrational for people to pay one dollar to download songs to their iPods or to watch wrestling matches on TV, even though they can't eat, drink, or protect themselves from the elements with a song or a wrestling match, then why judge it to be irrational to pay one dollar for another intangible source of satisfaction, "giving A what he deserves"?

One final note is in order. In Chapter 5, I reported that a number of evolutionary theorists attempting to explain how tendencies towards cooperation could have emerged in early humans assign an important role to the emergence of tendencies to punish non-cooperation, cheating, free riding, or unfairness. Such theories are quite compatible with the possibility that the immediate or proximate factor that causes individuals to engage in punishment is an emotion, anger. After all, the immediate cause of running from a predator is not a rational calculation but also an emotion, fear. The considerable evidence of a *taste for punishing* in experiments, including the ones by Fehr and Gächter to which we return now, is accordingly quite consistent with those evolutionary theories.

Group contributions when there's a chance to punish

Now that we're a little clearer on the notion of incurring a cost to punish, and having reminded ourselves of where the tendency to punish might come from, we're ready to discuss Fehr and Gächter's experiments with voluntary contributions to a group fund in the presence of opportunities to engage in costly punishment. Recall that their explanation for declining contributions included the idea that high contributors felt exploited by free riders and wanted to punish them. Consider now the fact that some responders in the Ultimatum Game were willing to give up a small amount of money to impose even larger losses on "misbehaving" partners. Fehr and Gächter conjectured that if cooperating types in a voluntary contribution experiment could punish the non-cooperators by some means other than withdrawing their own cooperation, contributions could rise because the fear of punishment might induce the uncooperative individuals to contribute more, and the cooperators would themselves contribute more, rather than less, as free riding declined.

Here's how the amended game was played. As before, four subjects were put in a group and asked to make a series of decisions about keeping money or putting it into a group fund. As before, everyone would earn more (1.6 times their initial endowments) if they all put everything into the fund, and as before, each rational player trying to earn as much as possible for herself had the incentive to hold onto her money—except perhaps out of concern about punishment. This time, after each set of decisions about how much to contribute, the subjects not only learned the total put into the fund and their earnings, but they were also told how much each individual group member had contributed (although their actual identities remained unknown). Then each was given the opportunity to have money deducted from the earnings of others at a certain cost per dollar of such punishment (for instance, the punisher loses one dollar, but the person targeted loses four dollars).[4]

Before reporting their results, Fehr and Gächter walk their readers through the predictions of the economic reasoning under which each player simply wants to maximize her earnings. Suppose that the two stages of the game—contributions, followed by learning the results and punishing—were to be played one and only one time. Then if you played cooperatively but saw that one or more members of your group had contributed less than you, you might feel upset with them. If you were single-minded in your pursuit of earnings, though, you would spend no money on punishing them. And if they knew this, the possibility of your punishing them wouldn't induce them to contribute in the first place. Indeed, in this theoretical world in which you are all selfish and rational and know this about each other, you, too, know that no one will punish *you* if you don't contribute, so to earn as much as possible, you, too, won't contribute anything.

Suppose, now, that the game was going to be played several times with the same group of players. In this case, you might think that punishing a low contributor during some early periods would make sense as a way of increasing your earnings because your punishment might induce that person to contribute more next time. There's a problem with this reasoning, though. If you're presently in the next-to-last period of play and a group member has taken advantage of you by contributing nothing, whereas you contributed your full ten dollars, you might consider sacrificing a little money to punish that person, sending a signal that he/she had best contribute more "or else." But if you and they both know that you're a rational type who cares only about earning as much money as possible, your signal would do you no good, because the next period is the last one, and you and they both know that it wouldn't be rational for you to punish next time if they fail to heed your implied threat. Punishing in the next-to-last period is accordingly pointless: it doesn't constitute a credible threat. And if that's so, the same holds for the period before the next-to-last one—the person you target for punishment in the third-to-last period has no reason to think that you'll punish her again if she free rides in the second-to-last period, since there's no point in sending a signal at that point. And on and on the logic goes, exemplifying the principle game theorists call "backward induction" (reasoning from the last period backwards to the first). The predicted outcome of this "backward induction" reasoning—that is, that no one will contribute at all, even with the opportunity to punish—is called "backward unraveling," meaning that the joint cooperation that seems like a good bet for all at the beginning becomes logically untenable through a reasoning process that unwinds the chain of cooperation from the last period back to the first.

Accordingly, Fehr and Gächter argued, subjects should free ride just as much in the modified contributions game with punishment opportunities as in the original contributions game without those opportunities, if conventional economic theory were correct. But if considerable numbers of people are positive and negative reciprocators or conditional cooperators, as Fehr and Gächter themselves hypothesized, the opportunity to punish could make a real difference.

Having reviewed this theoretical logic, Fehr and Gächter report how subjects in their experiment behaved in actuality. In one treatment, subjects played twenty periods of a contributions game without change of team membership, the first ten with no punishment opportunities and the next ten with the chance to punish. Each had twenty experimental currency units to allocate each period. In the ten periods without punishment opportunities, the researchers observed the usual behaviors: around fifty percent of available money was contributed to the group fund in the first period, after which there was a fairly steady decline over the next nine periods, towards final contributions of around ten percent. When the ten periods with punishment opportunities started, however, there was more than the usual "restart" effect. In fact, first period contributions in the second ten periods were significantly higher than the highest observed before, suggesting that even before having seen others punish, at least some subjects feared that they would do so (contrary to the traditional "backward induction" logic).

What happened next was in even clearer contradiction to the traditional theory. Contrary to its prediction, many subjects incurred a cost to punish others—and far from being a random process of targeting reductions at others simply to blow off steam, there was a clear pattern of higher contributors punishing lower ones. As a result, instead of falling in the twelfth period, the average contribution rose because some low contributors raised their contributions after being punished, and high contributors felt no need to lower theirs. For the remaining periods, contributions rose, rather than falling (see the figure below), and those who failed to contribute at least the average amount for their group were often punished.

Contribution to Group Account in Fehr & Gächter's Experiment

Source: data in Ernst Fehr and Simon Gächter, "Cooperation and Punishment," *American Economic Review* 90, no. 4 (2000).

The last period of this experiment is of special interest because, from the standpoint of the theory of rational self-interest, the presence of costly punishing at that point would be strong evidence that some sort of taste or emotion is at work. Did subjects spend money on punishing low contributors even though there was no way to gain by inducing more contributions in the future? What the authors found is that the amount of punishment given in the last period was no less than in other periods, and punishment was still, as before, aimed mainly at low contributors. So, many subjects must have been punishing not just to send signals that would allow them to earn more later on, but as a visceral response to being taken advantage of (or, viewed differently, because the satisfaction of teaching those targeted a lesson outweighed the cost to them, just as downloading a song outweighs the money charged to the iPod user). Their finding has been replicated at least a dozen times by independent teams of researchers.[5]

What does it mean for the real world?
Given their controlled and somewhat artificial nature, it's natural to ask what experiments of the kind just described really mean for the world outside the decision lab. Skeptics want to know whether similar results appear if more money is at stake, if the subjects aren't university students, and so on. Many such experiments *have* been conducted with other subject populations and with more money on the table, and most find similar results. In fact, a number of studies suggest that if older adult participants differ from students in the decisions they make under similar circumstances, it's not by being more ruthlessly rational and selfish, but just the

opposite: the adults show greater sociability, trusting, and cooperation. Higher stakes, whether achieved by multiplying the money on offer to a small subject group of similar type or by conducting the experiment in a country where the same average payout equals several days' wages, typically make little difference.[6] Until now, though, there remain too few researchers and too little research funding to give assurance that every result mentioned above has been corroborated by such tests. So I'll discuss the results I've mentioned as if their replication in university labs is adequate while we wait for further data to come in.

Assuming the observations mentioned can be generalized, then, what do they imply about human nature and the organization of society? First of all, the voluntary contribution games are a nice metaphor or stylized representation of a lot of social dilemma problems—situations in which what's good for the group, and thus for its members when viewed collectively, delivers less to each individual member than she can hope to get for herself by acting individualistically. For example, I'd like others to refrain from throwing their garbage onto the streets and streams that I commute and fish on, but I'd like to have the option of throwing a little of my garbage onto the street or stream at those times when it's too inconvenient or costly for me not to. I'd like others to pay their taxes so the government can provide me with well-repaired roads and bridges, but I'd like to pay less taxes myself if my accountant can help me to get away with it. I'd like everyone in my company to put in maximum effort to improve the bottom line and thereby increase my job security and my bonus, but for my own part I'd love to get away with showing up late for work, stealing some time for personal shopping on my office computer, and enjoying a more leisurely lunch.

If we make the rational, selfish actor model our guide for what to expect of people, we'd have to conclude that these problems are going to be pretty intractable. We might all recognize on an abstract level that the inconsistency between individual and group interest puts us in a dilemma and that we'd be better off if we could foreswear acting selfishly and instead do what's good for the group. But if we were in fact as perfectly self-interested and rational as the *Homo economicus* model implies, then we could do no other than to free ride. And with everyone acting this way, the outcome for all would be one big mess. We'd end up using various costly measures, such as spending money to audit tax returns, imposing fines for littering, monitoring workers' use of computer and phone time, etc., to try to mitigate the problems, but we'd be expending a lot of resources this way, and we'd still be suffering losses from free riding type behaviors because eliminating them entirely would be too expensive. The money, time, and attention expended on detection and mitigation could have been used for better purposes had we simply found a way to be good team players.

Worse still, living with some background level of moral misdemeanors while wasting a big chunk of our potential resources on auditing and monitoring wouldn't be the biggest problem we'd face. The fact is that we couldn't even count on having a semblance of honest government, courts, or police forces there to referee our self-seeking populace, given that the personnel for those bodies, too, would have to be drawn from the same conniving stock. Who would bother to inform themselves on political matters or go to the polls, for instance, when these things take time away from making money and consuming the things bought with it and when the chance of any one individual being pivotal in an election is infinitesimally small?

The research just discussed suggests that we are in fact at least somewhat better team players than the pessimistic theory of selfish behavior would have us expect. A lot of us are willing to do our parts for the general good, provided that we expect enough others to do so and think the number taking advantage of our contributions without contributing is being held in check. We're *positive reciprocators* in the sense that when we observe others behaving nicely towards us and following rules, we tend to behave nicely and follow rules ourselves. We're also *negative reciprocators* in the sense that when we see others trying to take advantage of us by enjoying the fruits of our contributions without helping out themselves, we're moved to want to extract some cost from them (perhaps by gossiping and contributing to their bad reputations or perhaps by shunning them) even if we ourselves pay a price. Some of us go so far as to be "altruistic punishers" on behalf of others: when we see someone violating a social norm or rule and hurting others, we're moved to take action, sometimes even when we ourselves weren't the ones directly harmed. And the presence of these reciprocators has a salutary effect on everyone: free riders contribute more (follow more rules) to avoid being punished, and conditional cooperators contribute more (follow more rules) because they're reassured that others are also cooperating.

The resulting equilibrium of cooperation isn't a perfect one: many people still try to get away with free riding and breaking rules, resources are still spent on monitoring them, and the costliness of the process makes it necessary to stop short of catching every rule-breaker. Yet in well-functioning societies and organizations, we almost certainly see far more rule compliance than would be the case if no one were a willing cooperator or a willing monitor, whistleblower, and castigator of free riders.

Heterogeneity

The idea that not everyone is the same played an important part in Fehr and Gächter's explanation of what happened in the voluntary contribution experiments without punishment opportunities that I discussed a few pages back. We should note now that the same variation in behaviors was also present when subjects were equipped with the power to punish one another. Though many took it upon themselves to punish low contributors and though the presence of such punishment caused many of the individuals who are least inclined to do so to raise their contributions, variation in behavior from one subject to another was still very much in evidence. In most trials of the experiment, contribution levels remained somewhat varied, with the same individuals who contribute least in the absence of punishment still tending to be the lower contributors and with the higher contributors being the ones most likely to pay the expense of punishing to bring others into line.

One fact on which I've commented little so far is that while most punishment in these contribution and punishment experiments was directed at free riders or low contributors, not all of it was. The expectation that a low contributor would be punished can have an efficiency-enhancing effect, since it can induce a potential free rider to contribute, which helps everyone else and thereby raises earnings on average. But some participants perversely target the cooperators, as if to throw sand in the gears of society. The consequence is that contributions rise less than they might, and in the worst cases, the availability of punishment opportunities can even cause contributions to fall. The punishing inclinations of individual participants is thus quite varied, ranging from some who spend considerably to punish low contributors and others who incur little cost to punish—these two usually being the most common types—to a few individuals who punish indiscriminately and some who punish mainly high contributors.

Working with my own collaborators, I conducted several similar experiments with subjects at my university and also obtained the raw data of Fehr and Gächter's original study to look again at the decisions of their subjects. We found that it's typical for about twenty percent of all punishment to be targeted at groups' *highest* contributors, rather than the free rider low contributors. We also found that such "perverse" punishment came most often from the low contributors, that it tended to cause high contributors to reduce their contributions, and that it went a considerable way towards explaining why, even though contributions went up on average when punishment was possible, total earnings of the lab subjects were often not higher in the treatments with punishment than in those without it.[7]

Another research team that included Gächter, Benedikt Herrmann, and Christian Thöni conducted similar experiments at sixteen different research sites in fifteen countries in Europe, the Middle East, the former Soviet Union, east Asia, North America, and Oceania. They found amounts of punishing of high contributors by low ones similar to ours in their subject pools in places like Bonn and Copenhagen, but much higher amounts of this behavior, which they labeled "antisocial punishment," among subjects in sites including Riyadh, Athens, and Muscat. This suggested to them a link between norms of social cooperation and the quality of institutions across societies, one that may even contribute to explaining why some of the societies are more economically developed than others.[8]

One likely cause for low contributors to punish high ones in experiments repeated for a number of rounds or periods is that the low contributors believe the high ones are punishing them. (The experiments rarely let the subjects know exactly who is punishing whom, so the subjects are selecting their targets by conjecture.) Evidence that some punishment is indeed motivated by a desire for retaliation was found by Nikos Nikiforakis, who carried out an experiment like Fehr and Gächter's but added a third stage to each round or period, a stage in which subjects learned who punished them by how much and were given the opportunity to punish back, again at some cost to themselves. Although punishing back is as irrational as is punishing, under the assumption that everyone cares only about his or her earnings and knows this to be the case for everyone else, Nikiforakis found a great deal of counter-punishment—so much, in fact, that punishers retreated from punishing free riders, and the favorable impact of punishment on contributions was largely lost.

Nikiforakis's version of the game exacerbated the problems posed by selfish or antisocial behavior and raised an important concern because individuals can indeed punish back their punishers in some real world situations. But there are several ways that the problem can be mitigated. First, the environment constructed for his experiment tends to exaggerate the importance of counter-punishment because it only informs subjects of who has punished them and only allows them to punish back those same individuals. When subjects are informed of *all* punishment that *any* group member gave to any other group member and can condition further punishing on that information, some of the higher-stage punishing is directed at those who punished inappropriately in the first place, which tends to deter such behavior. Experiments since that of Nikiforakis have shown that opportunities to punish, taking punishing itself into account, don't necessarily exacerbate the problem of misdirected punishment, and they may even lessen it. There are also possibilities that a group might exercise some control over who can punish whom, or that the whole punishment function can be taken over by the group, which establishes rules of punishment under the control of the majority.[9] Some promising results along these lines are discussed below.

Tipping the balance towards the pro-social actors

So far, the experiments discussed have shown that the possibility of voluntary cooperation is not nearly as remote as in an imagined world of perfectly selfish people. Yet while conditionally cooperative people were found to be common, there were also usually a few troublemakers seeming to resist the drift towards cooperation. This is probably reminiscent of a lot of organizations you've been a part of, and maybe of society as a whole. Many people seem relatively neutral in their attitude towards cooperation but go along with their group's trend. Others show a more affirmative leaning towards cooperation, but they still look for assurance that others are joining in. A few people try to actively cheerlead for cooperation, engaging in moral exhortation or going first in the hope of establishing a cooperative pattern. But there are usually a few resisters, a few people who resent the societal "goody goodies" or even view a cooperative norm as a tyranny of which they want no part. The introduction of punishment opportunities by Fehr and Gächter had strengthened the hand of the cooperators compared to their situation without that tool, so my collaborators and I wondered whether there might be other mechanisms that could go even further towards neutralizing the influence of the least cooperative group members. In the end, we came up with several ideas to try out in the lab.

In one experiment, we changed the nature of punishment so that the money taken away from a targeted individual could be, and in fact had to be, transferred to another group member (but not to the punisher himself). This has the potential to improve the effectiveness of punishment (now punishment and reward) because not only is most of the punishment aimed at the free riders, but also there are rewards that tend to go to the high contributors, encouraging still higher contributions. Although misdirected punishment didn't entirely disappear when we conducted this "redistributive punishment" treatment, there was much less misdirected punishment when looked at in the fullest sense because in many cases in which a high contributor received some punishment, she received still more reward and was thus rewarded on balance.

Another device that we tried is withholding information about who contributed how much and also withholding the right to punish unless a subject chose to pay a fee to see the information and thereby obtain that right. We found that the more cooperative subjects (i.e., the higher contributors) were the ones most likely to pay for the information, and therefore the low contributors, who in our other experiments tended to punish perversely, were partly screened out of the punishing action. On balance there was considerably less misdirected punishment when knowing who had contributed what required giving up some money (the real world counterpart of which might be expending some time or effort to monitor others' actions).[10]

We also experimented with different ways of removing or isolating the more antisocial individuals. In one set of experiments, we let subjects have a say in who their fellow group members would be after learning how much others had been contributing in earlier periods. The high contributors ended up clustering together and persisting in high levels of cooperation; we discuss this experiment further, below. In still other experiments, we programmed the computer to group subjects together according to their contributing and punishing behaviors. When the high contributors were put together, they tended to go on making high contributions. All groups that contained some punishers of low contributors but no punishers of high contributors did well, also. The punishers of high contributors, who tend to be low contributors, were left to themselves in what, among ourselves, we dubbed "the dog group." In that group, everyone was so uncooperative that there was effectively nobody whose contributions one could free ride on.

An even more powerful way of achieving cooperation by removing antisocial individuals is an experiment treatment in which groups could vote to expel individuals to a low-earning secondary group. We started with large groups of sixteen subjects who were instructed to play a voluntary contribution game for fifteen periods. After each period, everyone learned the contribution of each group member and could cast votes, at a small cost, to expel whomever they wished to from the group. In the early periods, the lowest contributor or contributors tended to be voted out, and this induced everyone else to contribute much more. Contributions in the main group tended to approach one hundred percent of the available money, and overall earnings were higher, even when including the expelled individuals in the calculations.[11]

Finally, a particularly successful way to overcome the problem of perverse punishers was to let groups vote on who could be punished. We conducted experiments in which groups of four participated in a series of voluntary contribution games like those described so far, except that before every few periods of play, they voted (privately, without communication) on whether punishment should be permitted to be given to others in three categories: (1) those contributing above their group's average, (2) those contributing below their group's average, and (3) those contributing their group's average amount. Recall that the "perverse" type of punishment, that which is directed at high contributors, tends to come from a minority of about twenty percent of subjects in our subject pools. With this in mind, it might not be too surprising that majority votes rarely ended up permitting punishment of high contributors. What's remarkable is that in 160 separate votes, *no* group ever voted to permit such punishment, but most groups eventually chose to allow punishment of low contributors, and groups in which low contributors could be punished tended towards nearly one hundred percent contributions of member's endowments because there was almost always at least one group member willing to incur the cost of punishing free riders.

An interesting aside is that part of the exhibited evolution towards the choice of good rules in the experiment sessions with voting on who could be punished had to do with learning by example. In each session, we had sixteen subjects who were randomly assigned at the outset to form four groups of four. The experiments were set up so that each group voted, its members made their contribution and, if applicable, their punishment decisions under the rules they'd chosen for a few periods, and then the members of the group got at least two (in some treatments four) chances to vote again. In a departure from most experiments, we shared with all sixteen subjects immediately before each vote some basic information about what rules each of the four groups had selected last time around, how much their members had put in their group account, on average, and how much, on average, their members had earned. Thus, subjects could see if another group in their session was doing better than they were under a different rule, and this could influence their votes. Since earnings tended to be substantially higher in groups allowing punishment of low contributors, votes increasingly went in that direction. So the experiment not only demonstrated that people could solve their problem of cooperation through a combination of individual actions and group rule-making, but it also nicely illustrated how institutions might evolve in favorable directions through a natural and quite uncoerced process of diffusion of good ideas from one group to another. Similar diffusion from organization to organization, company to company, city to city, country to country, and so forth doubtless accounts for some real improvements in economic and social practices over both short and long spans of time.[12]

Talk is ~~cheap~~ effective

Researchers have found that one of the best ways to produce cooperation in decision-making experiments like the ones discussed above is to simply allow the participants to talk with one another. It seems that groups that talk the problem over are able to reach an understanding and often to follow through on it, even if there's no tangible enforcement device available to them.

In theory, talk should be cheap (i.e., lacking in much incentive to "put your money where your mouth is"). If I'm about to play the no-punishing version of the voluntary contributions game with you and two others, I could reason that what makes me best off is if all of you put your ten dollars into the group pot while I keep my ten dollars for myself. Can I say anything to the rest of you to help bring that outcome about? The obvious thing to do is to mislead you into thinking that I, too, am about to put in my ten dollars and that we have an agreement to that effect. If, after our discussion, we each go back to our seats and make our choices under the protection of anonymity—the procedure we used in the experiment I'll now discuss—and if someone proceeds to withhold their money, no one will know it was me. So if I'm truly self-interested, I'll promise to put in my ten dollars, provided that the others make the same promise. Then I'll return to my desk and make the decision I've had in mind all along: keeping the money.

This logic helps to make clear that if everyone had no goals other than to maximize their money earnings and no compunction about lying to achieve that goal, then talking before we made our decisions would make no difference. Talk would be cheap and ineffective (although it could have a temporary effect if there are to be a series of interactions, if those interacting don't know one another's true types, and if they're good at feigning trustworthiness for a while).

Introducing an opportunity to talk gets more interesting if some people are honest at least some of the time. If we were all thoroughly honest and we all pledged to put in our ten dollars, we could then count on doing exactly that and earning sixteen dollars, a gain of six dollars for each of us over the outcome if we're all dishonest. If three were honest and one not, and if the honest ones supposed it likely that all were honest, then the dishonest person could promise to put in her ten dollars and could make twenty-two dollars, while the others would be "suckered" and make only twelve. All would be seeing more earnings in that case than in the complete absence of cooperation, but very likely the three who got the short end of the stick wouldn't willingly do the same again. So when group members meet to talk in a world in which some but not all are the type who keep their word, one of the main things likely to be going on is that they'll be scrutinizing one another's faces, body language, and tone of voice for signs of trustworthiness.

Past experiments—including ones by Elinor Ostrom, who was awarded the Nobel Prize in Economics in 2010 for work on institutions and collective action—had suggested that letting subjects communicate before beginning to make their decisions tended to significantly increase cooperation in social dilemma experiments, including, but not limited to, the voluntary contribution game. We at Brown decided to see whether we could replicate this with our own subjects, then perhaps we could delve into the matter more deeply once we'd determined whether the qualitative pattern held for us. We accordingly conducted both a ten-period simple contribution game experiment and a variant adding punishment opportunities, in each case letting the subjects meet and talk for five minutes in their groups of four and then return to their seats and make their series of choices privately and anonymously, with no further communication after the first period.

The result was almost perfect cooperation—every subject contributing his or her full ten dollars—for the first eight or nine periods in most groups. In fact, three of the eight four-person groups had no "defections" whatsoever: all contributed ten dollars in each of the ten periods, including the last one. In two other groups, only one person "defected," in the last period only.[13] And those were the results in groups not offered punishment opportunities, opportunities that could perhaps have been fashioned into threats to keep in line any individual group member who chose to renege on their word by free riding. Since cooperation was so high in the treatment without punishment opportunities, the treatment in which they were included had no room for improvement. Its subjects achieved high cooperation, but no better than those allowed to communicate and lacking the opportunity to punish.

Raising the bar: Anonymous chat

Having determined that communication worked at least as "magically"—and mysteriously from the standpoint of conventional economic theory—in our subject pool as elsewhere, we were ready to dig deeper. What exactly accounted for these high rates of cooperation? Was loss of anonymity crucial? Even though your partners wouldn't know it was you if you defected,[14] once the group got together to talk, they did know you were in their group. And maybe you'd meet them on the way out, they'd insinuate that you were the one who'd betrayed them, and you'd want to crawl under a chair. Did the physical proximity of face-to-face discussion play an important part, letting people convey their honest natures or making them feel bound to their word by virtue of, say, the eye contact and the emotions triggered by it?

To investigate further, we designed new treatments that employed methods of communication other than face-to-face discussion. First, we held experiment sessions in which the actual decision stage was preceded by a stage in which the subjects could type into their decision screens amounts that they might "possibly" contribute, without this binding them to contribute those amounts. After sharing this information and letting the subjects adjust their entries for up to a minute, the binding decision screen appeared and subjects' real decisions were entered. Perhaps not surprisingly, this had little net effect. It wasn't that subjects just typed in any old numbers and ignored what others typed; a close look at the data showed that most were trying to use the numbers they typed to signal their intentions and to coordinate on mutually beneficial behaviors. The problem was that a minority of subjects showed no hesitation about using their "numerical message" to encourage others to cooperate while intending to defect themselves, so while cooperation rose in some groups, it fell in others.

In another set of sessions, the ten binding decisions were preceded every few periods by designated time during which the members of a group could exchange text messages in a computer chat room. While the words exchanged among group members might be much the same as in the face-to-face treatments, these subjects were prohibited from revealing their identities to each other. Unlike the face-to-face communication treatments, then, participants' anonymity was never compromised. In the chat treatments, contributions turned out to be substantially higher than they were in the treatments with only numerical messages and in those without any communication. Although there was somewhat less cooperative behavior in a few groups, which made average cooperation levels lower than in the face-to-face treatments, contributions were nevertheless impressively high, averaging nine out of ten dollars in several periods. Among the twelve groups involved, there were two that achieved perfect cooperation and three in which everyone contributed ten dollars until the last period.

The results in the chat room treatment suggested that the mere ability to verbalize a cooperative strategy and get members to state their commitments to it could make a big difference. Presumably many subjects were already inclined to cooperate and treated the others' words and then deeds as sufficient assurance that they would not be taken advantage of. Others were probably uncomfortable with going back on their word—at least not for the few extra dollars it would gain them in this case. Although talk *should* be cheap, if we were really all utterly self-interested and asocial beings, talk was rather effective in these experiments. This might help to explain why nations spend millions of dollars to transport their leaders to summits with those of other countries where each can "take the measure" of the other.[15]

Communication and the trust game

Because conflicts between individual and joint interests are central to so many economic, social, and political problems, it's worthwhile to consider yet another experimental game in which communication has also demonstrated surprising power. Used heavily by experimental economists to understand the nature of trusting and trustworthiness, the "investment game" or "trust game" was introduced in a 1995 paper by Joyce Berg, John Dickhaut, and Kevin McCabe. Two individuals—since you've probably had enough of "A" and "B" by now, let's call them Al and Betty—are placed in different rooms, and each is told that he or she will be matched with an anonymous partner whose identity will never be revealed. The experimenter gives Al ten one dollar bills and does the same with Betty. The simple rules for their interaction are read to both of them, both being told that the interaction will consist of precisely three steps.

In step one, Al decides whether to send his unknown counterpart all, some, or none of the ten dollars he was given by the experimenter. If Al sends something to his counterpart, it must be a whole dollar amount, so he has eleven options ranging from sending zero dollars to sending ten dollars. Al goes to a private spot, puts the money he decides to send (possibly nothing) into an envelope, and seals it.

In step two, as promised in advance, a subject appointed to the role of monitor by the experimenter takes the envelope, opens it in a private place, adds two dollars for each dollar that was placed in the envelope by Al, and brings the envelope with the tripled amount to Betty.

In step three, Betty, in privacy, opens the envelope, and if it contains money, she decides whether to send some, all, or none of it back to Al. Unlike money sent by Al to Betty, money sent by Betty to Al is not tripled but is simply given to Al by the monitor as is.

The experimenter assigns ten or more subjects to each role simultaneously, and envelopes are marked with numbers but not names. The procedure ensures that there's no chance that Al and Betty will ever learn each other's identities, and it encourages subjects not to choose actions they think would make a good impression on the experimenter, but rather those that they themselves think best. The monitor role adds an extra layer of anonymity between the subjects and the experimenter, whom there's a danger the subjects invest with some kind of authority.

Like the voluntary contribution game, the trust game is also a social dilemma because both Al and Betty can be better off if they cooperate with each other, but if each acts in his or her own material interest, such cooperation is in theory ruled out. The potential benefit of cooperation is clear from the fact that each subject begins with ten dollars and ends up with only ten dollars if Al sends nothing to Betty. Every dollar that Al sends to Betty is tripled, so the more Al sends, the more money there is to be divided between the two. If Al sends his entire ten dollars, Betty receives thirty dollars in addition to her ten dollars, so there are now forty dollars that can be divided between them. The extra twenty dollars created by Al's investment can potentially benefit both of them, provided that Betty chooses to send back at least eleven dollars, but not more than twenty-nine dollars, out of what she received. The dilemma is that if Betty is a rational, selfish actor, she'll keep anything Al sends her, sending back zero dollars. So if Al is also a rational, selfish actor, he'll send her nothing, and each will indeed end up with ten dollars only.

Contrary to the *Homo economicus* assumption, not only Berg and colleagues but also dozens of replicators of their experiment in a large number of both rich and poor countries have found that only a small minority of those in the Al role choose to send no money. A substantial, although smaller, proportion of those in the Betty role choose to send money back. If all second actors (Betties) sent back at least as much money as they received, then no special social orientation is needed to explain the first actors' decisions—they could simply have been anticipating reciprocity from their counterparts and acting in their selfish interests. But self-interest can't explain the actions of those counterparts who sent money back, and it would be strange if exactly half of the subject pool are of the *Homo economicus* kind and yet believe that random assignment in the experiment caused most of those on the other side of these interactions to be reciprocators. At the very least, the evidence suggests that most in the Al role believe that many other people, if not themselves, act like reciprocators.

In addition to being useful for understanding a number of real world social interactions as we'll further illustrate in the next chapter, the trust game also provides a good context for thinking about what communication might do under differing assumptions about human sociality. Suppose the procedure were altered so that Al and Betty exchange messages with one another before making their decisions but don't learn one another's identities, so rewarding or punishing each other's decisions after leaving the lab is ruled out. Then under the assumption that each is a strictly rational and selfish actor and that both know this to be the case, their communicating can't have any effect, because it's always in Betty's interest to keep anything received and so it's always in Al's interest to send nothing. However, when subjects were given such an opportunity to exchange preplay text messages in an experiment designed by University of Minnesota economist Avner Ben-Ner and me, the amount of money sent by the first actors increased significantly, and the proportion of received amounts sent back increased still more. In fact, the large majority of subject pairs agreed on exactly those choices that maximize both efficiency and fairness, namely Al sends ten dollars and Betty returns twenty dollars so that both Al and Betty end up with doubled earnings of twenty dollars apiece. And fully eighty-five percent of the Betties kept their part of the deal when entrusted with the money.[16]

It's interesting to note that the problem of trust can also be overcome when it's possible for the parties to enter into binding contracts, so an effective legal system is one way to encourage economic interactions that would otherwise expose people to what they might consider to be too much risk from untrustworthy counterparts in the real world. If Al and Betty agreed to the efficient and fair deal just described and could count on a third party to enforce it, then that would be the best way to go in a world with little trust, even if contracting itself were costly. (If each had to pay nine dollars for the services of the enforcer, it would still be worthwhile doing the deal and earning eleven dollars apiece rather than not doing it and earning ten dollars). But the ability to trust, which is fostered by widespread trustworthiness in a society, could save on these costs of contracting, so more might earn a full twenty dollars.

To investigate that issue, Ben-Ner and I let subjects in some trust game interactions first try to reach an agreement on what each partner was to do, then decide whether to spend some of their potential earnings on a contract that would provide assurance that the agreement was fulfilled by imposing a large monetary penalty on anyone who violated their part. While a small majority of those in the Al role asked for contracts, most of those in the Betty role did not—a difference indicative of the presence of some selfish bias and distrust. Nonetheless, pairs who carried out an interaction without contracts, as most did given the second actor's vetoing of the contract idea, often proceeded to exhibit both trusting (on the first actor's side) and trustworthiness (on that of the second actor), even though the threat of penalties was absent. And interacting without contracts saved the parties the contracting cost. Thus, having strong norms of reciprocity that make possible greater trust can partially and economically substitute for legal fees and court proceedings, although norms and an effective legal system are both complements and substitutes in a well-functioning society.[17]

Trusting your gut

Studies using the trust game have also generated interesting evidence about the role of the emotions in economic decision-making. When explaining their decision to rely or not to rely on another individual, people often talk about going with their "gut feelings." Stephen Atlas, at the time a graduate student in economics at Tufts University, performed a small test of the susceptibility of trusting decisions to emotional cues with me in a set of trust games for which we recruited participants from the virtual world Second Life. The avatar representing a participant entered a simulated lab room and read the rules of the trust game displayed in a series of printed instruction messages. The game structure was identical to the ones described above except that each participant started out with one hundred units of the local currency, Second Life Lindens, instead of ten dollars, and the player in the first role could send any whole number of Lindens between zero and one hundred. Unknown to the participants, lab rooms randomly varied from one another in one respect: whether they included a framed photograph on the wall or not, and whether that photograph, if present, was of a pair of playful-looking giant pandas or of a fish being filleted by a chef. The instructions made no mention of the photographs. Gut feelings must have come into play, however, because first decision-makers whose avatar sat in the room with the panda photo sent an average of forty-four percent more Lindens than did those whose avatar sat in the room with the fish photo (the former sent 70.4, the latter 48.9, out of one hundred). Subjects in the fish photo condition in turn sent somewhat less than counterparts in a room with no photo. Is this how "rational economic man" behaves?[18]

That not all is controlled by pure reason in such social interactions was also illustrated by experimental economists who had asked their trust game subjects to inhale a puff of unlabeled nasal spray not knowing that some were being exposed to the naturally-occurring hormone oxytocin, which is implicated in human social bonding (including the mother-child bond), while others had been given a placebo. The subjects exposed to oxytocin turned out to be significantly more trusting for reasons they could not know but that the observer might loosely refer to as "gut feelings."[19]

Self-interest is rarely absent

While much of this chapter and the previous one have emphasized social aspects of human nature and behavior that were typically downplayed in economics until recently, it would be a gross distortion to imply that either evolutionary reasoning or laboratory decision-making studies lead to a view of human actors as lacking in self-interest. The need to correct an oversimplified portrayal of people, if we're to understand better why our economic and social arrangements work as they do, shouldn't drive us towards an opposite position that would be even less realistic than the first one. The discipline of economics couldn't have achieved the explanatory and predictive successes it's had while embracing so caricatured a view of human nature if there weren't more than a small grain of truth in the idea that self-interest is a prominent motivator. In many situations, indeed, self-interest relegates other factors to negligible importance by comparison.

Neither the evolutionary and biological evidence discussed in the last chapter nor the research of experimental economists discussed in this one challenge the assumption that self-interest is a strong and often the dominant factor in human motivation. Hundreds of economics experiments have found support for theoretical predictions about how individuals and companies interact in competitive markets, and textbook predictions based on assuming that each acts to maximize its profits are routinely corroborated. In social dilemma conditions, we find efforts to cooperate despite the pessimism of pure self-interest models, but those efforts are in a sense driven by a desire to achieve a better outcome for both oneself and others. Few subjects show an inclination to "martyr" themselves if others refuse to do their parts, so cooperation routinely decays towards zero if tools like punishment opportunities aren't made available.[20] Seemingly fair proposers in Güth's Ultimatum Game and trusting first deciders in Berg and collaborators' Trust Game may for the most part be acting out of enlightened self-interest. At least a third of Trust Game second actors who were sent money returned none, under ordinary conditions.

To test whether the first actors (proposers) in the Ultimatum Game offered relatively fair shares to their partners mainly out of a self-interested desire to avoid earning nothing, as can happen if their partners reject their offers, researchers devised a new game or variant of the old one, the Dictator Game. In it, as in the Ultimatum Game, a first actor must come up with a way of dividing some money between herself and a second actor, but unlike the Ultimatum Game, the second actor simply receives any money given and is denied any say in the matter, which is why the first actor is referred to (though not in the instructions given to the subjects!) as a dictator. Would Ultimatum Game proposers who were routinely seen offering four or five out of ten dollars to their counterparts still be so generous if given the power of a dictator? To the relief of believers in the self-interest assumption, the average amount given was indeed less in the new game. But those viewing Ultimatum Game results as indicating a human penchant for fairness found some support in the new results, also, because most first actors did *not* offer nothing.

Subsequent results in the Dictator Game have nevertheless been more consistent with taking self-interest as a good first approximation for what we can expect of human behavior. The Dictator Game is, after all, about as artificial a situation as one can imagine. You volunteer to participate in an experiment in order to earn a few dollars, and you find your employer, the experimenter, asking you whether you want to give some of the money to a stranger. The immediate response of most subjects is likely to be that "this experiment must be about selfishness and altruism, otherwise why would I possibly want to give away the money I came here to earn?" When many proceed to give some money, a skeptic can argue that this is telling us something about cultural expectations (i.e., that in the United States or Britain or wherever the experiment is being conducted, people understand it to be undesirable to be thought of as selfish). Since the same individuals don't walk down the street handing out money, their behavior in the lab scarcely proves that they aren't primarily self-interested. When experimenters devised procedures to give the strongest possible assurance to first actors that their personal decision could not be identified by either the second actor or the experimenter, giving nothing became more common. And when the possibility of *taking* from the second actor was added to that of giving to him or her, considerable taking emerged and most giving vanished, perhaps because most of the first actors who had some moral scruples felt that they could adequately demonstrate their moral scruples by just not taking.

A bit horrified by seeing how readily they took to stealing from one another when offered that option in several experiments, I decided a few years ago to investigate whether subjects could come up with norms of ownership to prevent their laboratory society from degenerating into a lawless free-for-all. Most people aren't thieves, I reasoned, and what keeps them from stealing isn't only fear of the police or of social stigma but a sense of right and wrong. What's more, the issue is of first-order importance to society because the very possibility of being productive and meeting our material needs would be threatened if there were no constraints on theft. It's often easier to steal than to produce, and vast amounts of time and effort would be diverted from producing to stealing and to trying to counter theft if no one respected others' rights to their earnings. Such a diversion of resources would impoverish society as a whole.

While I won't give details of these experiments on theft and property rights, since my colleagues and I are still busy studying the results, it seems worth mentioning here that our trials of treatments in which subjects acted independently without possibility of contract or of a tax-funded policing system produced results rather more supportive of assuming human selfishness than of supposing fairness or rule-observance to be important concerns. Subjects were assigned to groups and asked to decide how much of an endowment of tokens to allocate to producing (a private activity), to stealing what others in the group have thus far accumulated, or to protecting their own accumulations from theft. The setting is once again a social dilemma, since highest total and average earnings are attained when all tokens are used for production, yet each individual can earn more—taking others' actions as given—by putting some tokens into theft. There were, to be sure, substantial numbers of subjects who refrained from stealing in the first round of play. But stealing became common in short order, with those having compunctions about the act presumably casting them aside once they saw others engaging in it.

As usual, the news from our property experiments is neither all favorable nor all unfavorable for the assessment of human nature. In a treatment in which subjects could tax themselves to provide low-cost protection from theft, most chose to do so, and stealing became less common. And in another treatment in which subjects could communicate in a chat room and reach agreements not to steal, it was far less common still. The communication results here are yet another piece of evidence that human sociality is real and powerful, since the rational self-interest model predicts as usual that the messages exchanged should be just so much cheap talk. The failure to overcome the social dilemma posed in the experiments in the absence of communication, on the other hand, is yet another piece of evidence that self-interest should *not* be discounted.

Heterogeneity in the real world: Some examples

One of the more prominent and less familiar messages of the research discussed in this chapter is that there's no one description of behavioral disposition that describes everyone equally well, and recognizing that people respond differently to a given situation is often a key to understanding the nature of group inter- actions. While this finding has been supported with a variety of evidence from laboratory experiments, how important are differences in the weights people place on individual versus social outcomes to an understanding of actual societies?

Heterogeneity of behavioral inclinations certainly seems pervasive, and more importantly, it appears that many social arrangements are set up with it in mind. If everyone would simply work their hardest for the sake of the group, businesses could pay each worker a fixed fraction of whatever profit their group generated, counting on teamwork to produce the desired response. But usually, at least some opportunists can be expected to take advantage of such a situation by not pulling their weight. If they lack the tools for dealing with these types, the morale of the more group-minded individuals will be deflated by seeing them- selves "suckered."

The more cooperative individuals are rarely entirely without defenses, though. When companies use profit sharing or group-productivity-based bonuses to motivate shop-floor workers, the dependence of everyone's pay on everyone else's work typically leads to social pressure being exerted on a slacker by other workers—an analogue of the punishment seen in the experiments discussed above. Profit sharing can be an effective way to raise productivity, since it gives workers incentives to keep an eye on each others' efforts, thus aligning their inter- ests with their company's. But apart from some cooperatives and worker-owned companies, almost no company relies purely on profit sharing. Companies instead make use of individualized motivating mechanisms, including the right to fire or to deny promotion to someone who shirks his responsibilities. They reward better workers not only with the same share of the profits their company or work team generates as everyone else gets, but with differentially higher wages, bonuses, or promotions. Even partnerships like law firms keep track of billable hours and of who handles which clients.

Based on such observations, the dynamics of workplace reward systems provide us with evidence about the inclinations towards cooperation versus selfishness and opportunism that ordinary people display. Use of firing threats and differential rewards for different quality of work would be unnecessary if opportunists and uncooperative types could be easily identified and excluded. So observed reliance on differential reward systems is indirect evidence that it's difficult for people, given their varying inclinations, to cooperate perfectly. But if everyone were a perfect opportunist, only individually directed incentives like individualized bonuses, raises, and firing threats would be of any use, so the real-world usage and success of profit sharing and other team-based incentives speaks to the existence of cooperative tendencies—including tendencies to perform peer-to-peer monitoring and to put social pressure on slackers.

The securing of property, a topic mentioned just above, provides another example of how heterogeneity plays itself out. Societies have embraced property rights for millennia, and the notion that this is evidence for the centrality of self-regarding behavior will be taken up in the next chapter. Accepting for now that people need confidence that they can possess the fruits of their labors before they invest effort in cultivating, planting, and harvesting, what gives them such confidence in practice? One part of the answer is that governments pay for police departments, businesses pay for private security services, individuals put locks and alarms on their homes and automobiles, and people caught stealing are subjected to substantial penalties. But this hardly seems to be the whole answer. Many refrain from stealing because they consider it wrong, and as in the communication treatment of our experiment, they persist in their resolve because they're assured that many others are also not stealing. People are induced to buy into the idea that stealing is wrong by religion, family, and school. Altruistic parents have incentives to teach their children not to steal, even if they themselves aren't religious or morally inclined, if they want their children to be successful, and they know that the penalties make stealing a bad gamble. Since most people refrain from all but the pettiest forms of theft and believe that many people morally disapprove of it, people with shakier moral beliefs refrain from stealing when there's a significant probability of being caught due to the stigma attached to it, which harms not only their self-esteem but also their chances of finding employment and doing business with others.

The main point here is that it probably requires only a relatively small number of people with firmly internalized moral norms against stealing to render stealing unattractive to a much larger number of people when there is a non-negligible chance of being caught, since the large majority of people will want to at least appear to endorse this norm and will thus be ready to jump in on the act of shunning or stigmatizing its violators. The stronger the social disapproval of stealing appears to be, the fewer resources need be spent on policing and private security systems. If the probability of detection falls too low, the strength of the norm itself will begin to wane, since families will have less incentive to inculcate it. And if everyone were quite confident that nobody truly viewed stealing as wrong, a much higher probability of detection and higher penalties would be needed to deter theft, since there'd be no stigma to reinforce the other penalties.

It can pay to be (or to appear to be) cooperative: An experiment
If evolutionary pressures shaped our species so as to give a great many of us helpful social sentiments, why exactly is it that we also have criminals, corrupt politicians, and policemen who take bribes? Why is there variation among us in the strengths of moral emotions and inclinations, much as we vary in thrill seeking versus anxiety and in whether we are outgoing or shy? Did evolution fail to complete the job of selecting from among alternative variants the one most fit for the niche that humans occupy on our planet? Or has it done us a favor by making us vary?

Despite the progress that's been made in our understanding of human nature and its origins, we're far from having good answers to such challenging questions. Still it helps, I think, to recall that evolution is not a force guided by lofty goals, but simply a process whereby what succeeds in reproducing itself is well represented, and what doesn't succeed disappears. In and of itself, evolution (unlike Santa Claus) doesn't care whether you're naughty or nice. During most of our history, cooperative tendencies could benefit your genes by benefiting your group's success and your own chances of being in such a group. But overly cooperative tendencies could also put the individual at a disadvantage. It's worth discussing in more detail one of the experiments we conducted because it helps to illustrate the pitfalls of too much cooperativeness and, perhaps, to shed some light on why human beings evolved to be somewhat, but not perfectly, socially minded.

In the experiment in question, we once again sat sixteen subjects at terminals in a computer lab and randomly assigned them to four groups of four without revealing who was in whose group. After having their task explained to them, the subjects began playing a group contribution game like the ones described earlier, in some sessions playing a game without punishment stages, in others a game with punishment stages. In either case, at the end of each round, the subjects were as usual shown only the amounts put into their group account by each of the three others in their group, without personal identification. This time, though, we paused the process after three rounds and showed the subjects the average amounts contributed to their respective group accounts by each of the other *fifteen* participants in the room (their individual identities still remaining unknown). Each subject was then invited to rank the others by order of preference as partners for the next three rounds, and the computer matched those indicating the greatest preference to be grouped together. Play then continued for a total of seventeen periods, but with another pause, another information screen, another ranking, and another regrouping after every three rounds.

Not surprisingly, the higher contributors were the most popular partners. Both high and low contributors indicated a preference for being with high ones. Since groups were based on *mutual* preference, this meant that free riders couldn't get into high contributor groups unless they'd adopted the strategy of pretending to be cooperative. The result was that in each session some groups emerged whose members persisted in putting all, or almost all, of their money into the group fund, and since there was no free riding and little or no punishment was needed, their members earned more than those in other groups. Every session had its "dog group" in which the least cooperative subjects were concentrated, contributing relatively little and thus earning little. But since most subjects perceived the advantage of obtaining a better reputation and entering one of the better groups, contributions were higher in sessions using this group formation process than in ones in which subjects remained in a randomly formed group.[21]

On a practical level, our experiment can be seen as a stylized representation of the way people form associations and partnerships and enter into business dealings in the real world. There are incentives to act in a cooperative and trustworthy manner so as to be favored to join a good team (for instance, a law firm or business partnership) and receive business from customers. Reputations are built and conveyed by resumes, informal word of mouth, or formal recommenda-tions. In the "dog group" are fly-by-night operators who specialize in one-time transactions since they usually fail to build up the trust required to capture repeat business—the bottom-feeders whom people avoid whenever possible.

Now, suppose that our experiment could be extended in the following way: we'd invite the top twenty-five percent of earners in each regrouping session back to participate in other sessions, letting the low earners drop off of our evolutionary radar. As we repeated the process, our subject pool would come to be populated by more cooperative subjects only. The prehistoric selection of our species may have worked in a somewhat similar way. People in groups that successfully coop-erated flourished in relative terms and had more offspring, while people in groups that didn't cooperate failed to snag the mammoths, were more poorly nourished and more easily picked off by disease and saber-tooth tigers, and generally left fewer offspring.

Given our particular experimental design, however, the selection process described would not perfectly select the most cooperative people. Although those who contributed the most money to their group funds tended to get into the best groups—that is, the groups containing more high contributors—and although average earnings in those groups were higher than in other ones, the *highest* earning players in many sessions were individuals who contributed their full ten dollars round after round, always getting into a high contributor group, but who, in the very last period, contributed zero dollars while some partners put in ten dollars. These tricky "mimickers" got up to a ten dollar leg up on their genuinely virtuous counterparts (a solo "mimicker" gets twenty-two dollars; her three counterparts get twelve dollars, for instance) in that period. An individual who calibrated her seeming cooperativeness and selfishness just right would thus make out a little better. (With twenty periods, the difference from one period alone is fairly small.) If we chose the top twenty percent of money earners to return to the lab, both fully cooperative individuals and clever mimickers would be likely to be called back. So we could be building up a mixed pool consisting of both full-fledged cooperators and of clever, opportunistic mimickers of cooperation.

Without going into details, the basic point that can be made is that, in our extended experiment at least, there are selection pressures at work both for the cooperativeness that would make others consider you a good partner and for the ability to get away with some cheating at opportune moments. In the real world, though, there's almost never a predictable last period of play, so what is precisely the best moment to cheat is more difficult to determine than in our lab. Some cheating attempts backfire, with the cheater being punished or expelled, so the rule of simply being cooperative might do quite well for long periods of time. Nonetheless, both the inclination to "just be cooperative" and the inclination to "appear to be cooperative but cheat whenever you can get away with it" might well survive selective pressures for an indefinite amount of time. It might even be the case that having a few opportunists in their midst during some of the millennia of human evolution made groups more adaptable in certain situations, and this factor may also have contributed to the mixture of types that was the outcome of the evolutionary process.

The "ecology" of moral types

In the last section, I discussed variation in cooperative or moral inclinations as if it were entirely genetically based. But undoubtedly differences in the environments people are exposed to are also a contributing factor. Herrmann, Thöni, and Gächter's voluntary contribution experiments in fifteen countries, which I mentioned earlier, showed considerable variation across societies. They convincingly showed the variation in laboratory behaviors to be correlated with cultural and institutional differences in the countries from which the subjects were drawn. Environmentally caused variability is almost certainly at work *within* societies, as well. Evolution has equipped almost everyone with a set of social sensitivities, including concern to be seen favorably by others, "social antennae" attuned to grasping and adhering (as needed) to group norms, and a tendency to internalize, to some degree, the external stimuli of moral socialization in which the individual is bathed in the early years of life. Those stimuli differ from family to family and from culture to culture.

Further complicating the matter, a given individual isn't necessarily molded by genes and socialization into any one type at all, but he or she may respond more or less cooperatively, more or less morally, depending on the particulars of circumstance. The outpouring of fellow-feeling in the immediate aftermath of 9-11 is an illustration of such "plasticity." A few years ago, social scientists using laboratory decision experiments provided another remarkable example by demonstrating that two groups of subjects, brought to their lab to play what was exactly the same social dilemma game from the standpoint of the decisions and payments involved, were far more cooperative in a treatment in which the exercise was referred to as "The Community Game" than in one where the experimenters called it "The Wall Street Game."[22] We might be on our "best" behavior at our church or PTA meeting but behave quite differently when trying to snag a business deal or get a better spot in the line to buy a scarce ticket or sale item. Even the subtle suggestion of being watched affected payments under a break room's honor system, while irrelevant photographs on a simulated wall influenced decisions on trust.

We end up in a social world that's neither the *dys*topia imagined by cynics—in which everyone behaves with thorough-going opportunism at every moment of every day—nor a *u*topia in which all are thoroughly cooperative and eager to work for the common good. We have a complex "moral ecology," with a near continuum of interacting types, ranging from more social-minded and cooperative to more selfish, and with the character or type of the person you're dealing with not marked on his or her forehead but only discernable, if at all, by careful attention over long periods of time, so that clues about reputation are of acute interest.

Whether or not it pays to cooperate depends in part on whom you're interacting with. We seek out more cooperative partners, but in situations in which selecting whom you interact with is difficult, we also design rules of the game that help protect us from the predation of more opportunistic individuals. Some of these opportunists must be assumed to be present even if which ones they are can't be said in advance—hence the maxim of the philosopher David Hume, a friend of Adam Smith, that "every man must be supposed a knave." We nevertheless manage to find some people whom we can trust and with whom we can build long-term, mutually beneficial relationships. And they, too, are present to some degree almost everywhere, so that (despite Hume's warning) our organizational arrangements need not assume everyone to be a knave.

How can we use the insights into human nature that we drew from evolutionary theory in the last chapter and from experimental studies of human interaction in this one to see what stands between us and a better world? I propose as our next step that we explore the extent to which those insights and the approaches yielding them can help us to make sense of the economic, political, and social institutions that we've inherited from the last few thousand years of accelerating social change. That will be the task of the next chapter.

Notes:

1. Game theory is a body of mathematical theory to which economists and many others have contributed. It studies, using abstract deductive methods rather than empirical observations, human interactions that can be represented as games of strategy.

2. Traditionally, economists using game theory assumed that decision-makers had the simple goal of maximizing their own money pay-off, like *Homo economicus*. Efforts to incorporate psychological and behaviorally realistic elements into game theory are relatively recent additions, although some early game theorists like Thomas Schelling—see, for instance, his *Strategy of Conflict* (1960)—had discussed such elements before greater formalism came to dominate the field. Recent treatments allowing behavioral elements include Colin Camerer's *Behavioral Game Theory: Experiments in Strategic Interaction* (Princeton: Princeton University Press, 2003) and Herbert Gintis's *Game Theory Evolving: A Problem-centered Introduction to Evolutionary Game Theory* (Princeton: Princeton University Press, 2006, 2009).

3. Though I've mentioned replications in many countries, I won't discuss the unusual results obtained when including members of surviving hunter-gatherer societies and others operating far from a market environment. Those results, obtained by anthropologist Joseph Henrich and collaborators, are interesting for drawing fully general conclusions about human nature, but they don't merit a long detour here given the kinds of societies on which most of our discussion focuses. See Joseph Henrich, et al., *Foundations of Human Sociality: Economic Experiments and Ethnographic Evidence from Fifteen Small-scale Societies* (New York: Oxford University Press, 2004).

4. A cost schedule having a low initial cost of deducting ten percent from the earnings of the person targeted and increasing costs for deducting additional ten percent chunks was used in their first experiments but was replaced by the simpler approach, corresponding to my description, in later replications

5. Fehr and Gächter's initial paper on this research, titled "Cooperation and Punishment," appears in the *American Economic Review* in 2000. In slightly earlier research, the same researchers and collaborators also demonstrated willingness to punish and a significant impact of anticipated punishment on cooperative behavior in two-person games of reciprocity meant to capture essential features of employment relationships. Many of the replications and extensions that followed "Cooperation and Punishment" are discussed in Ananish Chaudhuri's article "Sustaining Cooperation in Laboratory Public Goods Experiments: A Selective Survey of the Literature," in *Experimental Economics* 14, no. 1 (2011): 47- 83.

6. In a conventional economics experiment conducted in Western Europe, the United States, Australia, or New Zealand, the average subject earns something like $20–$30 for one to two hours of attentive participation, so in an experiment like the one discussed that includes twenty periods of decisions, earnings in any one period are in the $1 to $1.50 range. (When I discuss experiments having many periods, the $10 to be allocated in a given period to which I refer usually are dollars of the laboratory or experimental currency, having conversion values of between 4 and 13 cents of real money.) This means that both the cost of punishing others and the one-time benefit of free riding when punishment isn't possible is often a matter of small change.

Stakes that are ten times as high in relative terms can be induced by paying $20 or $30 for a single period, by raising earnings for a twenty period experiment to the $200 to $300 range (generally affordable to experimenters for small subject pools, if at all), or by conducting the experiment in a country in which average earnings are a tenth or less than those in a rich country. (Illustrative experiments have been conducted in Peru, Indonesia, Kenya, and other countries.)

7. The research mentioned here is reported in the working paper that is the background to: Matthias Cinyabuguma, Talbot Page, and Louis Putterman, "Can Second-Order Punishment Deter Perverse Punishment," *Experimental Economics* 9, no. 3 (2006): 265-279.

8. See Benedikt Herrmann, Christian Thöni, and Simon Gächter, "Antisocial Punishment Across Societies," *Science* 319, (2008): 1362-1367.

9. Experimental treatments that include fuller information about the punishment pattern and opportunities to direct higher-stage punishment freely include: Laurent Denant-Boemont, David Masclet, and Charles Noussair, "Punishment, Counter-Punishment and Sanction Enforcement in a Social Dilemma Experiment," *Economic Theory* 33, (2007): 145-167 and Kenju Kamei, Louis Putterman, and Jean-Robert Tyran, "State *or* Nature? Formal vs. Informal Sanctioning in the Voluntary Provision of Public Goods" (Brown University Department of Economics Working Paper 2011-3), which also compares group-determined punishment to that chosen by individuals acting independently.

10. Details of the treatments discussed in this and the previous paragraph are provided in Talbot Page, Louis Putterman and Bruno Garcia, "Getting Punishment Right: Do Costly Monitoring or Redistributive Punishment Help?" Brown University Department of Economics Working Paper 2008-1. A group of researchers obtained similar observations about costly monitoring when conducting field research on common forest management, reporting that conditional cooperators engaged in more monitoring than other group members and thereby helped to enforce cooperation. See Devesh Rustagi, Stefanie Engel and Michael Kosfeld, "Conditional Cooperation and Costly Monitoring Explain Success in Forest Commons Management," *Science* 330 (2010): 961-965.

11. Matthias Cinyabuguma, Talbot Page, and Louis Putterman, "Cooperation Under the Threat of Expulsion in a Public Goods Experiment," *Journal of Public Economics* 89, no. 8 (2005): 1421-1435.

12. Arhan Ertan, Talbot Page, and Louis Putterman, "Who to Punish? Individual Decisions and Majority Rule in Mitigating the Free-Rider Problem," *European Economic Review* 53, no. 5 (2009): 495-511.

13. To avoid an exaggerated impression, you may want to recall from note 6 that I'm referring here to dollars of experimental currency that were worth well under that amount in real money, although the amounts at stake were still not trivial.

14. Each individual's decisions were anonymous in the sense that a given group member was only identified to the others on their screens by a randomly scrambled identification letter B, C, or D.

15. Our communication experiments are published as Olivier Bochet, Talbot Page, and Louis Putterman, "Communication and Punishment in Voluntary Contribution Experiments," *Journal of Economic Behavior and Organization* 60, no. 1 (2006): 11-26.

16. As before, a subject engaged in several such interactions, with each in this case involving a brand new partner, to avoid creating incentives for cooperation. In view of the prohibitive cost (for our research budget) of conducting such an experiment with subjects earning up to two hundred dollars apiece, the dollars referred to in the text were in fact experimental dollars converted to money at the end of the session at a more modest rate. Still, each instance of returning twenty dollars of experimental money cost a second mover two dollars in real currency.

17. The trust games with contract opportunities are discussed in: Avner Ben-Ner and Louis Putterman, "Trust, Communication and Contracts," *Journal of Economic Behavior and Organization* 70, nos. 1-2 (2009):106-121. The games without opportunity to contract are presented in Avner Ben-Ner, Louis Putterman and Ting Ren, "Lavish Returns on Cheap Talk: Two-way Communication in Trust Games," *Journal of Socio-economics* 40, no. 1 (2011): 1-13.

18. In the event, sending money was a good gamble because recipients tended to return enough to make the sender better off. Details, including photographs, are in: Stephen Atlas and Louis Putterman, "Trust Among the Avatars: a Virtual World Experiment with and without Textual and Visual Cues," *Southern Economic Journal* 78, no. 1 (2011): 63-86.

19. Michael Kosfeld et al., "Oxytocin increases trust in humans," *Nature* 435, (2005): 673-676.

20. In fact, Gächter and Urs Fischbacher, in a paper published in the *American Economic Review* in 2010, found that even subjects who are "conditionally cooperative," that is who prefer to contribute to the group account in a voluntary contributions game if they know that others are doing so, typically conceive their ideal contribution to be just a little bit less than what others contribute. In other words, the subjects don't like to think of themselves as not doing their parts when others are, but they shade their behavior at least slightly towards their personal self-interest. The result is that after enough rounds of play, conditional cooperators each aiming to put in just a bit less than their counterparts find their contributions gradually declining, even if there are no outright free riders among them.

21. Talbot Page, Louis Putterman, and Bulent Unel, "Voluntary Association in Public Goods Experiments: Reciprocity, Mimicry, and Efficiency," *The Economic Journal* 115, no. 506 (2005): 1032-53.

22. As you guessed, they cooperated significantly less in the second version. Ross and Ward, "Naïve Realism in Everyday Life," in Edward Reed, Elliot Turiel, and Terrance Brown, *Values and Knowledge* (Mahwah, NJ: L. Erlbaum, 1996).

CHAPTER 7
The Economic Rules of the Game

In June 2006, Warren Buffet, then the world's second richest man, startled press and public by announcing that he would begin to give his wealth away before his death. By itself, the action was surprising only because Buffet hadn't previously been known for public philanthropy. The bigger surprise was his statement that he would be giving the better part of his fortune not to his children or to a foundation bearing his name, but to the foundation of the only man then richer than himself, Bill Gates. At the time, *Forbes* magazine estimated the two men's personal fortunes at around forty-two billion and fifty billion US dollars, respectively. Their combined fortunes surpassed the combined net worth of the 42.6 million households in the bottom forty percent of the US wealth distribution.[1] In fact, Gates and Buffet were each about *five hundred million* times as rich as the average person in the bottom fifteen percent of the world's population, and together they were worth more than the one billion poorest people in the world combined.[2]

Buffet's announcement came the same month that Gates announced plans to reduce his day-to-day involvement with the company he founded, Microsoft, in order to focus on his philanthropic work. Gates's and Buffet's generosity inspired cover stories in the leading news magazines. That a great deal of admiration was forthcoming, as opposed to head-scratching, amusement, or derision, is another indication of the complex human nature we've been discussing in the last few chapters. The episode perfectly illustrates what Adam Smith had written two and a half centuries earlier about the public's response to magnanimous acts: "[such] actions ... call forth our approbation, and we hear everybody around us express the same favorable opinion concerning them." About the benefactors' motivation for engaging in these actions, Smith had written that "[t]hey excite all those sentiments for which we have by nature the strongest desire; the love, the gratitude, the admiration of mankind." So why not announce your donations while still alive and get to enjoy all that praise?

But why do we live in a world in which such vast inequalities arise in the first place? Can human nature help to explain this inequality, too? I think the answer is yes. Human nature explains the world's inequalities by accounting for the fundamental features of economic organization.

Some might begin by seizing on the last chapter's theme of heterogeneity and noting that there are large differences in intelligence, drive, inclination to take risks, and what economists call "rates of time preference," psychologists capacity for deferred gratification or impulse control. All of these contribute to inequality. While Gates and Buffet aren't necessarily the world's smartest men, if you were to arrange the world's 6.6 billion people by a suitable measure of intelligence, you'd almost certainly find them near the high end of that distribution.

Intelligence isn't all it takes to reach billionaire-dom from average beginnings, and it certainly doesn't guarantee it. (How many Nobel Prize winners in chemistry and physics, or even in economics, have been billionaires?) Usually, a healthy dose of drive, self-confidence, and creativity are also required. Like intelligence, the attributes of drive, self-confidence, and creativity are not distributed equally. And the *combination* of high intelligence with extraordinary drive, ambition, and energy, unusually high self-confidence, and great creativity is sure to be considerably rarer than is high intelligence alone, since having one doesn't imply having the others. If we had measures for each of these attributes and created a combined index that took into account all four, let's say one with scores running from 1 to 10,000, then 90 percent of the world's people might fall in the 1 to 500 range, the next 9 percent between 501 and 1,000, and the remaining 1 percent might be thinly spread over the range of values going from 1,001 to 10,000, as in the hypothetical graph below. And if rewards in a market economy were directly proportionate to one's score on this combined index, people with scores above 7,000 or so, perhaps including Gates and Buffet, might be expected to earn many times more than "just plain folks."[3]

At first blush, this might seem to be a more or less adequate explanation of the inequalities that we observe. But differences in ability can't be the whole explanation because in our discussion so far, we've merely been *assuming* that rewards in the marketplace are proportionate to scores on an imagined index of intelligence, drive, and other attributes. We've neither explained nor justified why that sort of proportionality has to hold. In asking "Why not a better world?" we're implicitly asking whether that proportionality is really necessary more than we're asking whether people can be made to be more homogeneous in their abilities and qualities—although more equal access to "possibilities of becoming" is also a relevant concern.

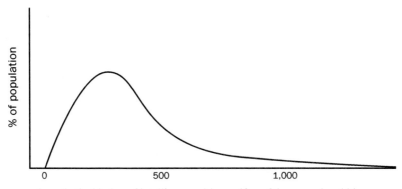

hypothetical index of intelligence, drive, self-confidence, and ambition

Consider a few simple facts. In the United States today, you can become wealthy if you're at the far right tail of the distribution of abilities to play the game of baseball. But that wasn't the case in the United States a hundred years ago, when baseball players made relatively modest livings. Nor would an ability to play baseball, if one could even acquire it there, bring wealth to a resident of Iran, Sudan, or Afghanistan. Similarly, had a person with Bill Gates's aptitudes been born into a society of reindeer herders in Lapland or of whale-hunting Inuit in Alaska any time in the last thousand years, he might have been a pretty successful herder or hunter, but he could hardly have built up thousands of times the wealth of his average contemporary. There's no reason to think that there were not many Inuit and Laplander's of exceptional intelligence, drive, and creativity, but wealth differences on millions-to-one scales didn't exist because of the ways their societies were organized and the ways in which they interacted with nature. Even in today's world, being one of the world's most talented poets or mathematicians or linguists or banjo players or pizza chefs won't win you a spot on anybody's richest list. Clearly, it isn't being outstandingly good at something that, in and of itself, brings wealth.

What explains why a person of extraordinary baseball-playing skill can remain poor in Afghanistan but become rich in America? What explains why a great poet is unlikely to get rich in either country? It won't come as a big surprise to anyone who's had a high school or introductory college course in economics that one thing we need to have in hand if we're going to explain these things is the concept of demand. The graph above, showing the frequencies of people having different levels of skill, dealt only with *supply*. Simply put, the reason it's not enough to be a rare ballplayer or a rare could-be techno-entrepreneur on the extreme right tail of the relevant distribution of talent is that there also has to be a *demand* for the things you're potentially talented at—winning baseball games or coming up with attractive software innovations. If you're the next Joe DiMaggio, but you lack a set of people wanting to see good baseball played because you happen to live in Lapland or Teheran or because it's the year 2487 or the year 24 and no one alive has ever heard of the game, then your skills won't fetch you anything. Customer demand for baseball and all its marketable accoutrements has grown over the past hundred years in the United States, explaining much of the growth in ballplayers' earnings.

But scarce supply and a strong desire to watch baseball are still not enough to explain high player salaries. It also takes rules of the game—not rules of baseball, but rules of economic life. And this is where human nature, not simply diversity of talent, comes in.

It's not impossible to imagine a world in which players competed to play on the best teams simply for the joy of playing and the pride of showing off their skills. High tech innovators might hone and use their skills to benefit millions of technology users, all for the pleasure and glory of being the first to bring out products capable of winning the acclaim of millions of people and getting their pictures on the cover of magazines, as Buffet and Gates did when they made their announcements. Many people do in fact contribute to free software development and similar projects without compensation. To understand why top ballplayers and innovators become rich, and not merely famous and blissfully pleased with themselves, we need to know why society isn't organized differently. Why can't each person do whatever work she enjoys or feels contributes the most or that some general planner or assembly of others judges it most useful for her to do, and then withdraw from the set of goods and services that society produces only her equal share—or an amount determined by her health, height, and other objective factors or by any criterion other than the supply of and the demand for her skills? To understand why we've arrived at a system that uses monetary rewards for effort and that ties those rewards to supply and demand, we need to know something about why we have the economic arrangements that we have. For that purpose, we'd do well to talk again about human nature, this time trying to understand its probable role in the evolution of our economic institutions.

Human nature and the economy

In Chapter 5, we recognized that as our genes' ticket to the future, we're designed to focus on the survival and reproduction of ourselves and our close kin, so we naturally value bread in our own mouths more than that in the mouths of strangers. We've seen, though, that the conditions under which our psyches were shaped made us profoundly social creatures, inclined to reciprocate when treated kindly, angered by being taken advantage of, desirous of the approval of others, wanting to think well of ourselves and thus abide by the norms we share with others, and susceptible to socialization and cultural influences. And we've seen that there's variation in the strengths of selfish and social forces that's most likely accounted for by differences in both genetic and environmental factors.

With their brain power, dexterity, and strength, these varied mixtures of selfishness, kin-centeredness, and sociality served our hunter-gatherer ancestors well enough that they managed to expand their foraging ranges from Africa east to Australia, north to the Arctic, south again to Tierra del Fuego, and across the span of two oceans from Easter Island to Madagascar. The same basic features were adaptable enough to allow the human species to prosper even more in agrarian societies, reaching a population of hundreds of millions spread throughout the globe, whereas our closest non-human relatives have probably never numbered more than a few hundred thousand in any one species and have lived only in narrow ranges in Africa (gorillas, bonobos, chimpanzees) and southeast Asia (orangutans).

More recently, our species' physical characteristics and social qualities proved adaptable to still-more-different industrial and information societies. Within such societies, our numbers have grown into the billions, and the standard of living of some has risen beyond previous imagination. It makes sense to look at our diverse behavioral inclinations, along with the characteristics of the physical nature from which we wrest our livelihood, if we want to explain why we organize our activities and motivate our ballplayers, entrepreneurs, truck drivers, and hamburger flippers as we do.

Two organizational elements that have played central roles in the economic life of most societies for thousands years are the concept of ownership of property and the practice of exchange, giving rise to markets. Let's start by asking where these two economic commonplaces come from.

Possession

Anthropologists believe that during the hundred thousand years prior to the birth of agriculture, the vast majority of humans lived in small groups (bands) that subsisted by gathering wild plant foods and hunting and fishing for wild animals. There was some differentiation of roles by gender and probably some mild specialization as to leadership in questions of migration, hunting, battle, and ceremonial roles, with age and other attributes affecting who did what. Perhaps there was also some specialization as to who made the tools, quarried the rock with which to make them, or prepared skins for use as clothing. But such occupational specializations are likely to have been minor compared to those in later societies, and differences between one person's consumption and another's are unlikely to have approached those between managers and workers in modern enterprises, much less those between Gates, Buffet, and the rest of us. The relative lack of specialization, and limitations on the quantity and varieties of storable assets, meant that differences in wealth would have been small.

If ancestral humans hunted, gathered, and moved around in egalitarian bands, can we assume that the concept of property would have been alien to them? Not necessarily. Primatologists observing chimpanzees in the wild have found that when a chimp catches a monkey, a principal protein source, others of its group gather around with upturned palms, begging for their shares. If a close buddy of the successful hunter (the chimps live in groups that remain together for years, much like human hunter-gatherers) receives a particularly large share, another circle will form around that second chimp, begging him for shares. Similar behavior is observed when fruits and leaves are given out in the chimp houses of zoos. The chimps seem to act as if they "respect" the "possession right" of the individual holding the resource, begging, rather than grabbing, in the hope of winning a share out of sympathy (or desire to be rid of their annoyance).[4] In hunter-gatherer societies, most plant foods and smaller animals are treated as belonging to the acquirer, although there are elaborate rules for sharing large prey.

Biologist John Maynard-Smith used a model from game theory, the "hawk-dove" game, to describe what can happen when two parties violently clash over a resource. Each must choose between two behaviors—call them "fight to the death" and "flee." If both choose "fight to the death," both are likely to suffer severe costs—perhaps one will be killed; the other maimed. If both choose "flee," neither gets the resource, so a valuable opportunity is lost to them. The best overall outcome (in terms of average gain or sum of benefits) is for one to choose to fight, and the other choose to flee, in which case the one willing to fight gets the resource without either one suffering the cost of actual fighting. The question is: How do the parties, or nature which instills in them some instinctual tendency or other, coordinate strategies so that undesirable "fight"-"fight" and "flee"-"flee" outcomes are avoided?

An instinctual willingness to defend a piece of territory, a nest, or a burrow hole can be found in many animal species, and noting this, Maynard-Smith suggested that the propensity to defend the territory one has already staked out is just the sort of coordination device that can cut down on the incidence of bad hawk/dove outcomes. If birds of a certain species instinctively know that the bird that built the nest will fight to the death to defend it from an intruder, and if intruders back off once they see an occupant acting like the builder, there will be fewer fatal fights, though birds *without* nests may die before they locate an unoccupied spot on which to build one. It's easy to see how the rule that it's the builder that fights has evolutionary advantages over the alternative rule that it's the builder that flees, since the latter reduces incentives to build well.[5]

The coordination device of a mental algorithm that might be called "the possessor will fight" didn't need to be invented out of whole cloth. It's a natural extension of the self-interest that must be built into every complex organism. Since food is critical to an animal's survival and since a large part of its energy is devoted to procuring it, it would not be very adaptive to meekly allow it to be snatched from its mouth by just any competitor under just any and every condition. So an instinct to appear prepared to fight to protect it unless the interested party displays an obvious advantage of size and strength or is enmeshed in ongoing relations of reciprocity with the possessor is likely to have arisen in most animals. All that needs to be added to get coordination on both sides is the tendency, when the next potential meal you come across is already in a competitor's hands, claws, or beak, to search elsewhere.

Like chimps, early humans couldn't "go it alone" in the wild, so many of their notions of property, especially at the level of "real estate," are likely to have emerged initially at the band level. Groups were probably more likely than individuals to be the entities clashing with one another over access to resources like clumps of nut-bearing trees. But groups living in the same general area for long periods of time would have had blood and other relations with neighboring bands, since females tended to move between bands as males looked for mates outside their immediate group (an ape instinct attributable to genetic benefits apes didn't need to understand). Closely related bands speaking more-or-less the same language could therefore have worked out a *modus vivendi* whereby they would either avoid heading for the same grove at the same time or would find a way of sharing and of avoiding a conflict should they happen to find themselves there. But unrelated groups, such as ones traveling a longer distance because their accustomed stomping grounds were suffering from greater population pressures or from drought, might sometimes enter your group's area and find the groves, stands of seed-bearing grasses and plants, and streams and ponds attractive, at which point fighting might ensue. Defense of a delineated territory against potential intruders has been found to be a universal trait of chimpanzees in the wild, so ownership of a rudimentary type goes far back in the history of our species and its predecessors.

Exchange

Even before the inclination towards possessive feelings had fully solidified into a concept of property, the emergence of exchange among groups is likely to have begun as a consequence of variation in environments that naturally gave rise to differences in what economists now call comparative advantage. If one group's habitual domain is visited by few large wild animals but includes a rich vein of just the sort of obsidian needed to make good arrowheads, whereas another group's domain includes forests containing many deer and other game but little of that stone, the forest group might offer meat and skins for the quarrying group's arrowheads. Adam Smith considered a "propensity to truck and barter" to be an element of human nature in its own right, and watching second graders bargain as they exchange treats might seem to support this, but the obvious advantages of trading would have been enough to account for its appearance once the band had learned to approach the neighboring band without an immediate outbreak of violence and with implicit recognition of one another's rights to their territories. The quarrying group would be able to reduce the time spent hunting for smaller, scarcer animals in its own domain, the hunting group could increase its hunting success by using better arrowheads than it could fashion from the materials in its range, and both could enjoy better diets with less time expenditure.

Exchange doesn't make for a market if there are only two traders. But once a number of bands having good hunting ranges became aware of a number of bands of superior arrow-makers, which might happen in part because of the splitting off of new bands from the initial ones over time, competition would begin to emerge, causing the number of arrowheads that would be exchanged for an animal of given size to become relatively uniform and responsive to changes in the supply of or demand for either good. Add competition to exchange, itself the natural outgrowth of differences in comparative advantage, and you have supply and demand as determinants of price. When demand grows without change in supply, for instance, some would-be buyers who would otherwise go without have an incentive to offer more, and once the sellers see this, the other buyers must follow. When supply grows without change in demand, some would-be sellers who would otherwise be left with unwanted items have an incentive to accept less, and once the buyers see this, the other seller must follow.

Evidence on the extent of prehistoric trade is still somewhat sketchy. In *The Origin of Virtue*, Matt Ridley reports that pierced sea shells, used as beads, were traveling more than four hundred miles inland from the sea by thirty thousand years ago.[6] But this doesn't mean that some beachcombing tribe operated a wholesale distribution network stretching for hundreds of miles. It could simply have been that fluid and unintended chains consisting of dozens of neighboring foraging bands occasionally exchanged the shells for other items in the course of their bartering encounters, with the members of bands furthest from the point of origin having no idea who produced them and where and with a given shell taking twenty to thirty years to make its way so far inland. In some cases, the goods may also have moved as a result of conflict and plunder, rather than of trade.

For most bands during pre-agrarian times, trading is likely to have been a small supplement at most to a largely self-sufficient way of life. Where trading was only occasional and on a small scale, market forces causing barter terms to adjust to changes in supply and demand and to converge to a common ratio in a given region would have been weak. Property rights might also have been relatively weakly defined except in unusually rich environments, such as on the banks of rivers having copious stocks of fish, where ownership of nets or canoes and perhaps even command over slaves might have made some wealthier than others and increased their desire to make sure others accepted the legitimacy of their claims.

The first privatization

Although concepts of possession and practices of exchange have existed for tens of thousands of years, the fact that people wrested their livings from nature in small groups during the long era of hunting and gathering would have put a premium on within-group cooperation. The varieties of storable wealth were also limited, and the absence of permanent structures, the need for mobility, and the narrow range of goods would have placed limits on how much could be accumulated. Thus, inequalities of wealth would for the most part have been modest, and rewards of social status and mating opportunities would have been at least as important as were differentiated material success as ways of calling forth the efforts of group members. The notion of *private* property was rudimentary and subordinate to rights of access belonging to the group.

All of this changed with the coming of the Neolithic or agricultural revolution, which began about eleven thousand years ago and led to an increase in the quantity and varieties of wealth, new possibilities for storage, and large shifts in the way goods were distributed and in the role of material incentives in motivating effort. Before agriculture, when it took the joint effort of a band to corner and kill a mastodon, it may have made no sense to try to grade each hunter's performance and parcel out more meat to the more effective ones because individual performance was hard to assess, and inequalities in the group could have caused resentments that would weaken the required group cohesion. But when nearly every adult in a Mesopotamian or Chinese agricultural village was a wheat, rice, or millet farmer, there was little advantage to tilling the fields as a group. The fact that staple crop cultivation is, and insofar as we know has always been, a family rather than large group activity throughout the world is probably attributable to the lack of critical scale economies and to the greater ease of providing incentives for effort on a family scale. Even gathering of wild plants had been a more individual or family-based activity than was hunting of large game. While work parties, in which families come together to harvest the crops in one member's fields, then the next, were still common in some agrarian societies until recent times, such practices almost never carried over into communal ownership of land and crops.[7]

Economists discussing the strong incentive features of family farms sometimes take for granted that family members can resolve their internal collective action problems. A traditional family could easily contain ten or more individuals, so it doesn't go without saying that the usual analysis of social dilemmas and free riding wouldn't apply to it. Yet the idea that free riding is more easily attenuated within families than in groups of unrelated individuals does appear to be a reasonable approximation to the truth, one whose accuracy is in part attributable to the genetic and biological factors discussed in Chapter 5. Families not only play a central role in the evolution of property, as discussed in this chapter, but also in the transmission of economic culture from one generation to the next, which is important to the next chapter's discussion of the origins of global inequalities.

The situation of animal herders is similar to that of farmers. A group could watch over a herd of animals together, with possible time savings. But if the group's members were to own these animals in common, their vigilance with respect to each individual animal would be likely to be lessened. I might rise early in the morning to check on a goat that appeared ill yesterday if it's one of my five to thirty goats, but none of us is likely to do this if we own three thousand goats jointly, since loss of any one goat means almost nothing to any of us individually.

Consider the Maasai, a herding people who live in the Rift Valley in Kenya and Tanzania. Well known to the outside world for their exotic appearance—long, braided, tied-back hair, face paint, elaborate beads, ritually mutilated earlobes, ubiquitous spears—Maasai herders might appear to a naïve observer to be enmeshed in one of the most communal societies in the world. Yet the animals they herd are not communal property. Instead, they belong to individual families, the males varying in rank and number of wives according to flock size. If you're asking yourself whether those practices spread only recently from neighboring farmers or townspeople, there's evidence that they go back thousands of years. The separation of the flocks of Abraham and those of his nephew Lot in Genesis Chapter 13 is attributed to the fear of competition over pasture. "Let there be no strife between me and thee and between my herdsmen and thy herdsmen, for we are brethren. ... Separate thyself from me," says Abraham. The fact that Abraham possesses one flock, and Lot another, is taken for granted by a text which may be derived from oral transmission beginning three thousand years ago.

While the different tasks to be performed *permitted* more private control over land and animals to emerge, those productive resources might not have become possessions of the individual family solely because of the incentive benefits. As with other steps in the progression towards more private property rights, not everyone may have favored private ownership of land and animals to the same degree, and emerging differences of power may have played their part in the movement towards these institutions. Less able, or less energetic, or simply unlucky farmers and herders might well have preferred a more group-based arrangement, while those in the opposite situation had more to gain from privatization and might therefore have used the resources at their disposal to push for the change. Because privatization served the self-interest of more powerful families, the self-interested side of human nature was thus contributing to the evolution of more private property and production arrangements, not only through the incentive advantages that self-interest imparted to them, but also through the inclination of those in stronger positions to push for and defend the change. Disparities of power were also evident within families insofar as male supremacy over women was on the whole greater than in preagricultural societies.

At the same time as family units were becoming more independent in producing the goods they needed, the growing population densities of agrarian societies were making protection from marauding beasts less necessary and protection from marauding people more so. The concept of private property was congealing, but it was only as effective as the social recognition and protection accorded it—a point to be emphasized again below. In place of the band, larger and more formalized social arrangements, first at the village and then on still larger scales, were emerging. Increasingly, farmers were pressed to contribute some of their resources to finance rulers, tax collectors, and priests who imposed order and interceded with supernatural protectors. Both the concept of private property and differences in occupation and social class are taken for granted in the 3,700-year-old Code of Hammurabi.

Following centuries of city-state growth, city-state also began vying with city-state, slowly building up empires that confronted other empires with armed soldieries. Monopolization of the tools of force (now far more sophisticated than the weapons of prehistoric bands due to the progress in metal-working that specialization within urban societies had fostered) allowed social and economic stratification to grow further by increasing the powers of rulers and putting the redress of grievances out of reach of those on the bottom of the social hierarchy.

Trade and money through the agrarian age

In addition to priests, rulers, and soldiers, the ranks of the specialized occupational groups in urban societies included builders, artisans, and merchants. Long distance trade, involving merchants travelling long distances and setting up outposts in territories in which they traded, is clearly documented in the early civilizations of Mesopotamia, with merchants from the south known to have set up small trading communities in what are now northern Iraq, Turkey, and Syria, hundreds of miles away. While the typical farming or herding family was economically self-sufficient compared to counterparts in the foraging band or later industrial society, many individuals also used some goods they didn't themselves produce, for instance salt, simple tools, and probably some items of pottery more easily made on a larger scale. Certain materials, including metals, woods, ivory, and animal skins, which were used, for example, in the making of weapons and in the decoration of temples, palaces, and elite houses and graves, were regularly procured and transported over long distances. In some cases, the goods in question were procured by force and distributed to common people in exchange for unpaid labor or military service; so use of such items needn't always imply growing reliance on markets. Market exchange was nonetheless on the upswing. Precious metals began to be used as a common currency among traders and rulers, if not among the masses. Eventually the coining of money began.

Despite ongoing change and political turbulence, agricultural civilization maintained a degree of continuity for three thousand years. Even if we fast-forward to late medieval times, in fact, observed changes might be judged as modest in that most people still earned their livings in agriculture and animal husbandry. Use of money had spread considerably, to be sure, with even peasants and laborers likely to purchase a variety of goods, such as tools and household utensils, saddles, horseshoes and footwear. They likewise purchased items like soap, candles, and tea, using money earned from selling some of their own products and services. Well-worn trade routes now linked Eurasia from the Atlantic coast of Portugal and Spain to the Pacific coast of China, with well-travelled extensions to the North Sea and the Baltic, through the Sahara to west Africa, through the Nile and Red Sea to east Africa, to Persia and India, and into southeast Asia. With increased local and international trading came increased competition and the emergence of more uniform prices at given places and times, responsive to changing scarcities and levels of demand for the goods in question.

While skipping this rapidly to the end of the preindustrial era glosses over a vast amount of detail, this very brief foray into the origins of the modern economy is enough for our purposes, because it's only with the industrial revolution of the nineteenth century that we see the next truly decisive stage in the emergence of property and trade. We'll return to a few other aspects of economic history when discussing global economic inequalities in the next chapter.

Changing individual/society relations: The industrial revolution

During the millennia of agrarian civilization, the dominance of agriculture and animal husbandry as sources of livelihood had caused the preagricultural band to be replaced by the household in day-to-day production and by the city-state, kingdom, and empire in the provision of order and defense. Now, the industrial revolution was about to shift the locus of both production and political order again.

Consider first production. Depending on how we look at it, transition to an industrial economy caused responsibility for production to become both more individualized and less so. It was more individualized in the sense that the individual became more independent of the family in earning a living, in a sense continuing an "atomizing" trend: from hunting band to farming family, then from farming family to wage-earning individual. But production, as well as consumption, became *less* individualized, as well. First, the typical individual now produced only a small fraction of her material needs, relying on market exchange to obtain almost all of what she consumed. Second, large companies (as well as large government and non-government organizations), involving far larger numbers of individuals than had hunting bands or agricultural villages, became important units of production and service provision. The companies themselves had dual characters, being hierarchical power centers, from one point of view, but webs of connection between thousands of legally independent economic agents (shareholders, lenders, managers, workers, customers), from another.

Implicit in the last point is the fact that in modern economies, the congealing of property rights that were linked to the family in agrarian societies became more concentrated in the individual in industrial ones. Of course, the family-centric character of property was often an individual one in practice, given patriarchal domination of most families (like the biblical Abraham's and Lot's) in the agrarian age. But individual property rights grew further, including more common ownership of property by women. Indeed, it was felt necessary to ultimately accord even corporations, which managed considerable quantities of property, the status of "legal persons."

On the societal level, the birth of industrial capitalism was associated with the revolt of urban merchants and manufacturers against the constraints both of feudalism and of the medieval guild system. In fighting for freedom of action with respect to inherited position and the relatively unrestricted political and economic power of monarchs, the merchant and manufacturing classes (and unlikely allies like Napoleon, whose armies helped end the agrarian age across a broad swath of Europe) used a rhetoric of liberty and equality that gradually came to acquire much wider implications than initially intended. By and by, notions of equality before the law and in the marketplace were fostered, and the idea of government "of the people, by the people, and for the people" emerged. Activists from every social class, gender, and ethnicity came to enter the political space being created by these trends and to push notions of equality and democracy closer to realization. The nation-states that were the dominant providers of law and order in the advanced industrial societies were in many respects continuations of the kingdoms and empires of their agrarian predecessors. But on an idealized level, they could also be conceived of as kingdoms turned on their heads, with the citizens as rulers and with those governing doing so as public servants.

As with the organizational arrangements that had marked foraging bands and agrarian societies, both technology and a human nature still relatively unchanged from that of preagrarian days were at work in shaping the arrangements of industrial civilization. A band having perhaps two dozen adults had been needed to bring down a mammoth or defend against a giant cat when the tools available consisted of rocks, clubs, and spears and when someone was needed to watch over the embers of the fire at night in case a torch had to be lit to shoo away a predator. Farming and animal husbandry, on the other hand, could be done by smaller numbers, and the family, a circle of individuals tied to one another by blood, had provided sufficient labor-power and a strong link between effort and reward. With factory production and other nonfarm activities of the industrial age, enterprises of much larger scale than either family farm or foraging band became desirable.

The social impact of large-scale production was different from what might have been expected, though. It was now possible for personnel to be brought together for their work shifts without having the enterprise serve as a unit of consumption, residence, or defense. Such a radical separation of spheres was possible because, after thousands of years of larger-scale polities and associated cultural and religious orders knitting together and maintaining the peace over considerable expanses of territory, people could move about their business with a general sense of security. Commuting ten or twenty miles to spend the day foraging with your band, then returning to a home miles away in the evening, had been not just a technological but also a social impossibility the last time cooperation in production above the scale of the family had been a general requirement because in preagrarian times, relations between distant groups were usually either nonexistent or hostile.[8]

Organization and incentives

With regard to incentives, motivation, and the organization of work, the picture is more complex. On the one hand, the optimal scale of production activities had done a complete pendulum swing and then some, from the moderately large numbers in hunter-gatherer bands, to smaller family units for farming and crafts, to often very large numbers in industry and other modern sectors. Provision of incentives can be difficult in large teams because many workers don't have measurable individual products, but rather they bear a difficult-to-establish share of responsibility for the output of the larger workgroup to which they belong. Which worker, for instance, should be credited with producing a given ingot of steel or bottle of aspirin emerging as an end product from a large mill or production line? Hunting bands had similar problems (who in particular drove that bison over the cliff?), but they could solve them more easily because their members were relatively few, lived together morning and night, and could easily identify and sanction slackers.

With the productivity of an individual being difficult to measure, and with cooperation in large organizations becoming key to valued productivity, why didn't the form of productive organization also swing back to band-like sharing rules in large modern organizations? There *are* some worker cooperatives, production enterprises jointly owned and controlled by workers. Some of them successfully use profit sharing to motivate high levels of effort, which is also promoted by worker eagerness to make sure their partners are working hard. Social pressure on any laggards works like the punishment in last chapter's cooperation experiments, and there's also the option of expelling any die-hard free riders. For the most part, though, what we see in the large scale sectors of modern industry and services is an emphasis on contracts structured from the top down between company and worker.

A company hires and has the power to fire a worker, who, if thus dismissed, has at least some hope of finding another job, rather than wandering off into the bush to be attacked by wild animals, as might have befallen someone expelled from his hunting band thirty thousand years ago. The company deals with the problem of work incentives in ways touched on in the last chapter, including keeping an eye on workers (through a chain of managers and supervisors if the company is large) and trying to determine who's pulling their weight and who's not. A variety of reward schemes are used; for example, those believed to be most productive are given bonuses or promoted to higher-paying jobs. Pay across the board is often made a little higher than the minimum required to attract the worker in order to make keeping the job an attractive goal and thus give the worker an incentive not to shirk effort, or at least not to do it too noticeably. Kindnesses might be offered to the worker in the attempt to trigger reciprocity in the form of worker effort and loyalty. These arrangements are clearly responsive to the self-interested outlooks that workers can be presumed to have by virtue of being human, yet elements like the bonuses just mentioned also reflect the social elements of human motivation.

Factors other than incentive arrangements have also been at play in the choice between the worker cooperative model and the capitalist firm. Since the scales of modern enterprise are often far larger than those of preagricultural bands, full reliance on output sharing supported by mutual monitoring may be more challenging. Mutual monitoring is more difficult in a large workforce spread out over multiple workshops, offices, and other sites. More importantly, most large enterprises have far more scope for specialization of roles than did prehistoric foraging bands, and this specialization has lent itself to greater degrees of hierarchy and inequality. Enterprise structure became more pyramidal than was the division of labor of the band in part because industries could employ many workers performing relatively repetitive physical or clerical tasks for each specialist in decision-making and because the responsibilities of the decision-makers (a.k.a. managers) required more training and above-average cognitive skills. Also, having wealthier investors, rather than workers, own the company helped shield the workers from bearing its financial risks, though by no means from the risk of layoffs when demand declined. Finally, as had been the case with the move to private farms and flocks the choice of organizational arrangements in the industrial era wasn't made in a way that gave equal weight to the interests of all who were affected. Those who stood to benefit the most—firm owners and top managers—also played a larger part in shaping the system's organizational arrangements, since they controlled the financial resources with which to set up enterprises and fund their operation.

Property rights, trade, and inequality

Now that we're discussing the large earnings differences between workers, managers, and financiers in the modern corporation, we're about ready to close the circle and return to the question of inequalities that we'd set out to explain at the beginning of the chapter. Let's try to pull together the strands of our discussion.

We began by suggesting that conventions of territoriality, which probably emerged in species long predating ours as a solution to the "fight or flee" dilemma modeled by the hawk/dove game, provided the general platform on which the concept of ownership arose. Fully private property was limited in the earliest foraging bands, in which rights of access to a territory or a stand of valued plants were more the preserve of the group than of the individual. But once territoriality and sufficient intelligence existed, exchange followed as a natural outgrowth of different resource endowments.

A major jump towards the privatization of property came with the transitions to herding and agriculture, in which responsibility for production shifted to the family. Trading continued to develop, facilitated in part by larger polities and denser populations, with specialized groups of merchants coming into being in early towns and cities. The emergence of precious metals as means of exchange, eventually stamped into coins, helped traders to transcend the limitations of barter.

We need to focus a bit more explicitly on the role of the supply-demand relationship. As trade grew, that relationship came to play a greater role in shaping the terms of trade—in monetized economies, prices. As we've seen, determination of prices by changes in supply and demand was essentially automatic once enough competition existed. But from antiquity to the late medieval period, countervailing forces were often present. In some cases, trade was controlled by rulers, and there were efforts to fix prices or rates of exchange between goods at customary levels. Development of markets in labor as we know them today was slowed by various factors, including the lack of scale economies in many activities, the resulting self-sufficiency in labor of small peasant and artisan families, and the reliance on slavery and indentured servitude where additional labor was needed. There was widespread disapproval of the practice of charging interest. And total trade volumes were small in comparison with those of the modern world, since households were still providing themselves with many of their requirements.

These barriers to the growth of competitive pricing have diminished since the industrial revolution. The growth of modern capitalism was accompanied by the declining intervention of political authorities in the operation of markets, the abolition of slavery, greater specialization and trade, increased economies of scale in production, and relaxation of controls on interest followed by innovations in credit and capital markets. Where before most people had been largely self-supporting farmers purchasing a still relatively small proportion of what they consumed, now the large majority of people were employed in specialized jobs, receiving their earnings in the form of money with which they purchased a wide range of goods and services in the market. The scope for custom and authority to determine prices and wages narrowed, and with competition between ever more sellers and buyers, market exchanges increasingly took place at prices determined by the immediate balance between the available supply and the level of demand for each good and service, including labor.

While historical processes help to explain the origins of property and of exchange at prices determined by demand and supply, they don't foreclose the possibility that alternatives could have emerged. In fact, there were trials of alternative schemes during the nineteenth and twentieth centuries, but each failed to achieve a comparable degree of success in raising prosperity while avoiding totalitarian controls over people's lives and thoughts. Alternative forms of enterprise, such as cooperatives, were perfectly legal and entirely possible for workers to join, yet they never rivaled numerically employment by capitalist firms, due to factors including financing difficulties and limited worker tolerance for risk.

Overall, the evidence from recent experimentation and competition of differing economic systems suggests that private property and trade, which emerged over tens of thousands of years as principles of human economic interaction built on prehistoric underpinnings, harnessed human energies more effectively than any alternative by providing incentives that appeal first and foremost to the self-interested aspect of human nature. The further freeing of private property and trade from competing social constraints during the transition from the late medieval economy to early modern capitalism was associated with unprecedented acceleration of technological change and unparalleled growth of productivity, convincing the majority of observers that these core elements of economic life might be wisely regulated and harnessed for the greater good but should not be rejected lightly. As the English economist, Alfred Marshall, whom we quoted in Chapter 2, wrote:

> If competition is contrasted with energetic cooperation in unselfish work for the public good, then even the best forms of competition are relatively evil, while its harsher and meaner forms are hateful. ... But [the economist] must not decry competition ... until he is sure that, human nature being what it is, the restraint of competition would not be more antisocial in its workings than the competition itself.[9]

Even primatologist de Waal, while pressing the case that humans are an empathetic and social species, says, "No matter how much brainwashing we engage in and patriotic songs we sing, we will always think of ourselves before we think of society. If any good has come out of the Communist 'experiment,' it is this clarification of the limits of solidarity."[10]

The scale of inequalities

Books have been written about the rapid increase in inequality in countries like the United States during the last few decades.[11] For our purposes, it's important to address not so much the reasons for the most recent uptick in inequality, but why inequality grew so sharply from the preagrarian to the agrarian and from the agrarian to the industrial ages. Recent trends can then be placed in a longer-term context.

Inequalities were constrained in hunter-gatherer days by the small scale, limited specialization, and strong need for group cohesion in such societies. Those constraints began to be relaxed in early village and herding societies, but initially inequality was probably limited by small production surpluses and by the need to protect whatever property one amassed from theft or spiteful destruction by others. The gap between rich and poor grew as new political structures emerged to give legitimacy and protection to property and as polities grew from villages to agglomerations of villages to city states and empires.

Economic theory predicts that as markets and competition increase, the earnings going to a resource's owner will come ever closer to equaling the net contribution to the total output of society that can be attributed to it. An individual's income should accordingly come to equal this net, or "marginal" product, times the quantity of each resource she contributes to the economy at a given point in time.

The earnings from both human and non-human inputs will vary with relevant qualitative features like skill, for workers, and soil quality, for land; so the labor earnings of, say, a fund manager or brain surgeon may be greater than that of a street sweeper or farm worker due to differences in the kinds of labor they contribute. However, the convention that individuals can own *non-human* resources greatly magnifies the scope for inequality when there's no limit to the amount of such property any one individual can own. If we add to this arrangements by which the fruits of one person's labor can become the property of another, for instance through institutions like slavery, the scope for inequality is further expanded.

Concentrations of wealth, clearly evident in the numbers and kinds of goods with which people were buried, the sizes of their tombs and burial mounds, and the scales of their palaces and dwellings, increase in the archeological record as populations under common rule and with extensive trade interactions grew during the agrarian age. What happens to inequality as agrarianism is left behind in favor of an industrial society? Some factors should lead us to expect industrial capitalist societies to have less inequality than agrarian ones, other factors to expect them to be more unequal.

Favoring greater equality are reductions in transportation costs and elimination of other barriers conferring monopoly power, abolition of slavery, disappearance of feudal and hereditary privileges, and expansion of education. But favoring more inequality are increases in the scale of operations of some companies in industries, including media and entertainment, financial services, various kinds of manufacturing, and software and telecommunications. Competition is imperfect because companies can achieve quality advantages that are difficult to imitate and because customers have limited time to investigate the quality of each variety on offer and they accordingly use brand names as shortcuts for forming quality expectations. Once a company achieves sufficient brand recognition and cache that customers are willing to spend a small premium to purchase from it rather than competitors, repeat purchases by many millions of customers at this small premium is sufficient to generate vast profits that can be plowed into further advertising, expansion of product lines, and investment in productive capacity. International competition, the continued presence of vast numbers willing to work for very low wages in poor countries, continued relative scarcity of the best trained and most capable workers, rising political power of the rich in some democracies, and declining bargaining power of workers relative to investors and consumers are among the factors blamed for the growing inequalities of the most recent decades. These will be discussed again in our final chapter.

Division of labor: The requirement of coordination
In explaining why property rights and markets were the lynchpin of the industrial economies of the past two centuries, I've given the incentives of producers much of my attention. But an equally important weight needs to be assigned to the advantages of markets as coordinating devices. To make this point, it's worthwhile to call again on Adam Smith, whom I've quoted before mainly as a social philosopher with insightful things to say about human nature. In fact, however, Smith's main contribution to economics in its narrower sense was his discussion of how the division of labor underlies economic progress and how that division of labor is fostered by markets.

In *The Wealth of Nations*, Smith contrasted the output of a medieval blacksmith producing small quantities of things like nails, pins, horseshoes, and knives to the quantity of output produced by a factory specializing in making only one of those items, pins. The owner of the pin factory assigned each of a dozen or more workers to specific parts of the pin-making process. As Smith writes, "one man draws out the wire, another straights it, a third cuts it, a fourth points it, a fifth grinds it at the top for receiving the head" and so on. With each worker becoming highly skilled in his particular portion of the production process and having no other responsibility than to repeat it over and over, he calculated that the number of pins produced per workman per day exceeded what an unspecialized blacksmith could produce by a factor of several hundred or even thousands. One of the reasons productivity rose so much in specialized factories, Smith said, is that as people focus on narrower and narrower tasks, there's an increased likelihood that highly specific tools—ones ideal, say, for sharpening a pin but not a knife—would be designed. And such tools would be affordable by an enterprise making nothing but pins but not by a blacksmith for whom pin-making is one of dozens of activities. Smith's argument that specialization lies behind rising productivity, including the fostering of technological change, remains a basic tenet of economics.

What's the connection between specialization and markets? As Smith saw it, the most immediate one is that the dramatically higher productivity of a specialized pin factory couldn't be supported by the demand for pins in a single village or town, since that village or town could provide only enough business to support one or two general-purpose blacksmiths. Since a factory owner and workers can't eat the pins they make, the only way to make a living from making large quantities of pins or of any other specialized commodity is to be able to exchange them for other goods or for the money with which to buy other goods. A market substantially larger than that of a single village or town makes that possible. As transportation costs and other barriers to trade fall, more high productivity and specialized production became possible. This is the meaning of Smith's famous remark that "the division of labor is limited by the extent of the market." That single observation captures the core thrust of Smith's book, which advocates for the reduction of trade barriers as the most important way to increase the standard of living of a country's people.

The logic of Smith's argument is clearly incomplete insofar as one can imagine ways to coordinate a large-scale division of labor other than trading in markets. Why couldn't pin makers deliver their pins, and nail makers their nails, to a central distribution bureau that would pay them money, or some other form of claim on consumption goods, and then see that their items are distributed to wholesale and retail outlets where those needing them could obtain them using that currency? The bureau, or some other body acting on behalf of society as a whole, could work out the number of factories of each type that are needed and could set payment levels for goods delivered in a manner that fairly takes care of the needs of each worker. This seems to have been what Marx and Engels had in mind, and it's what centrally planned economies like the Soviet Union of the 1930s to '80s attempted to do.

Pro-market economists, such as Friedrich Hayek (1899–1992), argued that running an economy by using central planning, rather than markets, would be impossible. One could say that their argument was no more than half right, since the economies of the Soviet Union and even Mao's China managed to survive for decades, sometimes achieving fairly impressive growth in their output of steel and machinery and in the expansion of literacy and health care. Still, doubters of central planning were right in anticipating that it couldn't match the efficiency or the degree of compatibility with individual liberty exhibited by market economies. The volume of detailed information needing to be passed up to planning authorities, and the processing of that information into efficient directives to enterprises, exceeded the bureaucrats' capabilities. The information was always dated by the time a plan was passed back down the chain of command.

Beyond the fact that the process of central planning would have been daunting had accurate information always been available, it was observed that enterprise managers lacked incentives to deliver truthful information, so the planners never received it. This is because managers were judged by how fully they achieved their planned output targets, and this meant that they could raise their chances of success—thus raising the bonuses they'd end up receiving—by providing the planners with understated reports of capacity and overstated reports of need for workers and materials. The inevitable planning errors that resulted from the lack of reliable information, as well as crude calculating procedures, led to gray market barter among enterprises and to inefficient self-sufficiency schemes within them such as factories designing and building their own equipment so they wouldn't have to depend on the planning system to deliver equipment to them, but thereby denying the economy the benefits of specialization. The system also scored poorly on creating incentives for innovation. Finally, central planning requires a bureaucratic process that's largely unneeded when markets are used. Not only does the extra layer of bureaucracy represent a costly waste of human resources, but it inevitably concentrates large amounts of power in the hands of those controlling the state, while making possible the exercise of petty power by thousands of middle- and lower-level officials.[12]

Sociality and cooperation

So far in this chapter, I've provided a thumbnail sketch of the evolution of property- and market-based economic institutions in which the self-interested strain of human nature has played a leading role. I motivated that discussion by referring to some of the most extreme examples of inequality in today's world and suggesting that, while differences in ability, drive, and other characteristics are often among the visible causes of inequality, understanding why such differences translate into inequalities of income and wealth requires us to explain why property rights and markets hold the place that they do in our economies.

Although the core roles played by property and markets seem to mesh well with the strong strain of self-interest in human nature, even in a market economy people's social natures can't be ignored. Not only could we easily provide examples to demonstrate that people get much of their life satisfaction and meaning from living and interacting with others. The narrower goal of explaining the functioning of our economic and political institutions is itself unattainable without reference to sociality.

We've already made reference to the roles of reciprocity and of kinship bonds to explain the effective operation of hunting bands and of agrarian and pastoral family units. We've also encountered sociality in our discussion of the modern employment relationship. While modern businesses take the individualization of rewards and contractual relations to great lengths, they often still attempt to treat workers with respect and to offer levels of pay and job benefits that might trigger loyalty and willingness to provide more effort. Doing so appears to bring out more effort from some workers, not only because of the implicit threat that they'll be replaced by others if they fail to give their all. In the early 1980s, the University of California at Berkeley economist, George Akerlof, argued that workers' innate sense of reciprocity underlies a "gift exchange" relationship between employers and employees that explains important features of labor markets and of the macroeconomy. Akerlof's article has spawned numerous studies, including a large number by experimental economists using a design called the "gift exchange game," the findings from which have by-and-large supported his thesis.

In the 1990s, the Yale economist, Truman Bewley, set out to investigate why, during recessions, American companies prefer laying off a certain number of employees to cutting all workers' wages and keeping on as many as possible. That alternative approach might seem more rational, since the entire workforce would still be on hand when the economy picks up again, and it might also be more fair and humane, since it spreads the pain around. After interviewing large numbers of managers and executives, Bewley concluded that the main explanation for companies' behaviors is the nature of the relationship between employees and firms. Employers, he wrote, believe that those who remain on the job will stop feeling that they owe the employer anything if their wages are cut. If a few fellow workers are laid off, those workers' pain "leaves the factory with them," while the remaining workers, feeling grateful for keeping their jobs, dig in and redouble their efforts. The role of the psychology of fairness had been left out of the economic theories Bewley had studied and taught for decades, he pointed out, but it sat front and center in the minds of top managers, and they were confident from experience that their reading of workers' attitudes was correct.

While not all such psychological inputs to decision-making enhance either efficiency or fairness, it can nonetheless be argued from even the most narrowly economic standpoint that our society would function poorly if people acted in a strictly self-interested fashion all the time. Complete self-interest would mean that people wouldn't hesitate to lie, cheat, and steal whenever the expected benefits to them exceeded the expected costs. Deception and theft could be kept in check, as we've already remarked, only through massive expenditures on surveillance coupled with draconian fines. The trend towards reliance on self-interest has led to a situation in which American businesses spend vast sums of money on crafting detailed contracts and on litigating cases of perceived nonfulfillment of obligations, whereas handshakes, trust, and honor might do the job more cheaply, as mentioned in the last chapter. Even now, there are times when they still do.

Trust and the economy

The importance of trust has received enormous attention from economists and other social scientists in the past two decades, with several using data on variation of measured trust in different societies to argue that those differences explain much of the difference in levels of economic development and so in standard of living.[13] The basic idea is that despite our increasingly sophisticated technology and the far greater complexity of our economy, many economic interactions can't take place unless one party is willing to trust another, because there are limits to the simultaneity of the transactions involved. For example, when I ask you to fix my car, it's impractical for me to stand next to you and hand you bills with each turn of the wrench, and even if I did, I'd be shelling out money without knowing whether you were providing me with the ultimate result I need. Typically, you fix the car, total up the cost, and I pay the bill before driving off again; so you did your work trusting that I'd pay, and I paid trusting that the work you did solved the problem and that you hadn't intentionally set off another problem to ensure my return in a month or two. Also, when I pay an insurance premium, I do it expecting the company to pay out to my family or me under stipulated states of the world, but not knowing for sure that it will happen. And when I shop online and click to submit my order, I know that my credit card will be charged, but I can only hope that the item will actually arrive and that it will turn out to satisfy my needs. The credit card company only hopes that I will ultimately pay them. And so on.

Of course, we build safeguards into most of these relationships, as well as building in expectations that there will be occasional failures. Companies set aside cushions of reserves. But the amount of transacting that takes place in the end is partly determined by the numbers of trustworthy people and companies that are out there, which varies across societies in a fashion well correlated with their levels of economic success. When my collaborators and I conducted the experiments on property and theft mentioned in the last chapter, we used subject pools in five countries, including the United States, Austria, and Mongolia. We found that our subjects in the United States and Austria did considerably more producing and considerably less stealing than those in Mongolia and that allowing subjects to communicate before making their decisions led to much higher degrees of cooperation and productivity in the first two countries. When seeking an explanation for our results, we took advantage of the survey question on trust that was mentioned in Chapter 4 ("Generally speaking, would you say that most people can be trusted or that you need to be very careful in dealing with people?"). In the most recent surveys, more than seventy percent of respondents in the United States and Austria answered "most people can be trusted," but only twenty-one percent did so in Mongolia. Per capita income in Mongolia is also several times less than that in Austria and the United States. Advocates of a link between trust and economic growth argue that such correlations aren't accidental.

Sophisticated safeguards are of some help in e-commerce and other areas, and the safeguard of formal contract and litigation is heavily used by businesses, but trust and honor have scarcely been dispensed with. People still value reputations for integrity in both their business and personal lives. Face-to-face negotiations are still important in business for the very same reasons such communication led to greater cooperation in our laboratory experiments. In person, people can make judgments of one another's trustworthiness, and when they give their word to one another face to face, the price they would pay for breaking it—in reputation, self-esteem, and conscience—is raised sufficiently so as to deter many an opportunistic breach of commitment. Similar things can be said about the roles of social dynamics within organizations.

Public goods

While self-interest and the profit motive can go a long way towards ensuring the provision of goods and services like TV sets and restaurant meals, our system also depends heavily on things that markets and profit motives don't address well on their own. The worker may purchase a car and the gasoline with which to drive it to work using money he earns from a private employer, but he ventures onto the road with a sense of security behind which stand a number of *public* services. He doesn't live in constant fear that his house will be ransacked or his children kidnapped while he's out, that he'll be held up by gangs of robbers at various points along his route, that he'll have to find his way over rough, unpaved terrain, or that he'll crash into other cars at intersections. He has a degree of security about such things because there are police forces that patrol his neighborhood and roads, because those roads have been built and maintained by public bodies, because traffic lights are in place, and because there are systems of laws, courts, fines, and prisons to impose costs on anyone who would steal his possessions, kidnap his kids, set up illegal road blocks, and wantonly run traffic lights.

He doesn't depend on police and courts alone for his sense of security, either. In most countries, he can expect that most of those who might otherwise have become thieves, kidnappers, and highway robbers have had it successfully impressed upon them by parents, schools, religious institutions, and civic organizations that stealing is wrong. He believes that most, if not all, people are disinclined to attack his house and car not only because of potential legal penalties, but because they buy into the same norms that he does, or at least they believe that many of those around them buy into those norms and would therefore think much less of them if they were caught stealing.

A critical point about things like road networks or legal systems and accompanying enforcement mechanisms is that they aren't well provided by private companies responding to the profit motive unless the process is facilitated by a government or other collective entity. Let's say that there are half a million businesses and twenty million individuals in a certain country who want roads they can drive on to move their goods around, get to work and shopping, and travel on their holidays. Private companies could in principle buy up the requisite land, build the roads, and charge people fees for using them. Some day soon much of this will be feasible, since every car or truck could be fitted with a small chip, could be monitored by satellites and roadside devices, and could receive a bill for road use, profiting the companies concerned.[14] Until quite recently, though, there was no feasible way for a road builder to profit from offering roads without setting up toll booths that reduce the net benefits of the roads to the users, especially if closely spaced. And if the supplier of a road or other public good asks the users to voluntarily pay for their share, some might do so, but probably most would not. Imagine a set of toll booths with some lanes marked "Contributing? Slow down here," and other lanes saying "Not contributing? Please proceed." Which lanes would be busy?

With the legal system, it's even more crucial that it be overseen by a body representing the public as a whole, since private companies might be good at delivering judgments in favor of the highest bidder, but not at the fair administration of impartial laws. Other examples of public goods include national defense, environmental protection and related research, monitoring of food and drugs, and setting and enforcing workplace safety standards. While the necessity of public provision is not as clear, most education is also provided publicly in most countries, and in many countries, the same applies to health care.

The way government overcomes the problem that prevents private companies from providing such public goods—that is, the fact that people can benefit from them without paying—is by using its authority to impose taxes, making paying one's share for road provision an obligation, rather than a voluntary act. That obligation is ultimately backed by the threat of fines or imprisonment, a threat underwritten by the government's status as the body uniquely empowered to use compulsion when needed to enforce its writ. Once the funds have been collected, the government can hire private companies to build the roads and supply other public goods, or it can do it with its own employees and equipment.

This view of government as something that can solve our collective action problems by imposing obligations under threat of force is misleading, though, if we fail to ask what or who government is. Through most of history, it might have been close to the truth to describe government as a sort of armed gang led by a particular "strong man" or faction that competed with other such gangs for domination over territories (though this discounts a bit the forces inclining even most emperors and kings to adopt a pose of service to their subjects). In more recent times, however, the ideals of a social contract between government and the governed and of democratic control of government by the citizens have been most widely aspired to. And while a democratically elected government can solve collective action problems like highway provision once that government is up and running, the very existence of a government that's reasonably honest and responsive to its citizens implies another collective action problem. If everyone is selfish, that is, the same presumably applies to the people who'll man the government. And who among the citizens will offer their time and attention to monitor those officials and make them accountable?

In addition, how are citizens to exert control over government policies or to convey preferences as to what those policies should be? It takes time and effort to become informed about public policy issues, to voice complaints about poor performance when it arises. With an electorate of millions, no one individual can hope to have much influence over the outcome of public debates, and no one vote has a significant chance of being decisive in an election. So having a responsive government is threatened by a gigantic free rider problem. Since there's no rational reason for a strictly self-interested individual to devote to policy matters even a smidgen of the time and energy that she could be devoting to generating, conserving, or spending her private wealth, it follows that in a world of strictly self-interested individuals, the only governments would be those gangs of ruffians most successful at suppressing their competitors.

Complex human nature to the rescue again

Put your finger on a collective action problem this thorny, and you can be pretty sure that it's not *Homo economicus* that you're most in need of. Fortunately, *Homo economicus* is just a fictional character, no more real than a centaur or Cyclops (and less interesting to boot). Our tax system looks as it does, and works tolerably well, because we're neither all pure opportunists nor all pure cooperators. If all of us were cooperative, we wouldn't need government, since we could spontaneously contribute to the cost of supplying ourselves with the public goods we need. If all of us cared only about ourselves, government wouldn't be of much help, either, for the reasons given above. But reality falls in between because in practice we've a mix of motives to draw on.

Citizens of mature democracies have reason to hope that despite the presence of *some* corruption, the *complete* corruption of government is not a foregone conclusion. Food, drug, workplace, and transportation safety authorities, for instance, are counted upon to take the safety of the public seriously. When a ceiling panel in a section of tunnel in Boston's "Big Dig" highway project collapsed and killed a motorist in the summer of 2006, for instance, the matter was the state's leading news story for months. Since elected officials worry about votes, this led to the immediate shutting down and inspecting of a half dozen tunnels, to tens of millions of dollars of repair work, and to investigation and fining of the responsible contractors. The system didn't work perfectly, but one avoidable death is far better than hundreds or thousands would be.

For this mechanism to have worked, it had to be the case that, contrary to their depiction as rational, selfish beings who would not go to the least bit of trouble to become informed or to cast a vote, many citizens do at least form impressions about how government is performing and do go to the trouble of voting. Being at a minimum curious about how their officials are performing, and getting a jolt of energizing anger out of evidence of their misbehavior, people pay to purchase newspapers and news magazines or to watch news programs or visit news websites. In the United States, although in some ways one of the most individualistic of countries, many people make voluntary contributions to support public radio stations. Public desire for information on the performance of government is a major factor permitting a group of semi-professional investigators, called journalists, to make a living by gathering information that people need to have in order to keep government honest and acting on their behalf. The most corrupt and inefficient leaders can thus expect to be voted out of office.

Even relatively egoistic motives, such as a politician's desire to be in the public eye, can have a salutary effect if the politician believes that what will raise his esteem is appearing to serve the interests of citizens, not being seen to get rich by taking bribes. The fact that people esteem those who act for the public good is evidence of their social natures, since pure opportunists, as mentioned earlier in connection with philanthropy, would scratch their heads over an honest public servant, wondering what's wrong with the poor fool. The positive emotions brought forth in others by moral action (Haidt's "elevation") and the desire "to deserve, to acquire, and to enjoy the respect and admiration of mankind" (which Adam Smith thought so important) combine to produce at least a few good eggs among our officials and public servants and a still larger number of public watchdogs, citizen advocates, and investigative journalists.

We know that policemen want good pay and promotions and that most do their jobs as expected mainly to keep their paychecks and to be able to look forward to a comfortable retirement. Yet in a well-functioning society, we can expect most policemen not to pull us over and demand our money after dark, and we're not shocked to hear of acts of heroism. The fact that thousands of policemen or firefighters travel great distances to honor another of their profession who falls in the line of duty speaks to the presence of emotions that a creature caring only about its pay check could never have.[15] A small dose of desire to serve the general good, mixed in with a large dose of desire to be respected and an environment in which respect is partly based on proof of commitment to social norms and interests, can go a long way towards generating "pro-social" behaviors, even in relatively self-interested people. This brings us back to Adam Smith's remark that "We desire both to be respectable and to be respected. We dread both to be contemptible and to be contemned."

More fully stated, the remark by David Hume that we partially quoted at the end of the last chapter is "[in] fixing the several checks and controls of the constitution, every man ought to be supposed a knave and to have no other end in all his actions than private interest." Yet James Madison may have been more on the mark when he argued that "If there be no virtue among us, no form of government can render us secure. To suppose that any form of government will secure liberty or happiness without any virtue in the people is an illusion."[16]

The interplay between the public and the private

The concept of public goods is well established in economics. But it's not too difficult to come away with the impression that they constitute a small subset of society's requirements and can be dealt with as just "a few special cases." I would argue that this is a wrong impression for several reasons.

First of all, there's a strong interdependence between the provision of public goods and the ability to produce private ones. This is made quite clear by comparing the situations of different less-developed countries. Those sufficiently lacking in basic physical infrastructures, such as roads and ports, and in basic social infrastructures, such as security of property and rule of law, see far less productive investment and activity. Strengthening both types of infrastructures have been a boon to countries like China. People's abilities to enjoy a wide variety of activities in their private lives also depend on provision of public goods like roads, beaches and parks, food and pharmaceuticals with reasonable assurance of safety, public security, drinkable water, and breathable air.

Many icons of entrepreneurship, including Bill Gates and financier George Soros, explicitly recognize that their success is not due to their efforts alone but to a vast social infrastructure that permitted them to receive education and experience and made it possible for them to reap returns on their investments. Whatever the gifts conferred by their genes and family backgrounds, such individuals would accomplish far less were large pools of talented associates and employees and a generally thriving economy not also part of the picture, and it would be hard to conceive of all of this being available without reasonably well-functioning social and political institutions. In many cases, one can also point to specific government investments, such as funding of military, space, and scientific research, which have generated spillovers in an array of high technology sectors.

More subtle interactions are equally important. The very concept of private property, which might seem on the surface to be the least public thing imaginable, is in fact meaningful only insofar as it signals collective consent. "[N]o one can have property in anything except as others acknowledge it. . . . There lies the paradox of all property: my right of property in a thing depends not upon my claim to it but precisely upon your readiness to admit my claim as privileged," writes John Taylor.[17] The internalizing of the social norm that one simply doesn't steal helps to make policing and the criminal justice system affordable; but just as surely, the presence of a reasonably effective policing and criminal justice system provides many with a critical incentive to adopt the norm and to inculcate it in their children.

Other "non-private" sectors

Although governments and corporations are the largest economic actors in the modern economy, many people are employed in and others spend substantial amounts of time interacting with non-government organizations that aren't owned by shareholders and that exist for purposes other than earning profits. In the United States, most hospitals and the majority of universities and colleges that aren't owned by governments are set up as nonprofit organizations, existing to render services to particular clienteles and receiving part of their funding in the form of donations. Absence of private owners and profit-claimants also characterize religious institutions, museums, orchestras, and other cultural organizations. Charities, foundations, and community organizations provide wide ranges of services based on voluntary donations and sometimes on volunteer labor. The nonprofit sector accounts for a significant fraction of the buildings, jobs, and services in all modern economies.

As with business and government, what makes the nonprofit sector work is again a mixture of self-interested and social motivations. Clearly the absence of profit *per se* doesn't mean that there's nobody in it for the money or for personal glory. Some people carve out well-paying jobs as "social entrepreneurs," innovators, or managers in the nonprofit sector. In the United States, there are tax advantages to making donations, which reduce but don't entirely eliminate their cost to the donor. Professional fund-raisers are well aware of other selfish, if not materially-acquisitive, motives for donating: to have one's name on a building or room or listed in a pamphlet or on a website; to have one's picture in the paper; to get to rub elbows with the famous; and so on. Fund-raisers embarrass people into contributing by sending them an initial gift (a nickel taped to the inside of an envelope or the pencils, small blankets or other items sent by some organizations) or by enlisting neighbors to make solicitations. Nonetheless, it would be excessively cynical to attribute all donations to self-interest, and as pointed out earlier, even when people do make donations "in order to look good" or to alleviate guilt over using the free pencil, this leaves the unanswerable questions of why a strictly selfish creature would ever feel guilt and why it should be that being charitable would be well regarded in any clear-headed, selfish species. Those questions are readily answerable, in contrast, using the realistic model of human nature we've continually referred to.

Applying moral standards

Our explanations of economic and social arrangements have given pride of place to the immediate needs to be met (food, protection), to the technologies for meeting them (hunting, agriculture, industry), and to proximate motivators of human behavior (material self-interest, desire for approval). As a result, there might be little reason to expect the arrangements adopted to measure up well against non-utilitarian standards like being just, providing opportunities for the cultivation of satisfying relationships, or contributing positively to our moral development. We should therefore feel little surprise when finding among the economic arrangements of the recent past institutionalized slavery, serfdom, and subjugation of women, and in the present such realities as child labor, human trafficking, and inequalities as vast as those with which this chapter began.

But we should be careful not to oversimplify. If the standards we're tempted to use to judge our institutions in moments of moral reflection are as deeply rooted in our evolved social natures as the last few chapters have suggested, then it would be surprising for them to have played no part whatever in the evolution of our institutions. Recent cultural and political developments, such as the successes scored by movements for equality between the sexes and "races," suggest that notions of justice can be quite effectively leveraged to bring about institutional changes that are in the self-interest of some groups and morally satisfying to others. While never separable from balances of arms and potential threats of force, heavy reliance on the rhetoric of justice throughout recorded history is consistent with the idea that notions of justice and injustice have exerted real power to affect sentiments and thus to influence support for or opposition to institutional rules.

Strengthened notions of individual rights are one example. As mentioned above, individual rights of property and freedom to enter and leave contracts were fought for by emerging merchant and manufacturing classes in the transition from feudalism to modernity that some call the "early modern period" and during the industrial revolution itself, with the protagonists doing this more out of self-interest than out of love of abstract principles. Yet the rhetoric of equality would ultimately help to fuel movements towards political democracy, universal suffrage, labor organizing rights, and much more.

Another example concerns changes in the domain over which notions of fairness and justice are applied. Principles of human worth imbedded in "Axial age" philosophies, from the ancient Greeks and Hebrews to the Buddha and Confucius, were often appealed to by people judging the justice of their rulers. Unfortunately, the idea that such principles applied to human beings in general, rather than to one's own group only, didn't carry much weight with the Spaniards as they slaughtered indigenous Mexicans and Peruvians, or with slave traders on the coasts of Africa and their customers in the Americas, or with the agents of King Leopold in the Congo. It seems that the ideals of justice and fairness that spring from the nature of human interaction in families and small groups took thousands of years to scale up to societal levels and that their application to the speakers of other languages and the believers in other religions is still working itself out in our own day. Comparing the era of colonization to the situation of today, an optimist might point to progress, but unfortunately, there are still far too many grounds for doubt. (The US invasion of Iraq in 2003 and Chinese coddling of African dictators during the past decade are two of the many possible examples.)

Some conclusions

Changes in the technological means of human survival, combined with continuity of a human nature formed during thousands or even millions of years of small-band living, seem capable of accounting for the way in which human economic life has been organized during the much shorter span of recorded history, though our discussion constitutes a quick sketch only, and numerous details remain to be worked out. While critical needs for cooperation in foraging band societies meant that a premium was put on curbing excesses of selfishness among our remote human and protohuman ancestors, the effectiveness of individually-oriented material incentives has meant a trend towards the focus of rewards on the family since the time that people settled down to support themselves in agriculture or focus on animal husbandry, with a further shift towards still more individualized rewards when people became specialized workers in diverse, non-family-based enterprises in the industrial age.

Yet people remain social animals, their psychological natures having had little time to change during a dozen generations of urban industrial life and another hundred fifty or so generations of life in agrarian states. The family was an effective unit of economic organization during generation after generation of agrarian and pastoral life because the strength of family ties (well explicable on evolutionary grounds) permitted the minimization of the incentive problems that otherwise exist when people share a livelihood from a common activity. In more modern societies, not only technology but also a socially-provided infrastructure of law and order, roads and transportation systems, traffic rules, policing, and more, make it possible for individuals to separate their working and personal lives so that much of the strictly economic side of daily activity can be organized through contracts using individualized material incentives. Yet provision of the public facilitators of private economic life would be impossible but for the fact that people remain receptive to moral norms and rules, with sufficient numbers inclined to play their parts as citizens and to demand honest performance from government despite incentives to leave the job to others.

If one starts from a pessimistic standpoint, recognizing the amount of selfishness (as well as stupidity) that can be found in human beings, it's possible to feel real amazement at how far we've come. Human ingenuity has been prodded, partly through the lure of material reward and the desire for acclaim, to achieve advances in our ability to manipulate nature that would have stunned all but the most recent of our ancestors. Material comfort and prosperity has been brought to hundreds of millions of people, although several billion still lag far behind. Political structures that once allowed arbitrary exercise of power for the benefit of rulers have been made to function more in the interest of ordinary people. And there are massive flows of resources into schooling, research, hospitals, and institutions of culture and of moral education. Two cheers for humanity! The glass is half full!

But of course, if one begins with a more optimistic sense of human potential, it's just as easy to see the half-empty part of the glass. For every individual enjoying a high standard of living in one of the world's rich countries, or as a member of an upper income group in a poorer one, there are another two living lives just a notch above subsistence, and two more living *without* clean water or access to health care, forced to engage in back-breaking toil, growing old while still young. Progress on getting educated elites and wider publics to embrace notions of universal rights have not prevented continuing outbreaks of genocidal strife between Serbs and Muslims in Bosnia-Herzegovina, between Muslims and Christians in the Sudan, between Sunnis and Shiites in Iraq, and even between Buddhists and Muslims in Thailand. The incentive and legal systems that we humans have had to rely on to achieve the progress so evident in richer and successfully developing countries are ones that make the world's wealth and income pyramids preposterously concentrated at the top, with a few thousand individuals controlling as much wealth as do the three *billion* at the bottom. But those same incentives also prevent many, however materially well-off, from devoting more time to human relationships and other dimensions of life. The most prosperous society in history is also the most materialistic, the most neurotic, and possibly the most depressed. And, thanks to complex environmental impacts, its way of life is unsustainable.

That the world is neither as bad as might be imagined nor as good as might be imagined, that it's neither a totally full nor a totally empty glass, doesn't make it a "Goldilocks" environment that we can happily call "just right." In the last chapter, I want to think aloud about what the light we've shed on our human situation suggests about the prospect of a better world. Before proceeding, though, I want to devote more attention to what I'm inclined to view as the most vexing problem of our time—why the gap between rich and poor countries is both so large and so persistent on a global scale.

Notes:

1. According to Edward N. Wolff, "Changes in Household Wealth in the 1980s and 1990s in the U.S." (Levy Economics Institute Working Paper No. 407, 2004), the poorest forty percent of US households had a combined share of US net worth of less than one-third of one percent. Using the estimate of average US wealth provided in James B. Davies et al., "The World Distribution of Household Wealth," *United Nations World Institute for Development Economics Research* (2006), the combined wealth of these households adds up to $87 billion.

2. An estimate that the poorest billion had a combined wealth of about $92 billion can be derived from the fact that the share of world wealth belonging to the poorest 10 percent is estimated in Table 10a of Davies et al. (see previous note) at 0.03 percent (i.e., a 0.0003 share), and that the next 10 percent have a 0.09 percent share. Assuming modest inequality within that next lowest 10 percent, we can assume that the poorest 16 percent combined had about 0.075 percent of world wealth, which the authors estimate at $125 trillion. Hence, the poorest 16 percent, roughly 1 billion people, had combined wealth of 0.00075 x $125 trillion ≈ $93.7 billion.

3. Note that the distribution graph I've drawn here is purely hypothetical. While my intuition is that the distribution of attributes conducive to amassing wealth has a "right-skewed" shape of the kind shown, no important argument in the chapter requires that that be the case. Approaches, such as the "winner-take-all" idea used in Robert Frank and Philip Cook's *The Winner-Take-All Society: Why the Few at the Top Get So Much More Than the Rest of Us* (New York: Free Press, 1995), can generate highly skewed distributions of income and wealth even if the underlying distribution of talent has a symmetrical bell shape.

4. The idea of "respect of possession" is used by Jane Goodall and discussed by Frans de Waal in his book *Our Inner Ape: A Leading Primatologist Explains Why We Are Who We Are* (New York: Riverhead Books, 2006).

5. As usual, the organism isn't assumed to understand the incentive; rather, "incentive" in this setting refers to evolutionary payoffs from building good nests and burrows.

6. Matt Ridley, *The Origins of Virtue: Human Instincts and the Evolution of Cooperation* (New York: Viking, 1996).

7. Lack of scale economies plus incentive problems explains well why, after a quarter of a century in which farmers worked the land mainly as communal production teams, the restoration of household control over farming in China led to a remarkable production boom and to the sudden surfacing of a massive rural labor surplus in the 1980s. Attempts by left-leaning governments to foster group farming in countries, including Chile, Peru, Nicaragua, Mozambique, Tanzania, and Ethiopia, at various times between the 1960s and the 1980s, were largely unsuccessful for similar reasons.

8. Apart from factory towns in more isolated settings, a noteworthy exception to the rule of separation of community from work unit was the large scale state enterprise under Communism, especially in China under Mao. There, partly because of the difficulty of procuring goods and services on the market, the enterprise strove to provide apartments, food, laundry, health care, and other services to its workers. This suggests that markets might be a useful addition to political order and cultural

homogeneity in making possible the separation of residential, social, and work life that marks modern economies.

9. Marshall, *Principles of Economics*, p. 7.

10. Frans de Waal, *The Age of Empathy: Nature's Lessons for a Kinder Society* (New York: Crown Publishing, 2010).

11. Examples include Frank and Cook's *Winner-Take-All Society* (cited above); Kevin Phillips's *Wealth and Democracy: A Political History of the American Rich* (New York: Broadway Books, 2003); and Robert Reich's *Supercapitalism: The Transformation of Business, Democracy, and Everyday Life* (New York: Alfred A. Knopf, 2007).

12. For an excellent discussion of the problems of central planning by an expert on the Soviet system who expresses sympathy with socialist ideals, see: Alec Nove, *The Economics of Feasible Socialism* (Boston: Allen and Unwin, 1983). I discuss these issues also in my book *Division of Labor and Welfare: An Introduction to Economic Systems* (New York: Oxford University Press, 1990).

13. Knack and Keefer, "Does Social Capital Have an Economic Payoff? A Cross-Country Investigation," *Quarterly Journal of Economics* 112, no. 4 (1997): 170-192; and Zak and Knack, "Trust and Growth," *The Economic Journal* 111, no. 470 (2001): 295-321.

14. The method will not be without problems, though. For one thing, if one company owns all of the relevant routes, it will have the power to charge high prices, and if we regulate it, thus limiting the company's profits, it won't necessarily be more efficient than simply having government itself provide the service. Another advantage governments have had in supplying roads is their right to purchase lands deemed to be necessary, under the legal principle of "eminent domain."

15. A recent example: on December 30, 2010, the Associated Press reported two thousand law enforcement officers from around New England came to pay their respects to officer John Maguire of Woburn, Massachusetts, who died in a shoot-out while attempting to stop a department store robbery the day after Christmas.

16. Speech to the Virginia Ratifying Convention, June 20, 1788.

17. John Taylor, "The Ethical Foundations of the Market," in *Rethinking Institutional Analysis and Development: Issues, Alternatives, and Choices*, eds. Vincent Ostrom, David Feeny and Hartmut Picht (San Francisco: Institute for Contemporary Studies Press, 1993).

CHAPTER 8
The Origins of Global Inequality

Though the last chapter's exploration of the emergence of property and market-based economic systems was motivated by a desire to explain income inequalities, we considered there mainly what accounts for inequalities within given societies or countries. In this chapter, we'll begin to consider why so much of the world's wealth is concentrated in Europe, in countries such as the United States and Australia (whose populations are predominantly of European descent), and in a handful of other countries, including Japan and some small oil-rich states. Why is so much of the world's poverty found in Asia, in sub-Saharan Africa, and in Latin America and the Caribbean? Why does a world that contains thousands of production lines churning out streams of cars, jet aircraft, refrigerators, pharmaceuticals, and enough food to stock tens of thousands of football-field-sized supermarkets day in and day out also include poverty so acute that it leads to some feeling compelled to sell their children for less money than an American would pay for a haircut? What explains why the rich are concentrated in one set of countries, and the poor in another?

Let's first consider a few reminders about the depth of the gap between the rich and poor countries. We'll then set out on an explanatory journey, a journey through some surprising and unfamiliar terrain that will require the remainder of this chapter and much of the rest to complete.

How the other half live

Early in the morning of June 19, 2000, a customs inspector in Dover, England, heard suspicious noises coming from inside a locked refrigerator truck. Prying its doors open, he discovered that the sounds had been made by two men, both gasping for air and close to death. Upon peering into the airtight compartment, he saw the bodies of other individuals, apparently lifeless. The two survivors turned out to have fifty-eight companions who had already died by suffocation. Almost all were young men who'd been smuggled overland from southern China, hoping to enter England illegally in search of work. As the press was quick to point out, the victims were merely the most unlucky of tens of thousands of their compatriots seeking to enter Western Europe and North America every month. It proved difficult to find kin to claim their bodies because relatives already in England illegally feared deportation if they came forward.

What might prompt people to take such risks? Conditions for illegal Chinese migrants in the West are no holiday. Most work long hours in menial jobs at low pay, sharing crowded and dirty living spaces. Their illegal status means that they're subjected to indignities, including sexual harassment, with no recourse to external protection. Why would people make the long trek from China to endure such conditions when statistics show that China itself had the world's fastest growing economy during the two decades prior to this incident and has shown no sign of slowing down in the decade since?

One might like to think that the answer has something to do with a craving for freedom, but few, if any, migrants mention this when asked. The fact is that the reasons behind their migration decisions are largely economic. Despite China's high rate of economic growth, an average rural dweller in Fujian, a fast-growing province on China's southeastern coast, still lived on only $89 a month in 2003, according to official statistics. In the southern Chinese province of Guangxi, which borders Vietnam, the corresponding figure was $34. Fifty percent of Chinese rural households lacked running water, and significant numbers also lacked electricity. China's economy has been growing rapidly, but from a very low starting point and very unequally. With average incomes of around an eighth to a tenth of the US level, and with levels of inequality implying that many earn a small fraction of that average, sizeable chunks of its population still live in extreme poverty.

As we saw in Chapter 1, the hundreds of millions of abject poor in China are matched by many other hundreds of millions who can be found spread over almost the entire expanse of nations beyond Europe and North America. Two incidents, occurring nearly simultaneously and just few weeks after the Dover event, help to bring this home.

On July 11, 2000, heavy rains led to the collapse of a large heap of garbage in a municipal dump in Manila. The avalanche of trash buried at least sixty people alive. The dead were members of families that supported themselves by combing the dump for salvageable scraps and food, their dwellings being makeshift shacks on the dump's edges. Television cameras captured macabre footage of neighbors and rescue workers clawing through the rubbish heaps for any who might still be alive.

On the same day as the Manila dump incident, one of a continuing series of explosions occurred alongside a Nigerian oil pipeline. In that incident, 250 villagers who'd been trying to make ends meet by tapping into the line with jerry cans and scooping up the excess from the resulting leaks, were burned to death when the oil caught fire, perhaps due to a spark from some crude equipment.

Terrible as they are, such tragedies, affecting a few dozen of the poor here, a few hundred there, merely hint at the extent of quiet suffering that affects hundreds of millions every day. Attendees of a World Food Summit in 1996 pledged to cut the number of hungry people in half by 2015, but in 2000, the United Nations Food and Agriculture Organization (FAO) concluded that the target could not be reached before 2030. The FAO estimated that 826 million, or about fourteen percent of the world's people, were still malnourished. In a more recent report, *The State of Food Insecurity in the World 2009*, the FAO estimated that 1.02 billion people (about fifteen percent of world population) were undernourished and that the summit target of reducing the numbers of undernourished to no more than 420 million in 2015 would not be reached given recent trends. Such malnutrition weakens the defenses of its victims, especially children, against a variety of infectious diseases, contributing to the deaths of about thirty-two thousand children per day somewhere in the developing world. Severe malnutrition also stunts the growth of the body and causes irreversible harm to intellectual development.

There have been an almost unending series of campaigns and declarations aimed at ending extreme poverty, including the Millennium Development Goals declared by the United Nations and endorsed by 191 member states in 2000. Real progress has been made in some areas, such as reduction of child mortality from infectious diseases. There's also been a noteworthy reduction in the numbers of extreme poor in some countries, particularly fast-growing China and India, which together account for a third of world population. Despite all of this, the sorts of tragedies described above have continued unabated. Another oil pipeline explosion took place in Nigeria's commercial capital, Lagos, in December 2006, killing at least 269. In July of 2006, European officials estimated that some 1,700 would-be immigrants from Africa died trying to make their way in handmade boats to the Canary Islands, which lie sixty miles off the continent's west coast and serve as a gateway to Europe for those lucky enough to reach it. The pressure of rising demand on food prices, and shock waves from an international financial crisis for which they bore no blame, added to the misery of the poor in much of the developing world during 2007–09.

India, like China, has seen considerable economic growth in recent years, but it still holds vast numbers of extreme poor. A third of its 1.2 billion people are estimated to live on less than one dollar a day, another third on less than two dollars a day. Many of the poorest are small-scale farmers struggling to survive by growing crops for which they must purchase chemical fertilizer, pesticides, and seeds produced by agribusinesses, in many cases using money borrowed at exorbitant interest rates from moneylenders. When crops fail and moneylenders can't be repaid, some moneylenders have been known to apply brutal pressure, and some farmers have been known to find their way out by drinking pesticide to take their own lives. Some twenty-five thousand farmer suicides are reported to have occurred between 1997 and 2006.

How did it get this way?

Like most complex problems, there's no agreed answer either to the question of how living standards came to be so lopsidedly distributed around the globe or to that of what, exactly, accounts for *which* countries are rich and which poor.

An oft-mentioned idea is that the rich countries got rich and have stayed that way by exploiting the poor ones. We'll see that there's at least a small element of truth in this. Today, consumers in richer countries enjoy a somewhat higher standard of living because goods made in the developing world are cheap, given that wages there are low. But it's difficult to argue either that low wages in poor countries are a principal cause of the rich countries' wealth or that wages are low in poor countries *because* exporting to rich countries puts downward pressure on them. Those working in export-producing factories are rarely the lowest paid in their countries, and Japan, Hong Kong, Taiwan, and South Korea all saw their wages rise during their decades of export manufacturing, so much so that the jobs in question moved to lower wage economies like China, Vietnam, and Indonesia.

As for the past, estimates suggest that colonies were a net financial drain on those controlling them, and there's little correlation between past colonizing activity and present national wealth. This suggests that colonialism was more about national aggrandizement and geopolitical competition than about extraction of resources, although cases in which colonizers became settlers and took over the lands of prior inhabitants fit the resource-grabbing view from the standpoint of the settlers. In any case, countries that fell to colonization were already less technologically developed and usually had somewhat poorer people than did colonizing countries at the outset of colonization. Since the initial differences can't themselves be attributed to colonization, one would like to know what put the richer countries ahead in the first place.

Another explanation of who's rich and who's poor is dumb luck. The fellows who came up with the steam engine and other clever devices before anyone else did just happened to be English blokes, this theory would say. They could with equal likelihood have been Iroquois (of present-day New York State) or Tonga (of Zambia) or Tahitians. Once luck had struck where it did and the process had gotten rolling, the technical know-how spread first to neighboring countries, due to proximity and low cultural barriers, and to other countries populated by English speakers, due to shared language. The English and their neighbors and offshoots were simply lucky that the people who devised the steam engine were tea-drinking chaps with good English mums. But this, of course, overlooks the fact that European colonization began centuries before the industrial revolution and that there are important reasons why some were and others weren't really in the running to be the progenitors of modern industry.

A third hypothesis focuses on geography and climate. Countries in temperate latitudes, such as those of Europe, North America, and northeast Asia, may enjoy an advantage due to an invigorating climate, the challenges to human ingenuity posed by that climate, and the check on disease-bearing organisms afforded by annual frosts. Countries with seacoasts and large rivers permitting navigation and the loading and unloading of large ships can more cheaply engage in international trade. Tropical countries bear a greater burden of disease, and landlocked ones have higher transportation costs.

The idea that access to water transport helps to explain economic development is not easy to dismiss given that so much of the world's population and economic activity are located near major rivers and ports. But there are plenty of impoverished countries (Haiti, Guatemala, Mozambique) having ample access to the sea. There are also examples of both early civilizations (Mesopotamia, Egypt) and current centers of economic growth (Singapore, Mumbai) having hot climates, and much of the correlation between temperate climates and current economic development is attributable to historically recent population movements of Europeans to temperate latitudes like those of the United States and Australia.

A fourth possibility—and a scandalously politically incorrect one—is that Europeans, their cousins in south Asia, and perhaps the northeast Asians who joined them in being modern and industrialized during the twentieth century are simply smarter than Africans, Polynesians, and Amerindians (the pre-Columbian inhabitants of the Americas). Countries populated mainly by the latter groups will never catch up without ongoing charitable assistance, this largely unarticulated view would imply.

But in addition to being distasteful, such ideas are historically unsupportable. The ancestors of today's British, Scandinavians, and Japanese were cultural and technological savages compared with contemporaries in Greece and China twenty-five centuries ago, but not because of any genetic deficit. China and India contained the lion's share of the world's "super-poor" just a generation ago, yet today they include quite a few of its super-rich and many of its most dynamic entrepreneurs and scientists. People of African descent can be found in the top ranks of science, literature, statecraft, and the arts. Conversely, north Africa, the Middle East, and west Asia (including Afghanistan), contain some of the world's least educated and poorest people, who are nevertheless "white."

A ten thousand-year divergence

This chapter and the next will offer a quite different explanation of how the gap between rich and poor countries came about. It allows that exploitation has a part to play in the gap's widening, but instead of focusing on differences in character, genes, or luck, it puts the different historical experiences of the peoples of different regions at the center of its explanation of why some and not others had the upper hand as the world was knit together by exploration, colonization, and trade.[1] Ethnicity plays its part, not because of the innate superiority or inferiority of some groups relative to others, but due to the persistence of features of economic culture transmitted from generation to generation within families. We'll also find that unequal relations among groups tend to solidify and persist from one generation to the next thanks to the sort of in-group/out-group competition, discrimination, and exploitation we encountered in Chapter 5.

The approach to be taken assigns important roles to the process of diffusion of ideas and to the parts played in that process by geography, culture, and language. But unlike the "English blokes" explanation, I'll argue that by the eighteenth century, no informed observer would have expected the world's next major mechanical advances to be coming out of the Iroquois Confederation, and I'll offer an exploration of why that was the case.

This chapter's discussion builds on last chapter's recognition that human societies have gone through dramatic changes in way of life, understanding of nature, and economic culture over the last ten thousand years. The agricultural and industrial revolutions, in particular, led to marked increases in private rights over property and in the degree to which specialization and trade feature in economic life. Specialization and trade in turn promoted technological advances that increased productivity and population density. Together, private property, specialization, and technological progress caused both greater inequality within societies (a regrettable trend) and higher average living standards for societies as a whole (a desirable one), especially after the industrial revolution.

But the most important point for our present discussion is that these processes didn't occur in all human societies at once. *Differences in the timing of humanity's technological and social revolutions hold the keys to understanding a great deal of global inequality today.*

At the time that Spain, Portugal, the Netherlands, Britain, and France began a more than four century process of exploring and colonizing the non-European world, there were already considerable differences in levels of technological development and in social and political structures in different parts of the world. But differences between the soon-to-be colonizers and other old societies of Eurasia, such as the Ottoman and Chinese empires, were not yet very great. In fact, nearly half of the inhabited world by territory, and well over half by population, exhibited a patchwork of older and younger civilizations with significant urban populations. This band of regions stretched from Western Europe across north Africa, the Middle East, and south Asia to China, Korea, and Japan. In them, laborers in towns and cities, traders, merchants, officials, priests, and soldiers were supported by agricultural surpluses produced by farmers who still constituted the large majority of the population. These societies had been sharing with each other technological, scientific, mathematical, and cultural achievements by virtue of intermittent and occasionally more sustained contacts for more than three thousand years.

When the fifteenth century began, however, the people living in the other half of the world's inhabited area were either partially or totally unaware of the interchange of knowledge among European, Mediterranean, and Asian societies. Areas that had had little or no contact with Eurasian civilization included some in which agrarian civilization had made a largely, or even fully, independent, but chronologically later, start: west Africa, Mexico, and Peru. Other areas outside the Eurasian orbit were as yet untouched by any agricultural revolution, including Australia, New Zealand, portions of the Kalahari Desert, the upper Amazon River basin, and lands in the northernmost latitudes of both the eastern and western hemispheres. Finally, the half of the world that had had no pre-1500 contact with the civilizations of Eurasia included areas that fell in between with respect to population density and extent of agriculture, including most of North America, southern and eastern parts of South America, the Caribbean, southern Africa, New Guinea, and various Indian and Pacific Ocean islands like those now comprising Hawaii.

Put simply, the main thesis of this chapter is that the differences in accumulated social change that marked different parts of the world on the eve of the European age of exploration and conquest in the fifteenth century determined who got colonized. And colonization and its aftermaths, especially the industrial revolution, contributed to a dramatic magnification of the already existing inequalities.[2]

Let's think once more about the transition from life in hunting and gathering bands to life in settled villages, towns, and cities, this time paying special attention to the fact that not everyone was making the transition at the same time.

The domestication of humans

During their first sixty to a hundred thousand years after attaining fully modern physiognomy, *Homo sapiens* lived rather like other animal species, moving about in pack-like bands and living off the land. During the next ten thousand years, almost everything changed, for most of us. We might go on camping trips to experience again what living off of the land was like. But usually we bring along some critical manufactured items, such as flashlights, thermoses, and tents. Most often, too, we bring along the fruits of our agriculture, rather than hunting for nuts, berries, and squirrels in the wild. When we've had enough of roughing it, we come back *home*. Like well-bread dogs or cattle whose last wild ancestors are distant memories, we human beings living in our cities, towns, and villages are now a domesticated species.

There was little inequality among world regions during the first few thousand years after modern humans began to radiate outwards from Africa to the other continents. Even twenty thousand years ago, people everywhere, whether ancestors of today's British and Swedes or of Nigerian Ibo, Alaskan Inuit, or South American Guarani Indians, used similar tools made of stone, bone, and wood to clear brush, skin animals, and pound plant fibers and seeds into gruels and porridges. When hunters from Siberia made their way into Alaska and then southwards onto the American Plains some thirteen thousand years ago, they were probably quite similarly organized, and they still had many tools in common not only with closer cousins in Mongolia and Siberia, but also with more distant cousins in Western Europe, Africa, China, and New Guinea.

Unfortunately for what was to follow, however, technological parity hadn't prevented generations of separation from giving rise to differences in language, culture, and physical appearance that would play into "us"/"them" distinctions during contacts to come. Those who crossed into the Americas may have had their last ancestor in common with the ancestors of today's San (Bushmen) more than a hundred thousand years earlier, and periods of separation stretching into the tens of thousands of years stood between the inhabitants of eastern or southern Asia and their counterparts in Australia or Europe. What biologists call "genetic drift" combined with the selection pressures of differences in climate to generate noticeable differences in skin color, eye folds, shape of nose, thickness of lips, and hair color and texture. Languages also followed predictable patterns of drift and change, so groups lacking regular contact for thousands of years inevitably came to speak languages that were mutually unintelligible.[3]

Although differences in language and appearance were not yet matched by differences in level of material culture or technology twenty thousand years ago, the relative similarity that existed in this respect was not to last. By ten thousand years ago, humans in different parts of the world were starting to live quite differently from one another. Along the Tigris and Euphrates rivers in Mesopotamia, along the Nile in Egypt and the Indus in today's Pakistan and India, around China's Yellow River, and a little later in other clusters, perhaps half a million people had settled down to cultivate the soil with rice, millet, barley, and wheat and to raise domesticated pigs, ducks, chickens, goats, and sheep. Within a few thousand years, specialists had begun to record information using writing systems devised for religious and administrative purposes, and towns and cities had come into being. People had mastered ironworking and were using the technique to forge stronger and more precisely shaped weapons and tools. Use of tools of war had become the specialized occupation of soldiers. Trade in goods like iron, silver, copper, gold, salt, timber, and precious stones was being carried on over long distances. And like their crops and animals, the people of these emerging civilizations had become the domesticated creatures they remain today.

It's not easy to say whether the ordinary people of "civilized" regions enjoyed a higher living standard than those in the "uncivilized" areas that lay beyond. Based on the skeletal remains unearthed by archeologists and on comparisons of farming with foraging peoples in modern times, some experts assert that the farmers in densely populated states probably worked longer hours, consumed fewer calories, and suffered from more diseases (due to living closer to more people and animals) than their hunter-gatherer ancestors and contemporaries. For better or for worse, however, the civilizing process was changing the people it touched in profound ways.

Like the Ache or members of small New Guinea tribes a generation or two ago, foragers before the Neolithic may have divided humanity into the two hundred or so people they recognized and knew and everyone else, who if encountered was assumed to be dangerous and hence was either fled from or killed. Like some San groups in southern Africa, bands may have built up wider networks with other bands that might have helped one another in times of local ecological adversity. But typical interactions remained in the immediate band, and with only a few dozen people living off of a large expanse of land it would be common to see no strangers for months at a time.

In settled agrarian society, by contrast, you might encounter in a short span of time many thousands of people who either dressed like you or like a recognizable class of others (say, soldiers or priests or traders) and whom you could assume to be a member of your society, though they weren't known to you personally. You could assume that they followed well known rules and spoke the same language as you. You could pass them at a market center and, though not knowing them, could know that they were unlikely to attack you because they belonged to a common social order that could be counted on to punish such acts.

Members of agrarian societies were more specialized in their roles and more dependent on a larger number of others than were their hunter-gatherer ancestors and contemporaries. Much of the living world with which they came into contact had been transformed by human action. They surrounded themselves with goats, sheep, pigs, or cattle, planted vegetables in their gardens, and grew fields of grain, but all of these representations of nature were long-since domesticated descendants of once-wild animals and plants, with no living person recalling their ancestry. Compared to their distant descendants of today, these farmers in the eras of Sargon and Hammurabi, of Akhenaten and Ramses the Great, of the Buddha, Confucius, and Aristotle, may have been fairly self-reliant in many matters, but already the typical person depended on some everyday tools and goods that had not been produced by her own household and had instead been made by specialized craftsmen and acquired through trade or passed through a centralized distribution system.

The breaks between settled agriculturalists, pastoralists, and hunter-gatherers were the first deep cracks in the qualitative homogeneity of humankind, foreshadowing the gaps between today's "developed" and "developing" nations. But awareness of the gap was limited because people at opposite ends of the civilization/foraging spectrum rarely met. The first farmers probably still had some contacts with true hunter-gatherers, but as entire regions transitioned to agriculture over dozens of generations, those in the heartland of an agrarian region would have neither memory of nor contact with people like their foraging ancestors, since full agriculturalists and complete foragers would tend to be separated by belts of intervening peoples and lifestyles that shaded gradually from the one to the other. Civilizations knew rumors about strange beings in unknown lands, ones who might have two heads, might eat their children, and so on. The ancient Greeks' beliefs about India, which Alexander the Great took into his foray in that subcontinent, were of this kind. The Hebrews, originally shepherds with evident misgivings about agriculture, vaguely recalled a first man and woman to whom nature presented its bounty without need of tilling the ground—that need being an apparent punishment for past transgression.

Though this romantic Eden-like view would resurface occasionally in figures like Rousseau, by and large when "wild" people were encountered by "civilized" ones in early modern times they were viewed as subhuman. A Dominican missionary who was among the first Spaniards to live in the New World, Bartolomé de Las Casas, had to argue before a panel of leading theologians back in Spain that the native peoples of the Americas were human and had souls, something that settlers intent on simply enslaving the Amerindians vehemently denied. When Charles Darwin, during the famous Voyage of the Beagle a full three centuries later, saw the natives of Tierra del Fuego at the southern tip of South America, he wrote in his journal, "I could not have believed how wide was the difference between savage and civilized man: it is greater than between a wild and domesticated animal, inasmuch as in man there is a greater power of improvement. ... These poor wretches were stunted in their growth, their hideous faces bedaubed with white paint, their skins filthy and greasy, their hair entangled, their voices discordant, and their gestures violent. Viewing such men, one can hardly make oneself believe that they are fellow creatures and inhabitants of the same world." And these are the remarks of a gentle and humane man said to have allowed himself to argue with Beagle Captain Robert FitzRoy only over FitzRoy's defense of slavery.

We've already seen how the flip side of cultures, which bind societies together with shared languages, identities, and norms, is the ease with which those not sharing the same one tend to be viewed as "other," as not worthy of those considerations accorded to members of the group itself. If, in the twentieth century, people as ostensibly similar as secularized Jews living among Germans, Bosnian Muslims living among Bosnian Serbs, and Iraqi Shiites living among Iraqi Sunnis could become in their neighbors' eyes vermin to be exterminated or driven from their midst, it should not be surprising—though this makes it no less tragic—that people so culturally distant from the Age of Exploration Spaniards and Portuguese as were the iron and stone age peoples they encountered around the globe could easily come to be treated as less than fully human. Most tragically, the colonizers enjoyed considerable superiority in weaponry and technological knowledge but no countervailing superiority of moral sensitivity, making it easy for them to do as they would with the inhabitants of "backward" lands.

Different timings, different connections, different outcomes

By the late twentieth century, the number of people living exclusively by foraging had shrunk to mere thousands in a world with a population numbering in the billions. They included a small population, perhaps two or three hundred, living an isolated existence on tiny North Sentinel Island, off the coast of India. The islanders made world news for a day when a government helicopter, flying low to inspect for damage following the December 2004 Indian Ocean tsunami, found itself being fired upon by a local defender armed with a bow and arrows. For even a few hunter-gatherers to have survived to this day of helicopters, jet aircraft, and CNN would be truly amazing had the agricultural or industrial revolutions been a rapid and uniform affair. The seemingly incongruous fact of their survival to the present day, even in tiny numbers, is trying to tell us something.

That something is that the human transitions from foraging to settled agriculture and from the latter to urban, industrial society were not events that happened all at once and at the same time everywhere. Instead, they've been works in progress, with the last pockets of land untouched by agriculture and modern economic activities—in the upper Amazon, the rain forests of Borneo, the Kalahari, the Arctic, and tiny North Sentinel Island—only recently coming to feel significant pressure from farmers, ranchers, and foresters.

The first agricultural revolution began about 10,500 years ago in the Near East, and by four thousand years ago, village life had diffused widely, from the

Near East eastward towards Iran, Afghanistan, and the Indus, westward into Egypt, southward to Ethiopia, and northwest through what's now western Turkey, and into Europe. Agriculture and associated changes had similarly diffused from the probably independent sites of domestication in north-central and central China through much of the larger area that is China today, gradually working their way into all of east and southeast Asia. The agricultural clusters of the Indus Valley (today's Pakistan and western India) spread throughout the Indian subcontinent and into Sri Lanka and parts of Indonesia. Since no impenetrable barriers separated the societies of Europe, north Africa, and Asia, crops and animals domesticated in one part eventually made their way to the others—though the Chinese successfully guarded the nature of silk production for centuries, thus fetching high sums for the cloth from admiring Roman emperors. With a few similar exceptions, most inventions, including metallurgical techniques, ways of harnessing horses, writing systems, mathematics, construction methods, and eventually printing and gunpowder, also spread throughout Eurasia and north Africa.

In contrast to this pattern, societies outside of the Eurasian/Mediterranean region had little or no contact either with Eurasia or with one another for thousands of years. In sub-Saharan Africa, new groups of crops appear to have been domesticated about three thousand years ago by people speaking Bantu languages who spread them from west Africa to central, eastern, and southern parts of the continent. In what would come to be called the "New World," an independent agricultural cluster appeared in the Yucatan Peninsula, then spread throughout Mexico and into parts of what is now the US southwest and east, while another cluster arose where Peru and Bolivia exist today and then spread into parts of what are now Colombia, Chile, northwest Argentina, and western Brazil. A fourth agricultural cluster was spread by people speaking Polynesian and Melanesian languages, dispersing among the islands of the Pacific and Indian Oceans with an agricultural economy based on tubers, chickens, and pigs. A fifth independent center of domestication arose in New Guinea, including crops such as tubers and sugarcane.

These non-Eurasian clusters of agricultural diffusion differed from the Eurasian ones in having lacked contact with one another and with Eurasia; so many of their own innovations and those of Eurasia failed to come to one another's attention until European expansion and colonization started connecting the dots on the world map in the fifteenth century. That linking of regions previously separated for more than ten thousand years would cause the New World's maize, potatoes, tomatoes, squashes, and cocoa to reshape food systems in Europe and

Africa. The conquistador, Cortez, was amazed at the scale and geometric layout of the Aztec capital, Tenochtitlan, which was larger than any Spanish city of its day.

Overall, though, the inequalities of development before Columbus favored the much larger and more diverse Old World or Eurasian cluster of civilizations. Their crops, such as rice, soybeans, and wheat, were often more nutritious than the root and tree crops of New Guinea and the Pacific. They had domesticated large animals capable of pulling plows and carrying armed men, and the horses they rode into battle proved especially powerful against the Aztecs and Incas. Their longer history of cross-fertilizing civilizations had produced forms of organizational and technological know-how that made their advances into the world's other regions impossible to resist. The uneven match of technologies and modes of organization in large part explains who were the colonized and who were the colonizers.

Conditions for conquest

In 1492, two civilizations, centered in what are now Mexico and Peru, were surrounded by belts of semiagricultural tribes and beyond them by areas still occupied by foragers. The two belts of civilization had, at their centers, elaborate hierarchies, cities, and control over large expanses of territory. But those empires lacked contact with one another, and neither had been in existence for very long, so fifteenth century Spain's encounter with them might be compared to Spain going into battle against Sargon of Akkad—a powerful figure in 2200 BCE, but one ruling a new empire deprived of the succeeding thirty-seven centuries of technological and organizational progress. Neither indigenous civilization of the Americas had yet developed or heard of steel weapons and armor, nor of gunpowder. Neither had developed the wheel for transportation or the plough for farming, partly because the ancestor of the horse had gone extinct in the Americas, and there were no large beasts of burden. Almost certainly they would long since have obtained all of these things if Mexico and Peru, like Britain or Japan, had had steady sea or land contacts with Eurasia. In that case, Pizarro could hardly have overthrown the vast Inca Empire with only a few dozen mounted soldiers. But the overland route from Asia had long since disappeared, and before Columbus there was no seafaring tradition in either the Pacific or the Atlantic that bridged the distances between the hemispheres.[4]

Sub-Saharan Africa's geographic isolation was less complete. There was some overland trade by Arabs and Berbers from north Africa and some seafaring trade on both east and west coasts. But there were few places where sub-Saharan and north African cultivators lived in proximity, and differences in climate, soils, and rain patterns made north African crops unsuitable south of the Sahara. West African and Bantu agricultures reached high enough productivities to support populations giving rise to kingdoms in some areas, but these appeared relatively late,[5] were scattered, and left out large parts of the subcontinent that continued to hold less-centralized societies practicing less intensive forms of agriculture, pastoralism, and even foraging. Iron tool-making existed, with significant cities and trade in parts of west Africa, but the more recent technologies to have swept through Eurasia, including steel, gunpowder, and the printing press, were absent when Europe's colonial era began. Larger and more technologically advanced civilizations appear not to have arisen earlier in sub-Saharan Africa, due both to "bio-geographic" obstacles to more intensive forms of agriculture, including fragile soils and the threat posed by the tsetse fly and other diseases to draft animals, and to the usually "thin" nature of contacts with Mediterranean and Asian civilizations, itself partly due to the difficulty of traversing the Sahara.

The world's remaining farming peoples, in New Guinea and various Pacific and Indian Ocean islands, relied on relatively low productivity agricultural systems based on yams and other nongrain crops, and they enjoyed even less contact with Eurasia than did sub-Saharan Africa. Along with peoples of Australia, Tasmania, and parts of New Zealand who remained hunter-gatherers, the horticulturalists of New Guinea and Oceania had no cities, and what state-like political units they had were still rudimentary when European explorers arrived.

One cannot, of course, simply blame differences in technological sophistication for what would transpire after 1492. Africans, Europeans, and natives of the Americas were all human beings who might have worked together to build prosperous societies using the best of the world's technologies and drawing on the richness of all of their cultures. But three aspects of human nature featured in earlier chapters help to explain why this didn't happen. The first is the confluence of self-interest, acquisitiveness, and territoriality. Europeans coveted the silver and gold, the lands, and other resources of the Americas and other regions, so peaceful sharing was not to be. The second is the dark side of social cooperation mentioned above—the ease with which people label the out-group as "other"—a part of human nature that makes it possible for the same people to behave quite cordially with own-group members while subjecting those in an out-group to less than human treatment. The third aspect, working closely with the second, is the power and persistence of culture, which is nothing short of the societal source of the worldview and mental matrix within which individuals develop and operate. The tenacity of cultures is well illustrated by situations in which people of different origins—for instance Jews and Slavic-speakers in Eastern Europe, Tamils and Sinhalese in Sri Lanka, or Hmong and majority Lao in Laos—have lived side by side for centuries but retained separate identities, often incorporated into relations of exploiting and being exploited. That same tenacity has permitted Amerindians and Spaniards to live as near neighbors in places like Guatemala, Peru, and Bolivia for centuries, while still maintaining distinct identities. Such persistent ethnic cleavages, the rule rather than the exception in any number of other cases, help to explain why technologies and ideas often failed to pass from one people to another even after contacts occurred, which in turn explains why inequalities of development that need not have persisted nevertheless continued to reproduce themselves from one generation to the next.

The colonial era

The beginning of the end of the separation of the human worlds of Eurasia and those of sub-Saharan Africa, the Americas, New Guinea, Australia, and the Pacific, came when Europeans mastered the compass and improved ship designs and took to the oceans. Between the early fifteenth century, when Europeans began claiming relatively nearby Atlantic islands like the Canaries, Azores, and Cape Verde, and the end of World War I, when remnants of the Ottoman Empire, including Syria and Palestine, fell into French and British hands, European colonizers took over the large majority of the territory and population of the other continents, including parts of Eurasia itself. This colonization of most of the world by Europeans began as a conquest by "more developed" agrarian civilizations (after 1800, industrial ones) of "less developed" foragers, pastoralists, and simple agricultural societies. Then, after the colonizers achieved an even greater advantage over the rest of the world's societies, even some relatively advanced agrarian societies fell to them. Furthermore, even countries that Europeans didn't directly conquer, such as Turkey, Japan, and China, eventually found themselves to be in a new world due to the impact of European expansion, the ability of the colonial powers to control navigation routes, and the emerging technological superiority of the Europeans over the rest of Eurasia. (Why Europeans, not Ottomans, Arabs, Persians, Indians, or Chinese, were the ones to break out into world conquest and then industrialization will be addressed later.)

Just how European powers bulldozed their way over the globe varied from place to place. But the general contours of that variation are surprisingly easy to predict if a few key factors are considered.

The first factor is position on the foraging to intensive agriculture continuum and the differences in population density and political organization that go along with it. Less populous regions, which lacked large-scale states, were the most easily conquered and, where climatically suitable, were eventually settled by Europeans. The second key factor is disease. Indigenous susceptibility to European diseases (for instance, lack of immunity to smallpox in the Americas) lowered native population densities following contact and created more room for settlers. European susceptibility to native diseases kept Europeans out of the interior of Africa until medical developments mitigated the problem. The third factor is climate: climates that Europeans found attractive, when coupled with low indigenous population densities and lesser suitability for plantation crops, attracted settlers who crossed the ocean, bringing their crops from home. In contrast, in hotter climates suitable for plantation crops like sugar, the colonizers brought in non-European slave and indentured laborers, with small numbers of European settlers managing production and collecting the profits; Haiti and Jamaica offer examples. Finally, geographic remoteness caused some places, such as Australia, to remain unknown to Europeans a little longer and to be settled later and more slowly.[6]

Consider a few typical patterns, beginning with what are sometimes called the "lands of recent settlement," "neo-Europes," or "European offshoots." Europeans settled in large numbers in what are now the United States, Canada, Argentina, Australia, and New Zealand because they found those territories to be occupied mainly by people living foraging lifestyles or practicing relatively low-intensity forms of settled agriculture. Such peoples tended to have relatively small populations, and they lacked organized states and were poorly armed, by European standards. People wielding bows, arrows, spears, and boomerangs, lacking gunpowder, steel, horses, and governments, could not fight off the inheritors of the accumulated technological and organizational know-how of Mesopotamia, Egypt, China, India, Persia, Greece, Rome, Christian Europe, and the Islamic Near East.[7] Where indigenous peoples had been "thin on the ground" or were rendered so by diseases to which they lacked immunity, new countries emerged that were peopled primarily by transplanted Europeans and others whom they brought in to work for them.

The rest of the western hemisphere falls largely into one of two patterns. In the islands of the Caribbean (including Cuba, Hispañola, and Jamaica) and on the northeast coast of South America (for instance, Guyana), Europeans found incipient agriculturalists with relatively low population densities and without states. They quickly subjugated them, saw most of the island people die from disease and overwork, and then they populated their territories mainly with African slaves, with varying numbers of Amerindians from inland areas, Europeans, and laborers from India and other parts of Asia added to the mix. The Caribbean region experienced a different fate than the "neo-Europes" (North America, Australia, and New Zealand) because its climate made it attractive for growing on plantations what were then high-valued export crops—especially sugarcane—by using enslaved and indentured labor. Some areas that eventually became countries included aspects of both the "neo-Europe" and the "Caribbean plantation" models: the United States (with its southern plantations) and Brazil (with its northeastern ones) being leading examples.[8]

The other major pattern observed in the Americas is the one into which Mexico, Central America, and most of the Andean region of South America, including Peru, Bolivia, and Ecuador, fall. These areas had been homes to civilizations that had begun independently, but as late as six thousand years after the first agricultural revolution in the Fertile Crescent. Their progress in developing agriculture and civilizations was impressively rapid, if we consider that their ancestors may have reached these territories for the first time only about eight thousand years earlier, whereas modern humans may have lived in Mesopotamia for sixty thousand years or more before domesticating that region's wild plants and animals. But being *relatively* quick innovators wasn't good enough because the six-thousand-year head start enjoyed by Eurasia, and the geographic breadth and diffusion of technologies among its various civilizations, made it easy for Europeans to subjugate Native Americans. Compared to the more northerly and southerly parts of the hemisphere, however, these more densely populated parts of the Americas evolved differently after their conquest. This is because their indigenous populations were large enough that even after substantial mortality from disease, the successor societies remained majority indigenous in make-up, and aspects of their pre-Colombian cultures and languages survived the encounter.

In some of the American lands in which indigenous people remained numerous, settler and native groups remained largely separated. Colonists tried to establish Iberian-style societies with the help of indigenous labor, but large numbers of indigenous people lived apart, impoverished and with little benefit of education or engagement with international trends. These countries' societies remain poorly integrated after hundreds of years, with ethnicity, social class, and wealth remaining linked, and with early patterns of inequality being maintained even as lines of ethnic distinction begin to blur. In places like Guatemala and Peru, uneasy mixes of class and ethnicity have made political and social stability elusive right up to the late twentieth century, when struggles between guerilla armies and landowner-backed death squads, and often intertwined conflicts between national armies and drug lord mini-states, have reflected the old cleavages. One of Washington's recent political headaches, the crop of populist leaders that includes Venezuela's Hugo Chavez and Bolivia's Evo Morales, can be traced directly to the manner in which European and indigenous populations have interacted for centuries. Chavez, of mixed Amerindian, African, and Spanish descent, was raised in a thatched palm leaf house, while Morales, of the indigenous Aymara people, grew up herding llamas in Bolivia's Andean highlands.

One of the most startling pieces of evidence for the persistence of cultures and of cultural differences is the fact that, viewing the two American continents from Arctic north to Antarctic south, there remains a strong correlation between the ethnic origins of countries' populations and their levels of economic modernization and standards of living. The two richest countries, the United States and Canada, have only two to three percent of their populations descended from Amerindians, and relatively high-income Latin American countries like Argentina, Uruguay, and Chile also have low proportions of indigenous descendants. This contrasts with some of the poorest countries, including Bolivia, Guatemala, Ecuador, and Peru, which are all around two-thirds indigenous by origin. Mexico, where indigenous ancestors also have about a two-thirds share, is closer in its income to Argentina and Chile than to Bolivia and Peru, perhaps partly because its indigenous and European people are more fully intermixed—less than thirty percent of today's Mexicans are classified as Amerindian rather than mestizo, versus fifty-five percent in Bolivia and forty-five percent in Peru. Elsewhere, high representation of people descended from Africans brought to the hemisphere as slaves is also associated with low income: the hemisphere's poorest country, Haiti, is around ninety-seven percent African by descent, and Jamaica, whose average income resembles Guatemala and Ecuador at about four thousand dollars, is eighty-nine percent African-descended. As will be discussed more in the next chapter, the industrial technologies, organizational arrangements, and outlooks that spread easily to the United States and Canada from England and other European countries in the nineteenth century were clearly far less easily absorbed by these majority indigenous and majority ex-slave societies.

Austronesians and Papuans

In the Indian and Pacific Oceans, economies based on horticultural production of yams and other crops, on the raising of pigs, and on fishing had existed for several hundred to a few thousand years on islands populated by speakers of the Austronesian language family, which includes Polynesian and Melanesian languages. Although most developed moderately hierarchical social and political structures in which chiefs exercised considerable power, total populations were small, and neither cities nor high degrees of economic specialization emerged before the colonial era. Those living farthest from mainland Asia had almost no contact with other civilizations. Their long voyages across oceans that the great Asian civilizations rarely ventured far into were, to a large degree, one-way trips by fearless risk-takers.

The Austronesians' arrival in places like Hawaii, New Zealand, and Easter Island occurred not only after the apogees of the ancient Mesopotamian and Egyptian civilizations but even after the Roman Empire had risen and fallen. The carrying capacities of their islands are unlikely to have supported populations of sufficient scale to generate large amounts of technological innovation under preindustrial conditions, even if their agricultural bases had been more productive.[9] For these reasons, when discovered by expanding European empires, they lacked the whole panoply of Eurasian technologies, including grain crops, horses, cattle, ploughs, steel, and writing, and their island territories were easily conquered by Europeans.

Colonial rule had differing effects in different parts of Polynesia and Melanesia. In some cases, as in Hawaii and Fiji, colonial rule was associated with the adding of significant populations of Europeans and/or Asians to the indigenous one. After nine decades of British rule, for example, Fiji became an independent nation with an indigenous Melanesian majority, but with forty-one percent of its population being descended from Indians who came as laborers on colonial sugar plantations and another four percent being of other ethnic origin, mainly European and Chinese. Hawaii became a US state in which people of Asian origin, led by Japanese and Filipinos, account for more than forty percent of the population, and those of European descent (twenty-four percent) outnumbered descendants of the indigenous population (seven percent) and other Pacific Islanders (three percent). In other cases, such as Samoa, the local population was largely left alone except for a layer of foreign administrators, missionaries, and teachers. Thanks to relative ethnic homogeneity and absence of exclusive religious doctrines hostile to foreign influences, many of the smaller islands have exhibited relatively peaceful, gradual adoption of elements of Western-dominated culture and institutions. But economic modernization poses challenges due to small size, high transportation costs, and the distance still to be travelled in educating populations to the point of competitive participation in less scale-sensitive high technology sectors.

New Guinea, an island considerably larger than these others that rests on the same continental shelf as Australia, is today divided into an independent country, to the east, and a province of Indonesia, to the west. When Europeans encountered it, they found inhabitants related to the Austronesian populations of neighboring islands living in its low-lying coastal areas and relying on activities similar to the Austronesians for their subsistence. Europeans remained unaware, for four centuries after their first landings on the island, that the frequently cloud-shrouded and mountainous interior of New Guinea hosted a substantially larger population made up of genetically distinct peoples speaking an unrelated family of languages now commonly classified as "Papuan." The highlanders' numbers had grown relatively large through the long practice of an indigenous form of agriculture based on the cultivation of root crops, bananas, and sugarcane and on extraction of starches from sago palms. Despite evidence that Papuans—believed to have arrived in the region tens of thousands of years earlier than the Austronesians—developed agriculture almost as early as did the peoples of Mesopotamia, they were still living in small villages with little economic specialization when the Europeans discovered them in the early twentieth century.

Why didn't the long practice of agriculture produce an urban, state-level civilization in New Guinea as it had in Mesopotamia and China? One possibility is that the absence of protein-rich, storable grain crops conducive to the accumulation of surpluses prevented the rise of specialists in nonagricultural occupations. The island's rugged topography, an almost polar opposite from the river valleys that gave rise to the ancient civilizations of Eurasia, may also help to explain why no integrating culture or political structure came to unite its people. Instead, largely self-sufficient and often mutually hostile groups lived in separated valley clusters, speaking roughly 750 different, and in many cases mutually unintelligible, languages. Topographical barriers were a major reason why the Europeans who laid claim to the island in the nineteenth century were unaware until the 1930s that a million or more people lived in the highlands they'd supposed to be essentially unpopulated. Like the Austronesians and the indigenous peoples of the Americas, New Guinea's highland farmers were completely isolated from the diffusion of ideas taking place millennium after millennium among the civilizations of the Eurasian landmass.

As with others in similar technological and political situations, New Guineans were dragged into the modern world under terms dictated by the Western powers, which found ways to exploit the island's mineral resources and potential for export crops without building large settlements of their own. Emergence of the current state configuration is explained by European, not native, machinations: the Dutch controlled the western half of the island, so it passed into the hands of Indonesia upon the latter's independence, while the eastern half, at first split between the British and Germans, became a British and Australian protectorate before attaining full independent late in the era of decolonization, in 1975.

Sub-Saharan Africa

As we've seen, crops indigenously domesticated in west Africa reached most of Africa south of the Sahara by the early part of the first millennium, as people speaking languages of the Bantu family migrated to the east and south. Still other agricultural traditions emerged to the north in Ethiopia, Sudan, and Mali. But as with their Amerindian counterparts, agricultural practices spread through Africa mainly well after the growth of agrarian societies in Mesopotamia, Egypt, and China. Perhaps more important for African development than this later start was the fact that intensification of agriculture was inhibited by climate, soils, and diseases. Even today, the continent lags behind most of the world in agricultural production, due partly to problematic soils and climate. By the early second millennium, many small, and a few larger, kingdoms existed, but due to relatively unproductive agricultures and to diseases limiting cattle-keeping, population densities were generally substantially lower than those in Europe and Asia. In 1500, there were about 38 million sub-Saharan Africans, as compared to 248 million, or 6.5 times as many, Asians, with Asia having almost three times Africa's population density. Today, Asia still has five times Africa's population, despite African population growth rates that have exceeded Asia's for decades.

Although the barrier of the Sahara and of the unsuitability of Eurasian crops to sub-Saharan seasonal patterns and soils are rightly pointed to by Jared

Diamond,[10] contacts with ancient Egypt and Arabia and with later Arab civilizations, via both the Sahara and the east African coast, offered to Africa vastly more opportunities to acquire Eurasian technologies than had been the case for the Americas, the New Guinea highlands, or Australia. Due to the relative technological and political underdevelopment of Africa south of the Sahel zone (the lands at the southern edge of the Sahara) and Ethiopia, however, Arabs, and later Europeans, treated the subcontinent more as a source of slaves than as a partner for trade or political contacts. Thus, there was little exchange of ideas beyond the spread of Islam in the Sahel and Swahili coast, and most technological progress south of the Sahara in the millennia before the colonial era came instead from the unrelated southward migrations of the iron-using Bantu-speakers.

As a result of all of these factors, sub-Saharan Africans at the time of European expansion resembled Amerindians, Austronesians, and New Guineans in that they engaged in agriculture but made almost no use of ploughs, wheeled vehicles, or horses. Given its relative technological inferiority and the absence of states strong enough to organize resistance, in most regions, sub-Saharan Africa might be expected to have been an easy target for Europe's colonial expansion. Colonization was indeed what happened in the southernmost part of the continent after its coastline became a staging point for Portuguese and Dutch voyages to the Indian Ocean. Those who came ashore noted the hospitable Mediterranean-like climate, found the land to be suitable for a European-style agriculture, and judged the indigenous population to be thin on the ground. After beginning settlement there and conquering a succession of islands and coastal trading points elsewhere in Africa, however, Europeans didn't penetrate most of the continent's interior because its tropical climate and diseases, especially malaria, made it too inhospitable for settlement or even for the long-term posting of soldiers and administrators. It was also clear that Africa was not an empty continent that could be developed by Europeans without first expropriating large numbers of existing inhabitants.

Several factors worked together to change Europe's relative disinterest in Africa in the late nineteenth century. One was the development of quinine for the prevention and treatment of malaria—an outgrowth of colonization in its own right, since the usefulness of the bark from which it was extracted was only discovered by Europeans after its long use by the indigenous people of Peru. Another was an increase in the military superiority of Europeans over Africans, thanks to more accurate and powerful guns and the eventual inclusion of motorized transport and machine guns in their arsenals. Third was the competition for spheres of influence between Britain and France and the sudden interest of Belgium and Germany in joining the club of colonizers. With Africa's interior rendered more penetrable, concerns that the continent would be grabbed by competing countries if not by themselves led West European governments to rush into a "scramble for Africa" in the 1890s.

Africa's colonial period was a short one, and its demographic effects were much less far-reaching than those in the Americas, Australia, and New Zealand. Colonization's impact on African societies was as much the result of the intensification of economic and political contacts with outsiders and the drawing of Africa into "the modern world" more generally than of colonial status per se, and this impact continued in the era of independent states that were in essence also colonial creations. Independent African countries were poorly prepared to participate in international markets on advantageous terms, and their governments were extremely fragile and easily subject to capture by military officers, corrupt politicians, and movements pitting tribe against tribe. Since the 1960s, civil wars based on ethnic divisions and the attempts of local groups to control mineral resources have devastated many countries, almost a direct result of the fact that the national borders drawn around peoples lacking common precolonial languages and ethnic identities had only two or three generations to incubate national identities, a far cry from the centuries that the nation-forming process had taken in countries like France, England, China, and Japan.

The colonial era in Asia and north Africa

This brings us to those parts of Eurasia that were not busy colonizing the rest of the world in the fifteenth to nineteenth centuries, that is to Asia, the vast continent containing more than half of the world's population, to north Africa, long part of the Mediterranean world and in 1400 either within or under the influence of the Ottoman Empire, and to that empire itself. What happened to these homes of early civilizations when the world became a European stage?

Not much, in the beginning. Although Portuguese explorers succeeded in navigating around Africa's southern tip, reaching India in 1498 and China in 1513, the European powers were unable to conquer any major part of Asia for more than two centuries, and in several cases, they were successfully repulsed. For example, the Portuguese seized Muscat, in the Persian Gulf, in 1508, but they were driven from it in 1650 by the Sultan of Oman, who also took back from them his possessions in Zanzibar. Starting in the 1620s, the Dutch and Spanish controlled Taiwan, which at the time was only a lightly settled island divided between a small population of Chinese from the mainland and the members of aboriginal Malayo-Polynesian tribes. But the Europeans were driven out by a Chinese general in 1661. The Portuguese, Dutch, and English established trading posts and forts along the coast of India, but when the East India Company attempted to impose trade on the Mughal emperor in the late 1680s, their effort ended in failure. Japan famously and successfully refused to open its territory to trade with Western countries until effective threats could be brought to bear in the mid-nineteenth century, and formal European trading concessions were not granted by China until about the same time. While Arab and Muslim traders of the Persian Gulf and Malaysia suffered from increasing European domination of their trading routes, the major empires of Asia remained intact and still wealthy centuries after the Aztecs and Incas had fallen to Spain.

In north Africa and the Middle East, the Ottoman Empire also remained a powerful presence well into the eighteenth century, with only Egypt falling partly under European influence in the nineteenth. Persia also would remain an independent power throughout Europe's colonial period. These facts fit in well with our understanding of European colonization as the overwhelming of technologically less-advanced peoples by more-advanced Eurasian powers using tools in a sense acquired through the combined contributions of the whole array of Eurasian civilizations. While easily achieving dominance over non-Eurasians, the north Atlantic powers were still more or less evenly matched with other Eurasian societies at the time that they embarked on their overseas expansion, and accordingly they were unable to dominate those societies with anything like the ease with which they crushed the Aztecs and Incas, seized the lands of tribal and band-type societies in the rest of the Americas, Australia, and Oceania, and ultimately did the same south of the Sahara.

However, by the end of the eighteenth and the beginning of the nineteenth centuries, Europe's colonial successes, the build-up of its capital, markets, and sources of raw materials, and the technological progress spurred by military and naval competition among rival powers, had led to changes in the relative levels of technology, prosperity, and military might that put the Asian-based empires at a growing disadvantage, thereby rendering them susceptible to European conquest or bullying. Even then, it was generally the less unified (India) or less advanced (Malaysia, Vietnam) parts of Asia that were colonized. Turkey, Iran, China, Korea, and Japan never became European colonies. One Asian country—Japan—even succeeded in industrializing and becoming a colonizing power in its own right before the age of colonization was over.

Why Europe?

Why was it Europe, among the several Eurasian regions that shared the fruits of ten thousand years of agriculture and civilization, that ventured out to locate and map the remaining continents, to rule vast areas, to plant demographic shoots that became the majority populations in large parts of the Americas and Oceania, and to build a huge technological lead by launching the first industrial revolution?

The traditional story has it that Europe's outward expansion was motivated, more than anything else, by the desire to find trade routes to "the Indies," the sources of coveted spices and other goods. During Europe's early colonizing spree in the fifteenth to seventeenth centuries, the Mughal Empire in today's Pakistan and India, Ming Dynasty China, and the Ottoman Empire were the world's wealthiest states, but they showed no interest in far off lands. In a way, it was Europe's sense of inferiority, as well as the shifting political geography that saw the Mongols in the thirteenth and the Ottomans in the fifteenth and sixteenth centuries controlling the land routes from the Mediterranean to India and China, that led Europeans to break out into the Atlantic and then into the seas beyond.

An idea advanced by several scholars, including the medical researcher, scientific polyglot, and geographer, Jared Diamond, and the economic historian, David Landes, is that, contrary to intuition, Europe's political fragmentation was a decisive *asset*. They begin with the fact that China's Ming Dynasty Emperor Yongle sent a fleet of hundreds of ships, some of them among the largest masted wooden ships ever built, into the Indian Ocean between 1405 and 1433. Scholars who've studied the episode believe that Chinese ships visited and could easily have colonized much of what is now Indonesia, Malaysia, and East Africa, doing all this a half century before Portuguese sailors arrived there. But the emperor who succeeded Yongle decided to mothball this navy and to maintain his country's more traditional inward orientation. After all, for two thousand years Chinese dynasties had faced existential threats only from the nomadic tribes to China's north and west, never from the sea to its east and south.

Diamond and Landes contrast the position of the Chinese admiral who commanded the fleet just described, Zheng He, to that of European adventurers like Columbus who could knock on the doors of several European royal courts and, despite rejections, still find one monarch or another willing to support their ventures. Once the process started, competition between monarchies sharing no common overlord helped to drive it forward. European monarchs also exercised less total power in their own domains than did their Asian counterparts, which left greater independence and room for maneuvering to religious orders and to merchants operating in the region's cities and ports. Ironically, the relative *poverty* of Europe's late Medieval and early modern monarchs in comparison to the Ottoman, Mughal, and Ming courts may help to explain why it was the European rather than the Asian countries that began colonizing new lands in the fifteenth and ultimately gained world dominance in the nineteenth and twentieth centuries.

Exploration and colonization of other continents by Europe's Atlantic-facing nations almost certainly helps to explain why the industrial revolution occurred in northwestern Europe. The wealth generated by colonies created capital for investment, while the expanding international trade increased demand for European goods. Inexpensive raw materials were found, and the opportunities for out-migration helped to prevent wages from falling, contributing to the demand for manufactured goods and to the incentive to mechanize.

Agricultural revolutions, human evolution

This chapter began to sketch an explanation of why the world's regions exhibit such enormous differences in incomes. I've emphasized the already substantial differences in levels of technology and organization that existed on the eve of the era of European colonization and the implications of those differences for how the colonial era unfolded. I attributed differences around the year 1500 to differences in the timing and progress of the agricultural revolution in different parts of the world. As for *why* agricultural revolutions occurred at different times and progressed to different levels in different areas, I noted that soil, climate, and disease conditions were more propitious than elsewhere in Europe and Asia, and that the contiguity of the Eurasian landmass and periodic contacts among its many civilizations allowed for a build-up of technological and organizational capabilities that other regions lacked opportunities to learn from.

In his masterful and influential book, *Guns, Germs and Steel*, Jared Diamond provides other reasons for Eurasia's agricultural head start, as well. He argues that potentially domesticable animals were either nonexistent or went extinct too soon in places like the Americas and Australia, partly because humans had not evolved alongside the large animal species native to those areas, which made it easier for people to hunt them to extinction. He also asserts that naturally occurring large-seeded grasses capable of being bred into nutritious grain crops were more abundant in Eurasia, and agricultural diffusion was aided there by the existence of adjacent regions having similar latitude and thus growing conditions, whereas it was harmed by large changes in latitude and natural barriers (jungle, desert) in the Americas and Africa.

Since I lack expertise on some of the issues involved, for instance whether it's easy, difficult, or impossible to domesticate a zebra, I haven't commented on them. What's most important for my own purposes has been that agricultural revolutions occurred at different times and fostered different degrees of change in different regions of the world.

The approach I've taken in this chapter has been an evolutionary one in that it's emphasized incremental changes over long periods of time along with geographic variation in the transition from foraging to farming, an important step in human social evolution. There are also links to the evolutionary view of human nature on which I focused in Chapter 5, including the role that self-interest and territoriality played in the emergence of property- and market-based economic systems. Another link is the strong role of kinship, which featured in Chapter 7's explanation of family-based farming and herding economies, and which plays a central role in the transmission and resulting continuity of culture within groups as well as the barriers to the sharing of ideas between them. The hostility to out-groups that forms the "flip side" of within-group solidarity also plays an important part in explaining the unfortunate manner in which the clash between different societies has played out over the centuries of colonialism.

Finally, the evolutionary principle of continuity contributed importantly if so far mostly implicitly to explaining the opening of global gaps in development. To anticipate a theme of Chapter 9, just as reptiles retain organizational features of earlier vertebrates, mammals features of reptiles, and humans features of earlier primates, and just as the evolutionary process from fish to human involved a path of many steps rather than a single enormous leap, so changes in technology and social organization have tended to build upon and to preserve past features and to proceed in a step-like fashion. Property rights and markets were already present in the classical and medieval worlds and were built upon to develop modern economic institutions, and transitions from foraging to horticulture to intensive agriculture to industrial society display a step-like property.

The upshot, as we're about to see in more detail, is that while the people on any branch of the human family tree are undoubtedly as capable of mastering the same organizational tools and technologies as are those in today's most modern economies, getting from one social, technological, and economic state to another displays properties of continuity that make it difficult to skip transitional stages. We'll see that the people of societies with long-standing economic and cultural features of literacy, currency use, states, cities, and market economies have more easily transitioned into the institutions of industrial society than has so far proven to be the case for the foragers, herders, or horticulturalists who were less far along on this evolutionary progression when the industrial revolution began. And with the advantage of this perspective, we'll be able to obtain a better understanding of how and why the modest income differences of Columbus's day ballooned into the much larger global income gaps of today.

Notes:

1. Diminished attention to differences in character and genes here is not inconsistent with my greater attention to them in Chapters 5–7. I contend that such differences are important *within* any given population, but there may be no systematic differences in average character or average genetic predisposition (for intelligence, hard work, etc.) when we compare any two groups to each other.

2. Readers familiar with Jared Diamond's *Guns, Germs and Steel: The Fates of Human Societies* (New York: W.W. Norton, 1999) will recognize the similarity of my approach to Diamond's. Based on my own prior exposure to some of the strands of material on which he constructed his history, I had been working on related, but far more modest, research before the appearance of that book. Diamond's discussion is wide-ranging and masterful, and I've been a strong booster of the book since encountering it. The main differences in my treatment versus Diamond's are that I have very little to say about the "biogeographic" causes of unequal early technological and social development on which Diamond focuses, and I have much more to say about the impacts of unequal development prior to 1500 on social and economic history leading up to the present day.

3. Readers interested in the spread of human population around the world may consult Luigi Luca Cavalli-Sforza and Francesco Cavalli-Sforza, *The Great Human Diasporas: The History of Diversity and Evolution* (Reading, MA: Addison-Wesley, 1995) and Stephen Oppenheimer, *Out of Eden: The Peopling of the World* (London: Constable and Robinson, 2003). A fascinating presentation of Oppenheimer's reconstruction of the process titled "Journey of Mankind: The Peopling of the World" appears at http//:www.bradshawfoundation.com. On the branching and evolution of languages, John McWhorter's *The Power of Babel: A Natural History of Language* (New York: Times Books, 2001) is a good bet (or for those like me with more spare time for audio learning, McWhorter's superb Teaching Company course *The Story of Human Language*).

4. Polynesian mariners did spread eastward across the Pacific, with landings in the Americas impossible to rule out, but their long distance voyages were generally in one direction only, and they themselves lacked contact with core Eurasian technologies.

5. The Ghana kingdom of Mali and Kanem-Bornu in Chad arose about 1,200 years ago, the Zimbabwe kingdom about 900 years ago, and the Kongo kingdom in Angola and Congo about 700 years ago. Their dates of origin are therefore more like those of the Mexican and Peruvian civilizations than like the civilizations of ancient Egypt, Iraq, and China, which arose some 2,500 to 3,000 years earlier.

6. One can test for the simultaneous impact of most of these factors using multivariate regression analysis. In a study of this type titled "Determinants and Economic Consequences of Colonization: A Global Analysis" (2007, unpublished), Arhan Ertan and I found that both *which* non-European countries were left uncolonized, and the *date of colonization* of the others, are well predicted by (a) a measure of early development of agriculture or states or population density, (b) navigation distance (prior to the Panama and Suez canals) from northwest Europe, (c) whether the country is landlocked, and (d) ecological conditions associated with malaria. We

also confirmed that a non-European country's distance from the equator, a proxy for temperate climate, is a positive predictor of the number of European settlers.

7. Recent revisionist scholarship, some of it summarized in Charles Mann's *1491: New Revelations of the Americas Before Columbus* (New York: Knopf, 2005), argues for greater antiquity, greater technological sophistication, and greater populations in the Americas before Columbus. Maize-based agriculture had, for instance, led to substantial settled populations in parts of the present-day United States, including much of the eastern seaboard. Mann even argues that bows and arrows used with sufficient skill by Native Americans were a real match for the muskets of English colonists. But none of this fundamentally changes the conclusion that, especially after the reduction of their numbers by disease, the Amerindians could not possibly have staved off encroachment by the better-armed Europeans.

8. This notion and other ideas in this paragraph are discussed in: Kenneth Sokoloff and Stanley Engermann, "Institutions, Factor Endowments, and Paths of Development in the New World," *Journal of Economic Perspectives* 14, no. 3 (2000): 217-232.

9. A key element of theories of long-run economic development is that the rate of technological change is partly determined by the number of people in communication with one another. The idea is that important innovations are associated with rare "geniuses" likely to be found with the same frequency in any population. If only one in a hundred thousand people has such genius, then a society of only fifty thousand will on average know only one such genius every two generations, but a society of ten million will have about a hundred at any given time. With relatively frequent contact among populations, innovations can cross-fertilize one another. For this reason, a much higher rate of technological development would have been expected in a set of interacting Eurasian societies with combined populations in the hundreds of millions than in an isolated island society with far fewer people.

10. See again his *Guns, Germs and Steel* (1999).

CHAPTER 9
Winners and Losers in the Race to Industrialize

The discussion in the last chapter took us well into, and in some instances briefly past the end of, the era of colonization. But major technological and organizational changes that helped to transform the world of the early colonial era into the world of today have barely begun to be touched on. Inter-regional inequalities in the incomes of average individuals were considerably more modest before than after the industrial revolution, so we'll need to look again at that transformation of economic structure and its ongoing impact in order to better explain today's global inequalities.

Still, if you're expecting the uneven impacts of the industrial revolution to have erased any lingering effects of differences in the timing of the agricultural one, this chapter is going to surprise you. The way those inequalities are distributed geographically has built surprisingly directly on the inequalities that began with the transitions to agriculture in Mesopotamia and other regions. Even in the age of decolonization, and the post-World War II world in which an "international community" has committed itself to helping all countries benefit from the fruits of modern development, the differences initiated by the uneven timings of agricultural transitions and contacts between agricultural civilizations have lingered and have in some respects been reinforced. Industrialization has accentuated the income gaps between leading and lagging regions, but who lags the most and who's catching up is determined to a surprising degree by where they stood centuries *before* the first industrial mill opened in Manchester. The next sections explain why.

Divergence: How the industrial revolution widened income gaps
When Columbus set sail towards the New World, the average income of the richest region of the world (perhaps China, perhaps Belgium) has been estimated to have been less than three times that of the poorest one (Australia or Tasmania). It was a modest gap compared to what would come later. As Europeans plundered their new conquests and worked their island plantations with African and Amerindian

slaves and with indentured servants from India and Indonesia, the ratio increased somewhat, but the difference between highest and lowest regional incomes grew at a relatively slow pace until the late eighteenth century. Only after industrialization had taken off in a big way did the gap between the richest and poorest country reach nine to one, in 1870. During the twentieth century, it grew rapidly, reaching thirty-eight to one in 1960, forty-five to one in 1990. And it continues to climb. Economic historians refer to the growing gap between rich and poor nations as "the Great Divergence."[1]

Why was the income gap so small in Columbus's day, and even in Adam Smith's, and why has it grown so dramatically since then? The main explanation is that until the nineteenth century, no society had succeeded in achieving a high standard of living for more than a small minority of its population due to the inherent limitations of an agrarian economy. The average person living in the most advanced agrarian societies was still only a little better off than a member of a rudimentary agrarian, pastoralist, or even hunter-gatherer society. It took the large majority of the population to produce food and raw materials for clothing, with a small surplus allowing others to pursue other activities—many of the latter not particularly productive. The small fraction belonging to the upper classes brought the average income up, but only by a little.

The industrial revolution changed this by raising productivity in both agricultural and nonagricultural sectors and making it attractive for families to have only a few children and to invest in their education, rather than to have as many children as possible contributing as soon as possible to the family's livelihood. Instead of using the agricultural surplus mainly to support a high living standard for a few, a growing portion of society's output was invested in nonfarm productive sectors, where productivity rose rapidly, generating still more investible surplus. Productivity rose so rapidly that the majority of people in industrialized countries became prosperous relative to the ordinary people of the past. Since not all countries industrialized at the same time, those in industrial countries (for instance, Britain or the United States in 1925) had considerably higher average incomes than those in agrarian ones (say India of the same period).

Once industrialization was in full swing, it fostered successive waves of technological change, though these also left behind countries not yet participating in the process. Waterwheels powered the first industrial factories, fossil fuels those of the nineteenth century, then electrical power those of the twentieth. New technological developments revolutionized food production, health care, transportation, communications, household conveniences, and other facets of life, with progress from 1800 onwards rivaling the accumulated changes of the previous ten thousand years.

A mere hundred years ago, European immigrants were packing their life's belongings, boarding steamships to cross the Atlantic in a trip taking a week or longer, and fully expecting never to see or hear again the voices of family members left behind. Today, millions of educated workers cross the same ocean in a six hour flight to work on one or the other side of that ocean for a few years, return home for visits once or twice a year, and stay in regular touch with friends and family thanks to jumbo jets, fiber-optic lines, the Internet, and other inventions.

Progress in medicine and health care is even more remarkable. Not so long ago, a typical family lost a high proportion of its children in their first five years, and a woman's lifetime risk of herself dying in childbirth was more than one in ten, a level still seen in those countries having the greatest poverty and the poorest health care systems. But in most countries, this risk has shrunk towards as little as one in twenty to fifty thousand. Dozens of other examples can be found, together contributing to the effective doubling of life expectancy in a few short generations. Although some doubt technology's benefit to our quality of life, professing a willingness to do without jet aircraft and dishwashers, few, if any, would want to turn the clock back on the medical progress that's come with advances in scientific knowledge and technology.

To explain how income gaps between the world's various regions evolved during the two centuries from 1800 to 2000, we need to understand where industrialization spread to and when during those centuries. To briefly foreshadow: industrialization spread during its first century almost exclusively to societies with close cultural proximity to the leader, then to others in its general cultural and geographic sphere—Europe. By the last decades of the twentieth century, it was spreading rapidly among non-European societies, as well, but only among those that had been advanced agrarian societies before the era of European colonization or that had come to be populated by people from those societies. By the beginning of the twenty-first century, the old Eurasian agrarian societies (England, France, Germany, etc,) and their offshoots (the United States, Australia, and, in its own way, Japan) either had a huge head start over the rest of the world or a head start in catching up (China, Brazil), reinforcing the inequalities that had begun to open up before 1500.

The industrial revolution and the diffusion of ideas

The key to understanding why development in the agrarian age has been such an important determinant of growth in the industrial one is the by now familiar evolutionary theme that ideas and outlooks tend to change in an incremental process that unfolds over fairly long periods of time. It's not guaranteed that "once ahead, always ahead." Still, the relatively slow and cumulative nature of social change, like its biological counterpart, has given economic development a pronounced quality of persistence.

Economists Diego Comin, William Easterly, and Eric Gong have recently shown that countries that had more advanced technology 2,500 years ago tend to have more advanced technology and higher incomes today. An index of technological level five hundred years ago predicts income today still better. And both indices give even better predictions when the authors apply the early level of technology not of the land where the present country sits, but of the places that the current inhabitants' ancestors lived in—a procedure discussed in more detail below.[2] Technology and forms of organization are part of human culture, the "software" of the human phenotype that's as important in determining who we are as is the biochemical "hardware" of our genes.

Let's expand on our brief remark at the end of Chapter 8 about humans not springing directly from fish. In the history of biological evolution, we don't find life's early experiments with large, complex animals, the fish and amphibians, being surpassed suddenly by new lines of evolution that start afresh from simpler organisms. Once successful body plans were in place in the line of vertebrate animals, nature built on them, inventing reptiles, birds, and mammals on the basis of the existing vertebrate model—not from protozoa, fungi, or flatworms. Sudden spurts in previously simpler lines were certainly possible, but they were statistically far less probable than were incremental changes in already adaptively structured ones. It's no accident that earth's most cognitively sophisticated and creative species has as its most immediate ancestors the recent precursors of great apes, not those of sea slugs, geckos, or algae.

Something similar has been the case in human cultural evolution. Social and technological development has built on itself (Renaissance Italy upon Rome upon Greece upon Egypt and Mesopotamia) far more often than innovations from unrelated sources have emerged to eclipse the old. Michelangelo and Galileo weren't Inuit or New Guinea highlanders. A previously unknown land called America produced Eli Whitney and Thomas Edison, but they were descendants of transplanted

Europeans, not of the hunter-horticulturalist locals. The incremental character of social and technological change was already noted in the last chapter, where we saw that Eurasian civilizations, societies that were the first to develop grain-based agricultures and that benefited from ongoing, or at least periodic, contacts with one another over thousands of years, were still in the world technological lead in 1500, some nine thousand years after the transition to agriculture.

True, no one society's developmental lead has lasted forever. Again and again in history, the *neighbors* of a region's most dynamic society have taken its technological and organizational developments "to the next stage." The ancient Greeks learned much from Egypt and the Near East, but they were then able to take mathematics, science, and the arts to "higher" levels. Rome, heavily influenced by Greece, exceeded it in military and administrative achievements. Italy was at the forefront of European trade, science, and technology in the fourteenth century, but once-backward England, on Europe's periphery, leap-frogged ahead, with the rather late-settled Scandinavian countries soon joining the club of technological sophisticates, as well. In addition, Japan became the technological and military superior of its cultural mentor, China.

These cases of overtaking don't represent rising stars emerging from out of the blue, though, any more than human beings have sprung directly from one-celled organisms. In each of the cases of technological leap-frogging, the new leader was a neighbor that had had centuries to learn from those already on the frontier, to absorb the old civilizations' outlooks and ways before moving ahead.[3] Its population was usually not far removed, genetically or linguistically, from the leader. The shifting of the "cutting edge" to a culture on the periphery of the former center is thus not inconsistent with the proposition that historical change, from ten thousand years ago until the present day, has been incremental in character.

Grain domestication and animal husbandry followed after improvements in tool making, domestication of the dog, and indeed after tens of generations of experimentation with the germination of knowingly, if casually, broadcast seeds. Writing and formation of states followed grain domestication and animal husbandry. Mathematics, literature, and philosophy followed writing and states. Late medieval improvements of the plough, and other inventions like the telescope and the lateen sail, built on earlier technical achievements.

What of industrialization? It also built on knowledge of how to work with metals and chemicals, harness power, and calibrate hardness, thickness, and speed, knowledge which had been developing for thousands of years. And like previous advances, it occurred on the immediate periphery, if not in the center itself, of the most technologically advanced area of the world. If industrial methods had appeared suddenly in a Khoisan, Iroquois, Australian, Inuit, or Polynesian society that had not first gone through the stages of agrarian-initiated development from which the core Eurasian societies had benefited, then the principle of incremental change would have been astonishingly violated. But nothing of the sort occurred.

Initiation and spread

In Chapter 8, I briefly discussed why it was Europe, rather than another of the Old World civilizations sharing roughly the same technologies in the fifteenth century, that became a world colonizer and the birthplace of modern industry. Recent debate among economic historians has focused particularly on explaining why it was in England, rather than in Spain, Italy, or China, where the industrial revolution began. As interesting as these questions are, I find it at least equally important to look at the way in which the industrial revolution *spread* once it had gotten started. A major breakthrough can occur at any of a number of nodes that are close to the frontier of knowledge and practice at the time in question, but the principle of continuity in social evolution suggests that the spread of such a breakthrough will tend to follow fairly predictable patterns, occurring most readily between peoples who're in close contact and share similar cultural orientations.

In keeping with this, we should expect the industrial revolution to have spread most rapidly to areas having the greatest similarities of language, technological knowledge, and culture to England's. And this was indeed the case. The diffusion of industrial techniques in the late eighteenth and early nineteenth centuries from its starting point in England began primarily in other parts of northwestern Europe, especially France, Germany, and the Low Countries, and in the English settlements in North America. Later, South Africa and Australia, both colonies with substantial populations from the British Isles, joined in. Southern and eastern Europe, including Russia, were slower in coming to the industrialization table, but they nonetheless beat almost all non-Europeans. No country without a large European population industrialized during the first century of the industrial revolution. Before World War II, well over 150 years after industrialization began in Britain, only a single non-European (or European-settled) country, Japan, had achieved substantial industrialization.[4]

The Japanese exception is, naturally, of interest in its own right. When we investigate it, we find a country with a centuries-old tradition of agrarianism and cultural borrowing that had been sufficiently politically unified and technologically capable to have staved off Western colonial incursion for more than two centuries. Its leaders, clearly among the few in the non-European world of the time still able to act independently and having the human and financial resources with which to do so, were determined to achieve technological modernization and parity with the West as a matter of national survival. The country had long fostered a literate culture, a significant urban population, and extensive internal (including maritime) commerce, and it was advanced in preindustrial metal-working and tool-making. For Japan or an east Asian neighbor to have emerged as the first non-European industrializer is thus broadly consistent with the theme of persistence. It's the kind of exception that proves the rule.[5]

In addition to the fact that Japan's industrialization wasn't a complete break with the rule of incrementalism, since it occurred in what was already a relatively sophisticated Eurasian society, the transfer of industrial techniques to Japan also involved a good deal of hands-on training of Japanese apprentices by German technicians. More significantly, once Japan had begun to succeed in its quest, it went on to demonstrate the principle of incrementalism by virtue of the way in which industrialization radiated out from it to Korea, Taiwan, China, and southeast Asia, a process closely paralleling the one that had occurred during the first generation of industrial diffusion, when industrial technologies had radiated from England to its colonies, to Germany, and to much of the rest of Europe. It was as if a fire lit in England had spread mainly in England's neighborhood for a hundred years, but a single spark, escaping and igniting a patch of tinder in far off Japan, had begun the same process of spreading industrialization in that neighborhood a century later.

The strange thing about the late twentieth century race to catch up
We've seen that the gap between the richest and poorest countries has been growing since the start of the industrial revolution. But not all countries that were poor in, say, 1950 have grown poorer or have stayed poor in subsequent years. On the contrary, at least a few countries not originally in the club of industrialized nations have been successful in catching up in recent decades, and others appear to be in the process of doing so. Looking at east Asia, and perhaps south Asia, as well, one might feel optimism that the problem of underdevelopment is on its way towards resolution. The trouble is that the "race for development," and in particular the race to catch up on the parts of nations beyond Europe and its immediate offshoots, has also been looking very unequal in recent decades.

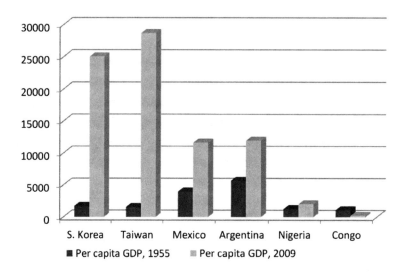

As the left-hand bars of each pair in the figure above show, in 1955, South Korea and Taiwan had per capita annual incomes, estimated by methods aimed at maximizing comparability of real purchasing power, of about $1,750 and $1,550, respectively, while Mexico and Argentina had incomes of about $4,000 and $5,500, and Nigeria and the Democratic Republic of Congo had incomes of approximately $1,250 and $1,100. In brief, the Latin American countries were substantially ahead of both the east Asians and the Africans, with the Asian countries only a small distance ahead of their African counterparts. By 2009, as shown by the right-hand bars, South Korean income per person was about $25,000 and Taiwan's was more than $28,000. Although average incomes of Mexicans and Argentines had also grown, they had fallen substantially behind those of their east Asian counterparts, with incomes of about $11,500 and $12,000, respectively. Meanwhile, the gaps with the African countries had grown further: Nigeria's average income was about $2,000, and Congo's had fallen to a heart-wrenching $231 in 2009. The right-hand bars thus show the incomes of the two east Asian countries towering over those of the Latin American ones which in turn tower over those of the two African countries. Controlling for inflation and population growth and measuring income in terms of its purchasing power, the incomes of the two Asian countries' people had grown at average rates of 6.1 and 6.7 percent a year, those of the Latin American countries at 2.4 and 1.7 percent a year, and those of the African countries at 1.1 and *negative* 3.4 percent a year during 1955–2000.[6]

What might account for the sharp differences in performance among different less-developed countries in recent years? Clearly, some have so far proven considerably less capable than others of catching up with the world's industrial leaders. During the late twentieth century, in fact, some countries had been catching up rapidly, some only slowly, and others not at all.

When we investigate who the winners and losers of the late twentieth and early twenty-first century development race were, a fact that might seem surprising but for the groundwork laid in Chapter 8 emerges rather clearly: countries that did better were ones peopled by members of societies that were also ahead in economic and social transformation as long ago as 1492. The world's income and growth leaders today—Europe, Japan, China, and India and the group that includes Canada, the United States, and Australia—are either ones with relatively advanced civilizations centuries ago or ones most of whose people today are descended from migrants from the relatively advanced societies of 1492. Oil-rich states, including Bahrain, Kuwait, Oman, and Saudi Arabia, although their income outlier status within their region is largely attributable to that resource, are not entirely exceptions, since their people's backgrounds lie also in an old Eurasian culture that was a world technological leader a thousand years ago. And many middle income countries, such as Turkey, Iran, and Argentina, are also either heirs of ancient civilizations or are essentially European offshoots.

Building and testing the hypothesis of continuity of economic success

The idea just stated—that differences that began for reasons of geography, climate, and soil condition during the agrarian age and that accumulated over thousands of years of contact or isolation help to explain which countries have been doing well and which poorly—was absent from the view of economic development that I learned as an undergraduate and graduate student in the 1970s. What I'd been taught in textbooks on the topic was that there are basically two kinds of economies, "developed" and "underdeveloped," and for an underdeveloped economy to become developed requires raising its rate of capital accumulation, participating actively in international trade, and avoiding "price distortions" like an overvalued currency, an unrealistically high minimum wage, or a ceiling on interest rates. "Developed" and "underdeveloped" referred essentially to industrialization, with differences in developmental levels of the preindustrial starting points almost never commented on.

The thought that what kind of preindustrial economy a country had mattered to recent economic development occurred to me after traveling and conducting research in east Africa (mainly Tanzania) for more than a dozen years and after having begun to similarly travel and conduct research in east Asia (mainly China). When I began visiting these African and Asian countries, the World Bank listed Tanzania and China as having virtually the same income per person. In those days, both countries had been following socialist policies, many of them pioneered by the Soviet Union, and I was struck by the difference in results. In trying to foster state-led industrialization, China had dramatically increased its industrial output, even if it performed poorly with respect to product quality and availability of consumer goods. In attempting to borrow elements of the Soviet and Chinese models, in contrast, Tanzania had mostly just crippled its economy, causing declines in the production of both food and cash crops, heavy indebtedness, disappearance of most consumer goods from its shops, and growth of black markets that outstripped the volume of activity in legal ones.

In both China and Tanzania, the vast majority of people were still farmers in the late 1970s, but there were marked differences in the intensive, irrigated rice and wheat production of China's densely populated provinces and the low-yielding rain-fed production of corn (maize), sorghum, and cassava in sparsely populated Tanzania. China's agriculture boasted extensive and, in part, ancient irrigation systems that contributed, along with local scientific research and modern inputs, to some of the highest crop yields in the world, whereas the vast majority of grain production in east Africa relied on replanted seed, with little use of fertilizer, which was too expensive for farmers to afford or for the country to import in substantial quantities. During the 1970s, China had completed the remarkable engineering feat of building a railroad over more than a thousand miles of rugged Tanzanian terrain to allow neighboring Zambia to export its copper without reliance on the railway lines of then white-ruled Rhodesia (now Zimbabwe), South Africa, and Mozambique. To partially repay its debt to China, Tanzania was awash in simple Chinese-made goods like thermoses, pots, pans, and flashlights—some of the only goods still available in its stores—some two decades before China became the supplier of choice to America's big box stores.

As an undergraduate, I'd taken a course on the anthropology of agricultural development in which ideas regarding correlations between agricultural intensification, population growth, and technological change associated with economist Ester Boserup were featured. Now, those and related ideas about processes of development over very long periods of time began to come back to mind. While China was still poor, it seemed to me to have far stronger developmental capabilities than the parts of Africa I knew, thanks to its large population, the dense concentration of that population in coastal areas, the solidification of a common ethnic identity and language over thousands of years, high levels of basic literacy, a tradition of respect for scholarship, and an evident capacity for state and enterprise administration, perhaps also stretching back to an almost unbroken history of Chinese states. Interlocutors in China could not have agreed more strongly, always politely correcting suggestions that China was in any way comparable to developing countries in Africa. In their view, China was in fact a very advanced society that had fallen behind during a period spanning generations, not millennia. Their deep-suited intuitions and my newly emerging ones were about to be supported by the continuation of the super-heated economic growth rates that were still relatively new when my thinking began running in these terms in the late 1980s and early '90s.

Initial tests

By the mid-1990s, I was beginning to expand my narrower comparison into a much broader one: that countries with advanced agrarian societies like China's, Korea's, or India's should be expected to have an easier time commencing an industrialization process than countries that until recently had relied on extensive forms of agriculture or horticulture, on nomadic herding, or on foraging, and that had lacked large scale polities—countries like Tanzania, Zambia, or Papua New Guinea. In crude terms, one could think of a continuum of societies mirroring the paths that European and Asian societies had themselves travelled in the past eleven thousand years: from foraging bands to societies of herders or agricultural villagers to densely populated agrarian civilizations to industrialized countries. The intuition is that while stagnation is common enough, backsliding several stages is not, so that societies situated on the advanced agrarian portion of the continuum should have an easier time adopting industrial technology and modern state organization than should societies in which foraging, horticulture, and herding have always dominated.[7] Fitting the countries of the Americas into the picture might be difficult, but it didn't seem impossible, since their current populations were descended to differing degrees mainly from people from Africa, from the American hemisphere itself, with its more limited experience of agricultural intensification and large states, and from Western Europe, which shared with China and Japan a long history of agrarian civilization. Possibly the divided origins of some countries in the Americas and the resulting social and political conflicts might negatively impact growth also, I thought.

Because the continuity of development framework sees agricultural revolutions as having led to subsequent developments of writing, cities, and states, my students and I put together two sets of data that made it possible to test parts of that framework: data on the timing of agricultural transitions and data on the appearance of states. For the first of these, we searched for estimates of the year in which a substantial group of people transitioned from reliance mainly on foraging to reliance mainly on cultivated foods, for each of what are about 150 present-day countries. What's now Jordan, for example, is believed to have contained significant numbers of settled farmers by 10,500 years ago, Italy by 8,000 years ago, Mexico by 4,100 years ago, and so forth. While most of our estimates are based on the expert archeological literature on the subject, in some cases we had to interpolate information about neighboring countries using our historical and geographic knowledge about likely directions of influence.

A second data-assembly exercise involved constructing an index of the presence of states, that is to say of political structures such as kingdoms, empires, or nations, all of which have much larger scale than the band or tribe. This index was constructed mainly by consulting the historical portions of articles about countries and regions of the world in the *Encyclopedia Britannica*, then assigning to each country a score for government presence, a second score for the degree to which such a government (if any) was domestically based, as opposed to being a foreign empire, and a third score for the proportion of the territory of the present-day country that it covered. For this variable, only the past two millennia were considered. Observations include, for example, that China had a homegrown empire covering much of its current territory during most of the years from 1 CE onwards, while Russia lacked any form of central government until 862 CE, and Swaziland had its first king in 1770.

We have data for both the agricultural transition and the state history variable for some 140 countries, including rich, poor, and middle income ones. The first testable implication of the theory of continuity of development is that how long ago agriculture began should help to predict how long what is now a country has had states (supra-tribal political organizations). We found, in fact, that there's a statistically significant positive correlation between the estimated years since agricultural transition and the index of indigenous states, whether the latter variable is measured for only the first fifty years after 1 CE, for the first five hundred years, for the first one thousand years, or for the first fifteen hundred years after the year 1. Thus, the frequently mentioned idea that agriculture led to the evolution of states is strongly supported by our data in what is apparently the first such test to be done using a large set of global observations.[8]

For a second exercise, we used data on the extent of urbanization in seventy-two countries in the year 1500, which was assembled by economic historian Paul Bairoch. We found that the estimated extent of urbanization in that year is also significantly positively correlated with both the number of years since countries underwent their agricultural transitions and with countries' state history indices.

Another factor long believed to accompany agricultural development and intensification is growth of population. During the 1960s, Boserup had hypothesized a general association between agricultural intensification, increases in population density, growth of specialization, and improvement in technology. When we checked for associations between our measures of early development and subsequent population density, we found that both earliness of agricultural transition and more extensive state history are in fact highly correlated with the estimated population densities of countries in the year 1500.

One last outcome that might be associated with improved technology, cities, and population density is income. If we use estimated incomes in around 1500, before the era of colonization, the correlation might not be all that strong since most improvements in technology resulted in larger populations more than in higher incomes prior to the industrial revolution. Nevertheless, average income might be somewhat higher in more "advanced" preindustrial countries, if only because of the higher living standards of various elites. When we checked correlations of our early development measures including years since agricultural transition and history of states using the best available estimates of per capita incomes in 1500, we found these, too, to be positively correlated. Thus, at about the time that Europeans were beginning to colonize lands bordering the Atlantic and Indian Oceans, it was countries that had had earlier agricultural revolutions and earlier-formed states that were the most urbanized, the most densely populated, and that had the highest incomes.

We then turned to the period *after* the era of colonization, investigating whether countries with earlier agricultural revolutions and earlier-formed states still had higher per capita incomes in the year 2000 and whether their recent rates of economic growth have been faster. By recent growth, we mean the rate of growth of countries' average incomes during the last four decades of the twentieth century, the period of the "race to catch up" among the world's former colonies, which is also a period for which the data on growth rates are relatively good. For both income level and income growth, the answer was positive, with strongly significant correlations. Countries with earlier agricultures and states have been growing faster in recent decades and have higher incomes today, all else being equal. So the pattern I'd glimpsed in my early comparison of China and Tanzania was supported when information on a hundred or more countries was pooled for analysis.

An age of colonization exception?

Despite the considerable evidence for persistence or continuity of economic development over very long periods of time, an important qualification may be in order when looking at the era of colonization itself. Our measures of very early development are good predictors of both the recent level of income and its recent growth rate, when only the correlations between any two of these variables are considered. But when several other determinants of income or growth rate are simultaneously controlled for by the method of multivariate regression, early agriculture and states are much better at predicting the recent growth rate of income than at predicting the recent income level.[9] And the correlation of income in 1960 to our measures of early development is quite weak.

Why is it that both the development indicators of 1500, *before* the age of colonization, and the rates of economic growth in recent decades, after the end of the colonial era, are highly correlated with very early development, while recent income levels are not so well correlated? The explanation appears to lie in the nature of the age of colonization itself. Some countries that were neither densely populated nor urbanized, countries that came late to agriculture and to states, were built up economically mainly by European settlers, while countries like India and China experienced no improvement in income levels between 1500 and 1960, their incomes even dropping due to the confluence of high rates of population growth and relative technological stagnation. One of the most influential scholarly papers of the past decade in the field of economic growth refers to this phenomenon as the "reversal of fortune."[10] However, when former colonized countries, ranging from those of Central America and the Caribbean to those of sub-Saharan Africa, Asia, and Oceania, confronted a new post-colonial era of relative trade openness and international development assistance after about 1960, it was the very countries having the most advanced development indicators before 1500 that experienced the most rapid catch-up.

Continuity and migration

The part played by migration in influencing outcomes after 1500 implies that checking for links between the early history that occurred in a particular place and the recent economic performance of the country in that place today is likely to yield imperfect or incomplete results. For example, if we want to use a theory of historical continuity of social capabilities to predict whether countries such as Australia or Canada or the United States would achieve strong economic growth or high levels of income in the late twentieth century, then checking how early the people who lived *at that time* in *the lands* that now constitute Australia or Canada or the United States began practicing agriculture and having indigenous large-scale states may be the wrong procedure. Most Amerindians began practicing agriculture thousands of years later than did the ancestors of the largely European-descended people living in the United States and Canada today. Australia had no agriculture before the arrival of Europeans, and Australia and the United States and Canada all lacked full-fledged states. We need to check, instead, when *the ancestors of the people who have come to live in Australia, Canada, and the United States today* transitioned to agriculture, states, and other correlates of social and technological advantage. The three countries are now mainly populated by descendants of people from old Eurasian societies, with the survivors of the indigenous, precolonial populations of their current lands constituting only small minorities. The strength of the Australian, Canadian, and US economies in the industrial era is well predicted by a theory of persistence of development when migration is taken into account, but would be a curious anomaly otherwise. Failing to account for the major migrations of the colonial era might explain the weakness of correlations between early development and level of income mentioned in the previous section.

To move from "case study" type observations like those of the last paragraph to large sample statistical tests, my students helped me to research the ancestry of countries' present populations by consulting a large variety of sources and constructing a spreadsheet or "matrix" identifying the proportions of ancestors of the people now living in each of 165 countries that lived, in the year 1500, in the territory that is *presently* each of those same countries. For South Korea and China, for example, our matrix indicates that in the year 1500, approximately one hundred percent of their current residents' ancestors resided in those same countries, while for Chile, only a little over a third of the ancestors of current residents were to be found within what are now that country's borders, with about fifty-five percent of present-day

Chileans' ancestors living in Spain. To take another example, about fifty-four percent of the ancestors of people of the northeast South American country of Guyana lived in the Indian subcontinent in 1500, thirty-nine percent lived in various African countries, and only five percent were Amerindians from Guyana itself. Most of the ancestors of present-day Taiwanese lived in China in 1500. And so on.

Overall, our research found that almost eighty-one percent of the world's people today live in countries that are more than ninety percent "indigenous," such as China and South Korea, while ten percent live in countries in which less than thirty percent of the people are descended from people present in 1500. For sixteen countries, which include Australia and the United States, less than ten percent of the current population's ancestors lived within the country's present borders in 1500. Nine percent of the world's people live in countries whose share of local ancestors falls *between* the thirty percent indigenous and ninety percent indigenous levels. This group includes Mexico, Peru, and Malaysia.

To test for continuing effects of early development on economic performance, my colleague David Weil and I, together with research assistants, calculated "migration adjusted" versions of the agricultural transition and state history variables discussed in the last section. For example, what might be called "migration adjusted years since agricultural transition" for, say, Guyana, averages together the years since agricultural transition for India and neighboring countries (fifty-four percent weight), the years since agricultural transition for relevant African countries (in all, a thirty-nine percent weight), and the years since agricultural transition for Guyana itself (a five percent weight), with the weights being the population proportions of each group among the current Guyanese people's ancestors. (Hence, more than ten times as much weight is given to the date of transition to agriculture in India as to the corresponding date for Guyana itself.) The same procedure was used to calculate "migration adjusted state history." We then redid past checks of whether early development (measured by time since transition to agriculture or by state history) is a good predictor of current average income, but now substituting the "migration adjusted" measures for the original ones.

We found that "migration adjusted years since agricultural transition" is considerably more highly correlated with countries' average incomes in 2000 than is the years since transition of each country when migration is not accounted for. The same holds for the adjusted and unadjusted state history measures, exactly as expected. Associating the developmental capabilities with the cultures *of people*, who can migrate, rather than with the boundaries *of territories*, which are fixed in space, dramatically improves the performance of a theory of economic continuity.[11] As mentioned previously, Comin and co-authors' measures of technology in 1000 BCE, 1 CE, and 1500 CE also do a substantially better job of predicting or explaining incomes today if adjusted, through a parallel procedure, using weighted technology indices for the actual ancestors of countries' populations. This makes sense if the observed continuity effects are the result of attitudes and capabilities slowly passed from generation to generation in cultures, rather than the consequences of strictly geographic factors like climate or soil.[12]

Mapping the world's remaking since 1500
The facing page shows a map of the world in which the shading of countries represents the proportion of their people today who are descended from people living in the same or in an immediately neighboring country in 1500.[13] Black backgrounds, seen in Europe, Asia, and most of Africa, denote countries almost all of whose present-day people are descended from people who lived there in 1500. Light backgrounds with small black dots, shown for the United States, Canada, Australia, New Zealand, and Argentina and Brazil, represent countries whose current populations are almost all descended from post-1500 migrants. Cross-hatching, seen for some Central American countries, the northernmost part of South America, and Chile, and a dark background with white dots, seen in the cases of Peru, Bolivia, Mexico, and South Africa, belong to countries with both large shares of descendants of indigenous people and large shares of descendants of migrants. (People of mixed ancestry are dealt with by estimating ancestry shares. For example, if a hypothetical country's current population were homogeneously "mestizo," the country would be treated as having some Amerindian and some Spanish ancestors.[14])

The map also provides information about who the migrants are, at least in broad-brush terms. This information is displayed by the pie charts appearing over each of thirteen regions. In most old world regions, descendants of migrants constitute a tiny share of current population, so the pie or circle is almost entirely filled by the shading indicating indigenous descendants. In regions with many descendants of migrants, such as the various parts of the Americas and Australia and New Zealand, the pie charts depict several different patterns. In the United States, Canada, Argentina, Uruguay, and Australia and New Zealand, the dominant population group consists of descendants of Europeans. In Mexico, Central America, and the Andean countries (Colombia, Peru, Bolivia), descendants of indigenous people are the largest group, with European descendants coming next.

In countries of the Caribbean, descendants of Africans, whose ancestors arrived as slaves, are the largest group.[15]

Sadly, for those who would prefer to see a world in which race or ethnic origin is irrelevant, the incomes of these different groups of countries significantly match up with the incomes now typical of the regions their ancestors came from and with the earliness of agriculture and states in the regions of those ancestors. Sub-Saharan Africa, and even the parts of the Americas in which large agricultural civilizations arose, had been later to develop agricultural societies and states than were the countries of Europe and Asia, and as discussed in Chapter 8, neither region had shared fully (for the Americas, at all) in the technological diffusion among the Eurasian civilizations. In line with these factors, the portions of the New World with larger current population proportions descended from indigenous Americans and Africans have lower incomes, while the portions with mainly European-descended populations have higher incomes. The pattern even holds in Asia, where Taiwan and Singapore, which were occupied by pre-state Malay and Austronesian peoples practicing low-intensity agricultures in 1500, are today relatively high-income countries. The explanation may at least in part be that these countries have seen descendents of people from China, one of the oldest agrarian civilizations of Asia, become their dominant population group.

Regional Ethnic Origin

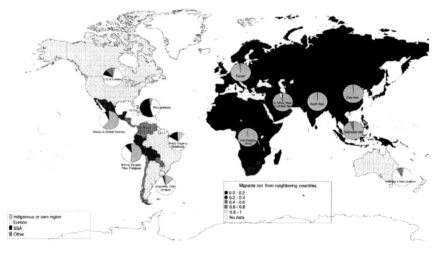

World map with shading for proportion of population indigenous and region pie charts indicating population shares of migrant groups (source: Putterman and Weil, 2010)

The relative incomes of ethnic sub-groups or minorities within countries are also fairly well predicted by the early state history or agricultural or technological development of their ancestors. Fijians of Indian ancestry have higher average income and longer state history than Fijians of indigenous (Melanesian) ancestry, but the Indo-Fijians' incomes are in turn exceeded, on average, by Fijians belonging to the tiny European and Chinese minorities, whose ancestors also score higher on early development measures, including state history. In Guyana, the ordering of average incomes for Chinese, Portuguese, east Indian, Black (Afro-Guyanese), and Amerindian populations also broadly coincides with their ordering for average ancestral state history. With only relatively minor exceptions, we found this pattern to hold for each of the ten countries in our sample that have the most diverse populations in terms of their ancestors' state histories—they include the two just mentioned plus Cape Verde, Panama, Paraguay, South Africa, Brazil, Trinidad and Tobago, El Salvador, and Nicaragua—and for the eighteenth most diverse country in our sample, the United States.[16]

It's important to recognize that each of the ethnically diverse societies just listed attained its diversity largely as a consequence of colonization, with slavery and indentured servitude often playing roles, as well. Partly due to this, the standings of the various ethnic groups in terms of income may not be attributable only to differences in skills, knowledge, or cultural attitudes passed down from generation to generation within each family; they may also reflect the way in which social and political dominance, slavery, and racism allowed for the perpetuation of economic power. Also, the high incomes attained by Chinese and other Asians in Guyana, Panama, Brazil, Trinidad and Tobago, and the United States could reflect the fact that those who left China to come to these places were disproportionately members of entrepreneurial families, self-selected for business-relevant skills and for inclinations towards hard work. But whatever the degree to which persistence of group differences is due to intergenerational transmission of culture, skills, and the like, which can occur independently of stratification and exploitation, versus being reinforced or even principally caused by the exploitation and racism, the main take-away point from our exercise is that the persistence of relative economic success from generation to generation, over hundreds of years, and both between and within countries, is of sufficient magnitude to merit first-order attention along with factors that more conventionally attract the interest of economists, such as the policies governing exchange rates and interest rate ceilings.

Neo-Europes, plantation economies, and cookie-cutter states

The statistical results just mentioned come from pooling observations from each of a hundred or more countries located in very different parts of the world. To make more concrete what lies behind these results, it's useful to talk about specific countries and groups of countries and to think about what their experiences were in early history, during the epoch of colonization, and more recently. For that purpose, I want to go back to the region-by-region type discussion employed in Chapter 8, this time focusing not on what made each region more or less susceptible to colonization in the first place, but rather on its transformation by the colonial era and its performance in the race to catch up. I discuss first three widely dispersed patterns, then two large regions deserving separate comment.

Let's consider first those areas of the non-European world that had limited or even no development of agrarian civilizations before the European expansion began. We've seen that those regions in which civilizations with cities and large-scale states had *not* yet appeared in the fifteenth century met with two different fates. One outcome—good for the country, bad for its indigenous people—belonged to the lands whose climates were temperate and not suitable to growing estate crops like sugar; think again of Canada and Australia. Those lands attracted European settlers who moved into agricultural and then industrial occupations in patterns that tended to be relatively egalitarian among the settlers, paving the way for their emergence as stable and locally controlled democracies during the eighteenth and nineteenth centuries. Their people, recently arrived from England, France, Germany, Ireland, and elsewhere in Europe, finding themselves with huge territories on which to develop their agricultural, mining, and industrial activities, quickly mastered and extended the technologies and organizational methods of the leading northern European countries, building countries in the front ranks of the world's income and wealth distribution—countries in which the descendants of the indigenous inhabitants were left to play marginal roles. These are the "neo-Europes" mentioned in the last chapter.

Another fate awaited islands and other territories whose climates and soils were suitable for plantation agriculture. These saw the importation of large numbers of African slaves and/or indentured laborers from India or Indonesia. When slavery and servitude ended and the plantation economy had ceased to be profitable, they tended to end up as poor economies relying on agriculture and tourism—think of Haiti, the Dominican Republic, Cuba, and Jamaica. Ironically, the latter countries once generated far more wealth than what is now the United

States, which had been thought by many, in the seventeenth century, to be "useful for little more than fur-trapping and food-crop farming."

A very different outcome emerged where local societies weren't as technologically and politically advanced as the leading Eurasian civilizations, but where populations were substantial and disease conditions were unwelcoming to Europeans. Much of sub-Saharan Africa, New Guinea, and some Pacific islands fit this description. There, colonization came late, didn't involve much settlement by foreigners, and laid over the existing societies a relatively thin veneer of "modernity," including some Western-style education for a few. New borders separated country from country cookie-cutter style, with little relation to prior realities, and governmental structures were stood up by departing colonial powers with no connection to the political institutions that preceded colonization. The average adult in these countries still has less than 2.8 years of schooling, compared to 5.6 years in Latin America, 5.9 years in Asia, 8.7 years in Europe, and 11.7 years in the United States and Canada. They were relatively poor before 1500, are poor today, and have been largely absent from the list of high growth economies during the past fifty years.

Spanish America

Another category of regions are those that had reached the stage of large scale agrarian states prior to their colonization, but had done so more recently and with fewer technological advantages. As noted in the last chapter, Mexico and the Andean region of South America are prime examples.[17] Productive agricultures capable of supporting large populations had been achieved in these regions, giving rise to large-scale states. However, their more recent development, their less advantageous biological endowments (no horses for transport and war, no oxen to pull plows), and their isolation from the technological cross-fertilization that had enriched Eurasia's societies meant that they were behind in the crucial technological dimensions mentioned in the last chapter. After Spanish conquest and the decline of the indigenous population from disease, substantial European settlement occurred, but rather than being pushed aside or dying out like the aboriginal populations of the United States, the Caribbean, and Australia, large native populations survived. Some of their members became a labor force for European plantations and mines, while others sustained themselves in relative isolation on more marginal land. In some places, such as Mexico, populations of mixed indigenous and European ancestry became the majority, while in others, such as Guatemala, Bolivia, and Peru, a larger fraction of the indigenous people retained separate identities.

As we've seen, the characters of the resulting societies differed from those of the neo-Europes for several reasons. One of these is the system of hacienda farming, in which the best land was owned by a few European land grantees employing large numbers of indigenous workers, who provided for their own subsistence by farming small tracts of inferior land on the margins of the estate. The wider and partly racially-based inequalities in these societies meant that even centuries after Spanish conquest, large fractions of their populations got little education and lacked the capital to improve their families' economic situations. Yawning social and economic gaps also contributed to political instability, and for long periods of time, governments devoted more effort to repressing resistance by the poor than to creating conditions for social progress. Because these countries had European elites who engaged in continuing commerce with Europe and North America, it's not surprising that they were able to establish some modern industries and to build cities in which relatively advantaged minorities pursued European lifestyles. But given their dual natures, it's also not surprising that their people's average incomes in the late twentieth century lay somewhere between those of Europe and of poorer developing countries. Although their weak performance relative to east Asia in that period's "race for development" might seem to be adequately explained by more conventional factors, such as reliance on natural resource exports and excessive foreign borrowing, underlying differences in social structure may provide a deeper explanation.[18]

If all European migrants were interchangeable, then some South American countries with relatively small indigenous populations and relatively temperate climates would be expected to have developed in a manner more like that of Canada and Australia than that of Mexico, Peru, and Bolivia. Well under ten percent of the people of Argentina and Uruguay descend from indigenous people, and nearly ninety percent descended from immigrants from Spain and Italy. Venezuela and Chile also had European majorities, although their indigenous population shares were a quarter or more. These Latin American countries with largely European populations did achieve higher incomes than most on the continent, as would be predicted by a theory of economic persistence. But their patterns of development were also somewhat different from those of the Anglophone neo-Europes, in part due to the Spanish pattern of land ownership and in part to a slowness to industrialize similar to that of Spain and Italy themselves.[19] Economic inequality within their societies also gave rise to political divisions, which in turn encouraged the adoption of the counter-productive economic policies associated with *import substitute industrialization*, to be discussed shortly.

Asia and the Middle East

In the previous chapter, we began to touch on the different responses of Asian societies, some of which were colonized by the eighteenth century, others only in the nineteenth and twentieth centuries, and others not at all. Some of these countries, including parts of Indonesia, Malaysia, and the Philippines, had population densities similar to those of the core pre-Colombian American civilizations or Africa, so domination by European powers was achieved but wasn't accompanied by large-scale European settlement. Portions, however, were appropriated for plantations of rubber, sugarcane, and other crops, giving rise to patterns of inequality (e.g., in the Philippines) that have invited comparison to Latin America.

India had been the site of civilizations whose influence had spread into southeast Asia and parts of Indonesia, and in the religious realm, to the east Asian regions of Tibet, China, Mongolia, Korea, and Japan. But the subcontinent had experienced a less continuous record of political unity than had China, perhaps partly due to lesser geographic isolation. Portugal established a trading presence on the coast in 1498, followed by the Netherlands, and England made the whole of India its colony in 1765. Both India's already substantial population and its climate and disease conditions discouraged any large-scale European settlement, nor was there reason to import laborers to India from other regions, so the colonial epoch left the population's origins unchanged. On the other hand, nearly two centuries of British rule transplanted European legal and political institutions along with railways and other infrastructures and Western-style education. Though some seeds of economic modernization had been planted, economic misery grew during the period, in part due to damage done to traditional handicrafts by the importation of European manufactures. High rates of population growth, helped along by crops from the "Columbian exchange," such as the potato, and by colonial public health measures, may also have contributed to deepening poverty.

Not all Asian societies became European colonies. The old empires of the Ottomans, Persia, and China, and the kingdoms of Thailand, Korea, and Japan, were never conquered, or at least they were never conquered by Europeans. (We've already remarked on Japan's late imperial conquests of Korea, Taiwan, and parts of coastal China.) This can be viewed as the continuation of the pattern previously noted:

lightly populated pre-state non-European societies were replaced by European ones (Australia, Canada); more densely populated but politically disunited or technologically laggard non-European societies were conquered and ruled (India, Indonesia); and societies that were Europe's technological equals in 1500 and that maintained unified political systems were never colonized by Europeans.

Even so, the era of European colonization saw all countries of the region, apart from Japan, fall substantially behind Europe in technology and standard of living. Why? It seems hard to escape the conclusion that the dynamic launched by Western Europe's colonial expansion and reinforced by the industrial revolution played a part in the widening of the gulf between Europe and the rest of Eurasia. Exactly what roles were played by reduced control of trade routes, competing imports, and population growth are not entirely clear.[20] In any event, by the early twentieth century, the income gap between Europe and its offshoots, on the one hand, and east Asia and the Middle East, on the other, had become larger than the one that had originally separated Europe from the pre-Colombian Americas. This is ironic in the extreme, given that Europe's expansion would probably never have begun had it not received mathematical and cartographic knowledge from the Muslims of Spain, Egypt, and Turkey, had it not appropriated the gun-powder of the Chinese, and had its taste for exploration not been spurred by pepper, tea, and other goods from "the East Indies."

Why didn't industrial revolution technologies and organizational methods spread quickly to Ottoman Turkey, India, and China in the eighteenth and nineteenth centuries? In colonies, such as India, indigenous manufacturing has been said to have been suppressed by the colonizers, not desirous of competition. But in Turkey, north Africa, and China, geographic, language, and cultural barriers, including dangerously unscrutinized beliefs in the superiority of their own cultures, seem to help to explain the failure to pick up the new advances earlier. By the late nineteenth century, they could no longer stand their ground in military contests with the West, and their standards of living had fallen from near parity with Europe's to resemble more those of the other countries that industrialization had left behind. By the 1920s, both the Ottoman and the Chinese emperors had been deposed by groups of young modernizers; the former Ottoman protectorates and possessions in north Africa and the Middle East had come under European control, and the one early Asian modernizer, Japan, had already annexed Korea and Taiwan, was about to annex Manchuria, and might have gobbled up mainland China as a whole had it not over-reached by challenging the United States.

The race to catch up: Strategies

A popular African proverb which the Tanzanian independence leader and president, Julius Nyerere, liked to repeat says that "when the elephants fight, the grass gets trampled." When the major industrial powers fought World War II, north Africa, southeast Asia, and numerous Pacific islands were among their theaters. When the Cold War was fought out between the United States and the Soviet Union, the trampled grass included parts of Asia, Central America, and Africa, as "proxy wars" were fought between the northern and southern parts of Korea and Vietnam, between leftists and supporters of the status quo in Guatemala, Nicaragua, and El Salvador, and between movements allied with east and west in Angola and Mozambique.

The early post-war decades nevertheless differed from the age of colonization, when there had been no states to organize large-scale resistance to Europe's territorial grab in parts of the Americas, sub-Saharan Africa, and Oceania. Within two decades of the defeat of Germany and Japan, virtually the whole world was organized into independent nation-states. Leaders of Asian, African, and Latin American nations wanted to strengthen their countries so that they could be more like elephants and less like trampled grass. The idea of "the developing world" was born, and within that world the "race for development" was the order of the day. Soon, dozens of countries were in the business of drawing up development plans and approaching multilateral and regional development banks for financial assistance.

The governments of "less-developed countries," including the many newly independent ones, tried to foster economic growth by a variety of methods. Some depended mainly on their countries' natural resources, with a few for whom that resource was petroleum ultimately achieving significant increases in income. But most chose their policies starting from the dual assumptions that economic success means successfully fostering manufacturing and that homegrown industries would be unable to compete with foreign imports absent some kind of protection or management of their economy. The three most popularly adopted development strategies of the post-World War II decades are described in brief in the next three sections.

Import substitution

The most popular strategy was known as *import substitute industrialization* due to its aim of replacing imported manufactured goods with manufactures made in the developing country itself. Methods of protection included tariffs and restrictions on import quantities. Both made imported manufactures more expensive, the first by slapping a tax on them, and the second by raising their scarcity. By doing so, they gave homemade manufactures the chance to compete for the market, even with higher production costs and/or lower quality. The drawback of these protective measures, apart from the fact that domestic consumers paid for them in the form of higher prices, was that while there might be ways of justifying their use for a few years, they were difficult to get rid of once in place. The protected home industries, if profitable thanks to their protection, acquired the political clout needed to see to it that protection continued. Tariffs brought in government revenues, owners of the businesses concerned could bribe officials or financially support politicians to keep the protective measures on the books, and the relatively high-wage workers in the protected industries became yet another interest group favoring continuation of protection. The problem was that without convincing evidence that they were temporary, protectionist measures reduced home industry's incentive to raise its efficiency. In industries with significant scale economies, moreover, the home market in many countries was too small to support more than one manufacturer of efficient size, if that. Lack of competition thus ensured monopoly profits, but inefficient scale and protection from competition ensured high cost. The net result was that living standards of domestic consumers were lower than they might have been had the country simply imported the goods in question, earning the hard currency required by exporting goods they could produce at lower cost.

Another problem associated with attempts to industrialize through protection was that of currency overvaluation and indebtedness to foreign governments and banks. Countries protecting local manufacture of consumer products rarely were able to reduce their overall reliance on imports. Although they might now have been producing more goods, such as bicycle tires, matches, and beer bottles, this meant that they needed to import the machines to produce them, plus whatever raw materials weren't available in country, as well as petroleum, gas, or coal to generate power. To keep such essential imports affordable, the governments in question often regulated the price of foreign currency, assigning a higher relative value to the home currency than supply and demand would have dictated. Rates of inflation in the developing country higher than those in developed ones (a byproduct of government deficits) further contributed to currency overvaluation, since with a fixed exchange rate overvaluation comes automatically from the difference in inflation rates unless the government devalues. The problem with overvalued currencies was that while they made imports to the developing country artificially cheap, they also made it unprofitable to export goods, and in this way they depressed the export earnings that the countries needed for buying foreign products, such as the inputs for the protected industries.

Countries caught in this situation thus experienced an excess in their demand for the foreign currency with which to buy imports relative to the supply of that currency which they generated by their exports. They addressed this shortage by borrowing heavily both from multilateral financial institutions, such as the International Monetary Fund, and from other lenders, including large foreign banks. This is what caused most developing countries practicing import substitute industrialization to be chronically indebted by the mid-1980s. When interest rates rose in the aftermath of the 1970's oil price shocks and the ensuing "stagflation" in the United States, it became impossible for the indebted countries to pay current debt obligations by borrowing more money. They were forced, instead, to accept demands for economic restructuring, including cutbacks in government spending, devaluation of exchange rates, and reduction of tariffs.

The debt crisis convinced most developing country policy makers that paying for a protected domestic manufacturing sector by borrowing was an unsustainable approach. Not only did it seem necessary to nurture the means of earning the foreign exchange needed to pay for imports, but working towards the export of manufactures seemed a better idea for small countries, since the scale and efficiency of their industries would not then be constrained by their home market size.

Putting heavy industry first: The state socialist alternative

A second and more drastic way of fostering industrialization was the one followed by Communist-ruled countries, including the Soviet Union and China. Rather than make domestic industries artificially profitable by imposing tariffs on imports, these countries put all industry under direct government ownership and control and then simply decreed what would be produced by sending compulsory production targets to state-appointed factory directors. Competition from imports posed no problem, since nothing could be legally imported except by state-controlled trading monopolies. Trade, other than that with other socialist countries, was kept to a minimum.

Having severed most links with world markets, large economies like Russia and China could for a time ignore their comparative advantage (what they produced relatively cheaply) when deciding which industries to promote. Unlike the non-Communist countries with import restrictions but private producers, they gave priority to producing machinery and raw materials, not manufactured consumer goods. Thus, dependence on imports wasn't a big problem for them, and some, e.g. China, didn't become heavily indebted. Their main economic problems, rather, were the inefficiencies inherent in running an economic system from the top down: poor information, weak incentives, difficulty fostering improvements in technique, inability to identify the assortment of products truly suited to the needs of producers and consumers, black markets, and illegal channeling of inputs towards unauthorized production. Poor feedback, partly a function of authoritarian political systems, exacerbated these problems.

While authoritarianism had direct negative effects on quality of life for most, Communist rule did rack up its achievements in some countries. Complaints about the availability and quality of consumer goods were common, but most Communist countries had substantially better outcomes than non-Communist counterparts at similar income levels, with respect to reducing infant mortality, raising life expectancy, increasing basic literacy, and providing technical and scientific education. Advancing the early stages of industrialization by building heavy industrial capacity was also successfully accomplished, in Russia and China, as a direct consequence of the ability to impose production plans by fiat rather than paying attention to market signals.

The outward-oriented strategy

Contrasting with the import substitution and the state-managed industrialization approaches was the outward-oriented strategy associated with South Korea, Taiwan, and post-Mao China itself. This strategy combined tariff and non-tariff protection of domestic industries, such as those used in the import substitution approach, with a thrust to expand exports of manufactured goods. Policies supporting that thrust included avoiding the overvalued exchange rates that made other poor countries' exports uncompetitive, offering tax credits and subsidies to successful exporters, allowing low-duty or duty-free imports of raw materials and energy for export-oriented manufacturers, steering low-interest credit from government-run or supervised banks towards successful exporters, and establishing export processing zones on which application of these policies would be focused. Containing wage growth by thwarting the formation or effective power of labor unions was another element present at least in the initial decades. A combination of many of these approaches had facilitated Japan's march to mature industrial status after World War II, and in addition to the countries mentioned, Hong Kong, Malaysia, Indonesia, Singapore, and Vietnam would follow some elements. Indeed, most Latin American, African, and Asian countries emerging from the debt crisis of the mid-1980s, from traditional Communism, or simply from slow economic growth attributed to excessive government regulation, were trying to emulate aspects of this outward-oriented model to whatever degree they could from the 1990s onwards.

The new mantras of economic development placed more faith in market forces, especially the power of the market-determined prices to signal what is scarce and should be used more sparingly and/or bolstered by greater production and what is less scarce and should be substituted, if possible, for more costly inputs. They also gave emphasis to the view that new ideas and information are constantly being created and discovered at the level of the individual or enterprise and that it's best to allow these micro-actors the freedom to pursue their ideas under the guidance of market prices and with the spur of competition. Producing for competitive world markets, rather than for protected domestic ones, would spur efficiency, it was argued, because only by increasing quality and reducing cost could the producer hope to compete successfully in foreign markets and because world markets let the producer tap into potentially vast demand, thus allowing them to produce on the most efficient possible scale.

Alongside the emphasis on market forces and price signals, however, the new consensus about economic growth also placed emphasis on the importance of education and, linked to this, of roles that government might play in an economy. The ideal was said to be not the withdrawal of government from the economy, but rather reducing government interference in areas handled well by markets while improving government's effectiveness in areas like education, health care, and the provision of public infrastructures.

The gaps within

While focusing on the differences between countries in this chapter and the last, I've mostly ignored gaps between rich and poor within countries, gaps that are often every bit as large as the international ones. Chapters 1 and 8 provided glimpses of that inequality in India, a country in which forty-seven percent of all children are estimated to be malnourished but where a growing middle class own automobiles, eat fast food, and even enjoy advantages that Western middle classes lack in the form of abundant and inexpensive domestic help.

The United Nations Development Program (UNDP)'s *2006 Human Development Report* estimated that the average consumption level of the top ten percent of Indians was seven times that of those in the bottom ten percent. Such a gap is actually modest in comparison to the gap in Canada (ten to one) or the United States (sixteen to one), but larger gaps are found in other developing countries. In Brazil, average members of the richest ten percent of the population were estimated to consume fifty-seven times as much as average members of the poorest ten percent in 2003, which helps to explain why, despite having an average income three times as great as India's, Brazil still had almost 13% of its people living on less than two dollars a day in 2003 and almost 4% living on less than $1.25 a day, the UNDP's most stringent poverty standard, in 2006.

Although there might be some benefits to a nation from having a significant middle class of educated professionals able to provide essential capabilities for a range of activities, including law and health care, deeply embedded inequalities may also stand in the way of improvement in the conditions of the majority and of the growth of the economy as a whole. Wide class divides have probably contributed to political instability in many countries, for example in Central and South America and the Caribbean. Such inequalities have also sometimes led to the adoption of counter-productive policies. Examples include the favoring of agricultural exporters at the expense of peasant farmers, and possibly even industry, or populist programs that tax and redistribute without fostering sustainable improvements in productivity and employment. Income inequality means that dollars spent on education and health tend to have less impact than they might otherwise have, since potentially talented individuals are unable to continue their educations while less talented children of rich families enjoy more education than they can use very productively. Numerous studies have found that countries with less income inequality have on average grown faster than countries with more inequality, after controlling for other factors.

Within-country inequality and the historical persistence of income
When looking at some countries, for instance India, one might suppose that there are no links to be drawn between within-country inequalities and the theme of long-run income persistence featured elsewhere in this chapter and in Chapter 8. Indeed, inequalities appear to be a natural consequence of the private property and market systems that were discussed in Chapter 7, and to the extent that that's so, explaining them requires no reference to differences in the timing of transitions

to agricultural and then industrial forms of economy. In other cases, however, there are strong indications of a link between within-country inequalities and the emergence of income gaps over long periods of time, including those associated with differences in the timing of transitions to agriculture and industry. This was demonstrated by the case studies of the ten countries whose populations are most diverse in terms of their ancestors' early histories, as discussed earlier.

In addition to those case studies, Weil and I also performed some other simple exercises to investigate whether differences in the rate of economic change over long periods of time account for within-country inequality of income in the much larger set of countries studied by us. We calculated the variance of two measures of early pre-modern development—state history and years since agricultural transition—for the ancestors of the populations of each of one hundred countries around the world. The degree of variation of state history or of the history of agriculture is treated as zero, for example, in China, since virtually all present-day Chinese are assumed to be descended from people already living in China in 1500. The degree of variation of state or agricultural history in Mexico, on the other hand, is high, since the Amerindian ancestors of today's Mexicans had shorter histories of states and agriculture than did the Spanish ones. Variation is likewise high in Singapore (Chinese, Malay, Indian) and Fiji (about half indigenous, half Indian) but low in Vietnam and the Democratic Republic of the Congo.

With these estimates of variation in early developmental backgrounds of ancestors in hand, we turned to the World Bank's estimates of the Gini coefficient, a common measure of the degree of inequality of incomes that ranges from a low of about 0.25 to .27 for countries with the least inequality, such as Sweden, Norway, and Finland, to highs of 0.58 – 0.60 in countries with the most inequality, including Angola, Colombia, Haiti, Honduras, and South Africa. When we lined up the Gini coefficients alongside our measures of variation of pre-modern development of current residents' ancestors for one hundred countries, we found the two to be positively correlated to a statistically significant degree. The more diverse in origin a country's people, as indicated by high variation of state or agricultural history among their ancestors, that is, the higher the Gini coefficient measuring inequality of current incomes. This supports the idea that the persistence of differences in technological and organizational capabilities over hundreds of years helps to predict not only differences between countries, but also some of the differences of income *within* countries. In other words, it seems that the phenomenon of descendants of people from "less developed" societies continuing to earn less than descendants of those from "more developed" ones and of this contributing to income inequality within countries where people's origins are heterogeneous, may extend far beyond the ten most heterogeneous countries that we had looked at in "case study"-level detail.

An interesting point to note is that Weil's and my study considered only migrations after 1500, a year we chose as a rough representation of the beginning of the era of European expansion. Other major migrations have occurred in world history, including the movement of Indo-Europeans into the Indian subcontinent, the southward movement of Han people in China, and the movement of Bantu people from Nigeria and Cameroon into central and southern Africa. These other migrations also leave marks visible to the present day, but ones not captured by our exercise.

Do the pre-1500 migrations also leave telltale legacies of inequality today? Evidently some still do. Some of the inequalities in India itself may be associated with the imperfect mixing of lighter-complexioned Indo-Europeans with darker-complexioned Dravidian-speaking groups that inhabited the subcontinent before their arrival more than three thousand years ago. In central and southern Africa, similarly, Bantu-speakers tend to have higher incomes than Khoisan and Pygmy peoples, whose ancestors were the original inhabitants. That the Bantu were both further along on the developmental continuum from foraging to agriculture than were the Khoisan and Pygmies at the time of their encounters fits perfectly with the pattern of findings I've been discussing. In southern China, non-Han minorities like the Miao, Yao, and Yi, who were likewise more "backward" according to such a developmental continuum at the time that the Han expanded into their territories, are economically disadvantaged relative to the Han majority. The same applies to "indigenous people" in Taiwan, Japan, and other Asian countries.

Greater historical divergence of languages is also associated with more inequality

As we noted earlier, groups of people separated from one another for a sufficient number of generations come to speak mutually unintelligible languages. Like differences in physical appearance, language has often been a factor dividing people when those from different places came to live alongside each other in recent centuries. Weil and I carried out some statistical exercises to investigate whether linguistic differences account for some within-country inequalities of income.

We began by recognizing that not all languages are equally distant from one another. Swedish and Danish, for instance, are essentially dialects of a single language. Those who speak only Arabic can't understand Hebrew, but the two languages belong to the same Semitic language family and share enough common roots that knowing one makes learning the other a little easier. The same is not true of Arabic and Navajo or of Urdu and Chinese. Linguists have constructed "language trees" that reconstruct how closely or distantly related are any two among hundreds of world languages.

Using such a "tree," Joshua Wilde, a graduate student assisting our research at the time, calculated measures of the distance between each pair of languages spoken by at least one percent of the ancestors of the people living in each of ninety-eight countries around the world today. For Guatemala, for example, since a large percentage of the people's ancestors were Mayan-speakers and another large group were Spanish-speakers, we had to calculate the linguistic distance between Spanish and the most common Guatemalan Mayan language. More than one percent of Guatemalans' ancestors are also estimated to be of African descent, so linguistic distances between African and Mayan languages and between African and Spanish languages were needed. We then calculated the *average* linguistic distance between the ancestors of any two randomly chosen people in each of those countries, taking into account the differing probabilities that a randomly chosen ancestor would be a Mayan speaker, a Spanish speaker, or a speaker of an African language. In Guatemala, this average linguistic distance is relatively large, since the probability is substantial of randomly choosing a Spanish- and a Mayan-speaker, and since these languages have no known connections. The average distance is smaller in the United States, where most (although by no means all) people's ancestors spoke Indo-European languages, and it's smallest in countries like China, where no external group accounts for more than one percent of the current population's ancestors.[21]

Having obtained these average linguistic distance measures, we then estimated a regression equation in which we try to explain the degree of within-country inequality today (measured by the Gini coefficient) using the average linguistic distance and the country's income. We found that linguistic distance is, like difference in state history, a strongly significant predictor of economic inequality.[22] What might explain this? Perhaps peoples from very different cultural and language groups tended to form economically stratified societies when they interacted, with the groups happening to have advantages in terms of skills or control over resources tending to dominate the others, and with language being one important method of marking and maintaining separation. It might even be the case that long after marital or extramarital unions between two groups had caused near-total genetic admixture and after one language had emerged as dominant, patterns of inequality established in the once linguistically diverse society still persist, as is suggested by the case of Mexico, where the large majority of people are now Spanish speakers identified as mestizo, yet inequality remains as high as in other Latin American countries with similar proportions of Amerindian and Spanish ancestry but less admixture.

Margins of error

Although continuity or persistence of technological and economic development predicts a surprising amount of the world's inter-regional and of countries' inter-ethnic group inequalities, it by no means explains all global inequalities. In the short-run, differences in policies and other factors lead to differences in economic success between countries with otherwise similar backgrounds. Over longer periods of time, there are some deeper anomalies that raise questions about how much continuity there really is. I'll consider first short-run departures from what the continuity framework would otherwise seem to predict.

An obvious example is provided by China, where economic growth accelerated following policy reforms that began in late 1978. That timing had more to do with the vagaries of the physical decline and death of Mao Zedong than with long-term historical factors. India's growth rate also accelerated after the adoption of more market-friendly policies, the timing of which could not have been predicted by very long-term factors. As a still better example, only half of Korea experienced the sprint to more developed status that the framework suggests for the country as a whole, and this is because the Korean peninsula was divided between Communist and non-Communist governments in the early post-World War II era. While North Korea can be expected to catch up eventually, there's no sense in trying to predict exactly how the succession to Kim Jung Il will unfold based only on Korea's history during the past two millennia.

Of course, the Cold War, the success of Communist takeovers in Russia, China, Vietnam, and Cuba, and short-term experiments with socialism in places like Mozambique, Chile, Nicaragua, or today's Venezuela are far from being fully independent from the phenomena we've been discussing. They stem in part from tensions between early and late developing countries and from the colonial experience that the developmental gaps discussed in Chapter 8 made possible. They also stem from class conflicts within former colonies and from the inequality-fostering nature of capitalism, features of the economic systems whose emergence we discussed in Chapter 7.[23] Details of geography (such as the proximity of North but not South Korea to the Soviet Union) and details of personality and timing (What if Lenin had failed to get back to Russia from Switzerland? What if the Kremlin leadership had deposed Gorbachev earlier on?), on the other hand, can't be expected to be explained by broad theories. They'll always lie within the margin of error.

Deeper anomalies?

Possibly the most serious challenges to the idea that persistence of gaps that opened up in the early millennia of the agrarian epoch explains the main contours of the world's regional inequalities today are those posed by the Middle East, including Egypt, Iraq, and Iran. Based on a straightforward reading of the early development and continuity framework, the three countries should be among the world's fastest growing, if not its richest, today, since Mesopotamia and the Nile River valley hosted the world's earliest and perhaps second-earliest agrarian civilizations, with Iran being the home of powerful empires in the heydays of Athens and Rome. Baghdad was also a center of Islamic civilization and a world scientific and technological center during Europe's Middle Ages.

Jared Diamond, whose ideas on the timing and significance of the world's agricultural revolutions were discussed in Chapter 8, considers ecological degradation to be one possible cause of Iraq's decline since ancient times. A different, although possibly complementary, explanation may be that rather than having a continuing history of civilization with a common linguistic and cultural identity, something that might be said to be true of China and to some extent of the remnants of the Greco-Roman world, Iraq, and Egypt saw successions of conquerors, including Greeks, Romans, Arabs, and Ottomans. The conquests added new populations to old and destroyed most links of identity and culture to the early Mesopotamian and Nile Valley civilizations. Cultural continuity in Iran was also broken by various conquests. All three societies became more influenced by Islamic culture, which originated in an area peripheral to the early civilizations, than by ideas emanating from their own ancient civilizations. Being at the cross-roads of the three Old World continents may ultimately have worked to the Middle East's disadvantage relative to the more remote positions of Western Europe, China and Japan.

Cultural resistance to elements of modern science and statecraft that many view as being too closely associated with the Christian West has been stronger in the Middle East than in Japan and elsewhere. The tense relationship with the Christian world going back to Islam's founding, to the battles over Iberia and France, to the Crusades and into the centuries of the West's technological rise, may act as a check on the modernizing of many Middle Eastern economies, with the independent power of ideology suggested by this well illustrating the fact that people are not simply the income maximizers of economics textbooks. It also shows that the continuity-emphasizing explanatory framework of this and the last chapter is incomplete.

Nevertheless, Egypt, Iraq, Iran, and other parts of the Islamic world may, before another generation passes, bring their civilizational heritages to bear and embark on new eras of progress. Egypt was an outlier among non-European countries in promoting a national strategy for industrialization in the nineteenth century, a strategy reminiscent in some respects of Meiji Japan's. Iraq and Iran both have relatively large educated populations, and their setbacks in recent decades are in part attributable to specific turns of political fortune and to religious and ethnic cleavages. The entire region may very well still hold the economic growth potential that we would have expected of it.

A few conclusions

Not long after traveling in continental Europe and returning to Britain, Adam Smith began to write up the findings from his inquiry into why some countries were richer than others. He argued that the most important cause of economic progress is specialization and trade—not necessarily international trade, simply exchange among any specialized agents, including wool producers trading with grain growers and both of these trading with manufacturers. As discussed in Chapter 7, the reasons why specialization is so intimately related to human productivity and the standard of living are that it allows individual enterprises and workers to become especially skilled at specific sub-routines within the productive activity of society as a whole, and it fosters innovations and technological improvements. Specialization among enterprises also allows specific activities, such as making steel, auto engines, or electronic devices, to be carried out on very large scales, permitting further specialization among tasks within the enterprise and capturing the productivity benefits of physical economies of scale. The immediate core implication of all of this for Smith was that barriers to trade, including unnecessary tolls, taxes, and tariffs, should be brought down insofar as possible, and that government should, more generally, avoid interfering in economic activity.

In the centuries since Smith wrote, his insight about the links between markets, specialization, innovation, and productivity has been born out through leaps in productivity and technological possibilities that he himself could scarcely have imagined. There's been plenty of debate between contending schools of economists, but those adopting the basic Smithian outlook of favoring freer markets and trade have been dominant, their views being even more ascendant in recent decades. A supporter of Smith's views would be justified in claiming that the profit motive and freedom to trade have played central roles in the economic growth that's decisively raised living standards for a quarter of the world's people and that seems poised to bring still more people into relative prosperity.

Still, the conclusion that countries that remain poor have inflicted that condition on themselves by wrong policies, especially too much government interference, is overly simplistic. Government investments in infrastructure and education have been indispensable in each recorded case of economic success. Political stability and rule of law have also been indispensable conditions for success. A stable and well-functioning political order is thus critical to economic development.

In addition, most, if not all, "late-developing countries" have used government interventions to overcome their relative disadvantage. This was the case at the time of US adoption of the protective measures promoted by Alexander Hamilton in the late eighteenth century, at the start of Japan's industrialization almost a century later, in Korea in the 1950s to 1970s, and during the growth surge in China under Deng Xiaoping and successors.

Finally, this chapter and the last one have highlighted the fact that the policies pursued, especially narrowly economic policies like the setting of exchange rates, are not the only determinants of economic outcomes. Historical factors going back thousands of years help to predict who the world's economic winners and losers have been in recent centuries and decades, presumably because the capabilities and economic cultures of societies are formed over long time periods and are transmitted from generation to generation. Both Australia and New Guinea, for instance, might let markets determine their exchange rates, keep tariffs low, and run balanced government budgets, but no one should predict that New Guinea will catch up with Australia's income level during the next thirty years simply by getting its exchange rate, tariff, and budget policies right. No country has transitioned quickly from a stateless, nonliterate horticultural society to compete well with the offspring of those who've been on the world's technological frontier for centuries.

Rather than leading to unmitigated pessimism about the prospects of those left behind, the findings of historical persistence that I've been discussing can be put to work in closing developmental gaps. I've argued that differences in recent rates of progress are partly traceable to the ways in which different climates, flora, fauna, and interactions with other societies set different cultural trajectories for recent millennia, not that different groups of people have different inborn potentials. The ultimate message, both of some of the more conventional recent investigations of economic development and growth and of the viewpoint taken in this chapter, is that the most important resource for development is the one found in human minds. Not only formal education, but learning by doing, not only information, but attitudes and ways of working with others, ways that become part of the fabric of a society, are keys to successful establishment both of stable and healthily developing political structures and of vibrant economic organizations and markets. More than anything else, finding ways to strengthen the capabilities embodied in people and in the networks, social structures, and organizations linking them is what overcoming historical inertia requires.

Notes:

1. In the paragraph, I use the numbers of Lant Pritchett's 1997 article "Divergence, Big Time," *Journal of Economic Perspectives* 11, no. 3 (1997): 3 – 17, which is also quoted in Chapter 1. Using the GDP per capita numbers posted by the World Bank in 2009, one finds that the ratio of average income in Norway to that in Burundi was more than 500 to 1 in that year.

2. Diego Comin, William Easterly, and Eric Gong, "Was the Wealth of Nations Determined in 1000 B.C.?" *American Economic Journal–Macroeconomics* 2 (2010): 65-97. The authors take their method of applying relevant information about the places of origin of a population's ancestors from the study by the author and David Weil, discussed just below.

3. Analogies from biological to social evolution are clearly inexact insofar as horizontal transmission (from neighbor to neighbor) is as common as is vertical transmission (from generation to generation) in the social sphere, a point extensively commented on by Robert Boyd and Peter Richerson in their classic *Culture and the Evolutionary Process* (Chicago: University of Chicago Press, 1985) and in their more recent *Not by Genes Alone: How Culture Transformed Human Evolution* (Chicago: University of Chicago Press, 2005). But the fact that culturally similar neighbors borrow and improve more readily than do culturally distant ones still gives the ideas of continuity in biological evolution considerable relevance to our discussion. In the examples cited, moreover, England had absorbed wave after wave of Roman and Germanic (including Viking and Norman) genes, both of Indo-European origin, into its earlier Celtic population, also Indo-European; Japan's genetically distant indigenous populations may have been outnumbered by Altaic-language speaking Asian mainlanders well before the steady flow of Chinese cultural influences to the island.

4. There was some industry in certain enclaves in Egypt, India, and China, but larger enterprises using technologies common in industrialized countries were often foreign owned. Note that transmission to nearby European neighbors was itself made easier by the closer cultural and trading relationships and proximity of European languages relative to those of some other regions of similar size (parts of sub-Saharan Africa, New Guinea).

5. Parallels have also been drawn between Japan and England as innovator island nations on the peripheries of their respective cultural zones. Other non-European countries that could have been candidates for early industrialization according to the persistence idea include Turkey, Iraq, Iran, and India, all home to ancient civilizations between which technologies diffused up to 1500. Each was probably disadvantaged by one or another set of political and other developments in the centuries before 1900—India, for instance, by Muslim-Hindu conflict and British conquest, among other factors—but details will have to be explored elsewhere.

6. The figures used in this paragraph and in the accompanying bar chart are rounded versions of those reported in the Penn World Tables version 7.0, available at the website of the Center for International Comparisons at the University of Pennsylvania.

7. More complete and systematic discussions of why this should be the case can be found in my article "Can an Evolutionary Approach to Development Predict Post-War Economic Growth," *Journal of Development Studies* 36, no. 3 (2000): 1 - 30,

and in Areendam Chanda and Louis Putterman, "The Quest for Development: What Role Does History Play?" *World Economics* 5, no. 2 (2004): 1-31.

8. The exercises reported in this and the next two paragraphs were conducted by Areendam Chanda and me and were reported in "Early Starts, Reversals, and Catch-up in the Process of Economic Development" which appeared in the *Scandinavian Journal of Economics* 109, no. 2 (2007): 387-413. Our check for a correlation between year of agricultural transition and experience of state-level organization is a crude one because we don't account for states present before the year 1, of which there was considerable experience in some of the areas adopting agriculture earliest. Including that information should only strengthen the correlation.

9. Income's level and its growth rate can be quite different. For instance, in recent decades China has had a much higher growth rate than the United States, but the United States has had a much higher level of income than China.

10. Daron Acemoglu, Simon Johnson, and James Robinson, "Reversal of Fortune: Geography and Institutions in the Making of the Modern World Income Distribution," *Quarterly Journal of Economics* 117, no. 4 (2002): 1231-1294.

11. See: Louis Putterman and David N. Weil, "Post-1500 Population Flows and the Long Run Determinants of Economic Growth and Inequality,*"* *Quarterly Journal of Economics* 125, no. 4 (2010): 1627-1682, and Louis Putterman, "Agriculture, Diffusion, and Development: Ripple Effects of the Neolithic Revolution," *Economica* 75, no. 300 (2008): 729-748. Work on a similar migration matrix applying to populations as of 1960 rather than 2000 is now ongoing, with a goal of seeing how the migration adjusted measures do in predicting recent rates of economic growth as opposed to per capita income levels.

12. This is not to argue that geography hasn't mattered, historically. The hypothesis that Eurasians obtained their technological advantage over native Australians, New Guineans, etc., during the ten thousand years before 1500 as a result of geographic and climatic factors remains a compelling one. But with the acceleration in movements of populations in recent centuries, traits originally owing to geographic factors have become mobile, causing the effects of geography to recede in importance in the medium run.

13. None of the countries, of course, had their present boundaries in 1500, but we treat an ancestor as having lived in a given country of today, say Bosnia-Herzegovena or Papua New Guinea or Chile, if the place in which they lived is now part of that country.

14. David Weil and I and our research assistants consulted studies that attempt to determine the share of ancestors of mixed populations by analysis of their DNA. For Mexico, for instance, the estimates consider sixty percent of the current population to fall within the "mestizo" category, and of the ancestors of those in that category, fifty-five percent are judged to have been Amerindian, thirty-five percent Spanish, and ten percent from various African countries, based on DNA analysis. See the Putterman and Weil paper cited in note 11 above and its appendices for details.

15. In the map's legend, SSA stands for sub-Saharan Africa.

16. Countries, such as Tanzania, Cameroon, and the Democratic Republic of the Congo, contain numerous ethnic groups, due to the manner in which colonial borders were drawn in Africa. But their ethnic groups tend to have similar state histories and were

often already living in 1500 within the present-day country's borders, so they don't appear in a list of countries with great diversity of ancestors' early histories.

17. Parts of Africa that had precolonial era kingdoms might appear to fall somewhere between this and the previous case. The kingdoms in question, for instance Buganda in present-day Uganda, were usually small and were combined by the colonizers with neighboring territories that lacked kingdoms. Because disease kept the colonizers at bay for generations and in the end precluded large scale European settlement, their fates fit better into the category above.

18. In an article titled "The Role of Governments and Market: Comparative Development Experience," the development economist Gustav Ranis argued that the duration of government protectionist interventions varied among countries due to differences in demands placed on governments. According to Ranis, Latin America's social heterogeneity meant that competing groups used governments to serve their particular interests, so governments became instruments for redistributing income and protecting entrenched interests. See: Gustav Ranis, "The Role of Governments and Market: Comparative Development Experience," in *State and Market in Development: Synergy or Rivalry*, eds. Louis Putterman and Dietrich Rueschemeyer (Boulder, CO: Lynne Rienner, 1992), 85-100.

19. Just why northern and southern Europe, especially Spain, differed so greatly in economic performance between the seventeenth and early twentieth centuries is a topic on which much has been written by economic historians and others interested in economic institutions and culture. In his 1998 book *The Wealth and Poverty of Nations: Why Some are so Rich and Some so Poor*, David Landes attributes characteristics of the hacienda system and of colonial institutions in Latin America to the manner in which Spain itself was "reconquered" from the Moors in the centuries preceding the age of exploration.

20. Population growth was perhaps partly fostered by adoption of New World crops and by new health and sanitary measures. Europe may have benefited demographically from the safety valve of emigration to its colonies, an option largely unavailable to Asia at the time.

21. Although there are large linguistic distances between the languages of China's majority Han population and those of some of its minorities, for instance ethnic Mongolians or Uygurs, the exercise discussed here ignores linguistic distance among groups that have lived within the present borders of a country for more than five hundred years, as have most of China's many minority groups. While accounting for such differences might be desirable, their existence probably doesn't affect our results much in the Chinese case since more than 90% of the country's population belong to its dominant ethnic group.

22. Details of the calculation of linguistic distance, the regression exercise, and of the results are shown in Putterman and Weil (2010; see again note 11 above). For readers without the requisite statistics training, it may serve intuition to simply state here that the estimation of regression equations allows one to assess the size, the sign (positive or negative), and the statistical precision or significance of the relationship of variable A and variable B, while at the same time controlling for potentially disturbing and simultaneous influences of variable C (or variables C, D, etc.) on variable B.

23. One might even argue for a degree of predictability, give or take a decade or two, with respect to the timing of pro-market reforms in countries like India and China. In particular, many non-European countries produced a generation of nationalistic, anti-Western leaders who followed policies antithetical to markets and international trade during the first thirty to forty years following World War II, and their passage from the scene in the late 1970s and the 1980s coincided with a worldwide swing of ideas towards freer markets and trade.

CHAPTER 10
Hope for a Better World?

Looking towards the future with a realistic sense of who we are and where we've come from, is there any part of our aspiration for a better world that we can continue to hold onto? Is there room for a more hopeful 2020 vision, or any prospect of a 2050 or a 2099 in which peace, prosperity, a livable environment, and a society that encourages real human flourishing might be realities?

One way of responding to these questions might be to push back a bit and suggest that the goalposts be moved to more modest settings. Maybe we'd be lucky enough just to *reach* 2099—to get through the rest of this century as a species without having suffered a nuclear holocaust, mass evacuations of continental seaboards in the face of a rising ocean, a drop of world population due to the spread of some deadly pandemic, or the vanishing of everything we know into a black hole thanks to some overconfident physics experiment gone haywire. Maybe instead of Armageddon, we'll merely be dealing with a terrorist bombing here, a civil war there, and we should allow ourselves to count that as a blessing. Maybe instead of moving New York, Mumbai, and Shanghai inland, we'll still be keeping an eye on polar ice sheets not quite fully melted away and bringing new technologies online to (further?) slow the progress of global warming and to fortify exposed coastlines. Maybe the world's economy will still exhibit large global inequalities, but the percentage living in extreme poverty will have fallen and the number living in relative prosperity risen. Maybe the world's political landscape will still resemble today's, and there will at least still be some vibrant and reasonably tranquil democracies, along with other countries still experiencing instability, unrest, and limited political rights. And maybe those would not be too bad a set of outcomes, considering that things could be much worse.

Still, I'd like to think it not too unrealistic to hope for at least a little more than this. My hope is that we'll have made enough progress in our *understanding* of the challenges that we face that, when we ask ourselves in 2020 or 2025 *why* we've been unable to reduce the incidence of war, of poverty, and of hatreds among people of different backgrounds, or why our abilities to live fuller lives haven't kept pace with our abilities to consume, we'll recognize that the answers turn not on the scarcity of *things* in the world around us but on the complexity of *our own natures*. We'll recognize, among other things, that the same institutional building blocks of competition and markets that have brought some of us so far by playing so effectively to the strength of our self-interest are also implicated in many of the shortcomings of our individual societies and of the global society still waiting to be born. We'll understand better how to tap into our desires to cooperate, to live up to our commitments, and to be part of something larger than ourselves, desires that also spring from durable features of our natures. With our understandings thus improved and continuing to progress further, with our commitment to change strengthened, and perhaps armed with technological capabilities still difficult to imagine, the prospects for humanity in the years beyond could well outstrip bare survival scenarios.

Looking back, we can see that the first advance to prosperity of a sizeable portion of the world's people was brought about, between the eighteenth and twentieth centuries, by a combination of competing nationalisms, of exploitation of the people and societies of technologically less-advanced regions, of commercial competition among nations and between industrial firms, and of prudent education of their children by families grasping its importance to their futures. Private ownership of resources and enterprises, and placing economic decisions in the hands of individuals and companies, gave rise to prodigious efforts to gain technological advantage and to powerful incentives to invest in the acquisition of skills. The resulting growth in our stocks of physical and human assets and in the bodies of technical knowledge at our disposal made it possible for more than just an aristocracy to enjoy ample food, shelter, and clothing. And the results of one advance after another in scientific understanding made possible the eradication of many infectious diseases and the treatment of previously debilitating and life-threatening conditions, causing life expectancy to rise by close to a quarter of a century within two to three generations.

But these processes fell far short of benefiting all to the same degree, nor were all of their results beneficial. Hundreds of millions of the descendants of those who populated the Americas and Africa before the sixteenth century have yet to see much of an up side to the losing hand that history dealt them in the years following 1492. While many millions of Asians have broken into industrial prosperity, and while many more now appear poised to join them, at least a billion Indians, Chinese, Cambodians, Burmese, Afghans, Thais, Vietnamese, Bangladeshis, Indonesians, Pakistanis, Filipinos, and other Asians remain too poor to eat three meals a day, too poor to avoid choosing between food and medicine, too poor to enjoy running water, electricity, and indoor plumbing.

Within the ascendant societies of Europe and North America, and among the economic winners elsewhere, as well, the benefits of economic progress have been enjoyed unequally, and often in a shallow, thoughtless way. Tendencies inherent in the joining of an economic mechanism of private ownership and profit seeking to a human stock varied in its health, education, and other attributes cause benefits to be distributed unevenly. The most clever, skilled, and hard-driven, those having title over scarce resources, those who inherited wealth or who had access to valuable connections, and those accepting greater risks and winning their gambles gain far more than others. And clever and talented individuals still face an unwelcome choice between doing what excites or inspires them and doing what will earn them a better living. In the United States, the average income of those in the top five percent of the distribution of income ($157,423) was about 950 times greater than that of their counterparts in the bottom five percent ($166) in 2000, and much of the difference could be attributed to differential advantages of upbringing, including parental education.[1]

Meanwhile, the central role of the profit motive, combined with the intimate link of profit to selling things, arguably contributes to a culture in which the real gain in human well-being that might have come with higher productivity and better health has fallen well short of its potential. Rather than be freed of material impediments to a richer life in the present, millions keep running on a treadmill with eyes glued to the brighter displays of opulence that are always on the horizon. The popularity of treadmills in the fitness clubs of middle class office workers, though a partial antidote to long hours of work without exercise, serves well also as an ironic symbol of this lifestyle.

Grounds for optimism

Despite these problems, one can easily find in twenty-first century humanity considerable grounds for optimism. After all, the rapid increase in human technological capabilities, coupled though it's been with large inequalities, an uninspired culture, an upsurge of depression, and growing environmental strains, might turn out to be a transitory phase, a sort of childhood of post-industrial revolution society on its way to something better.

The social and behavioral sciences, an optimist could point out, are inherently more complex than physics and chemistry because the human mind, based not only on the hundred billion neurons in the brain but also on their hundred trillion connections with one another and with the sense organs, endocrine system, and so on, is the most complex thing in the known universe. Human society, an interaction of millions of human minds—including the emotions that are inseparable from them—is several orders of magnitude more complex, still. No wonder progress is slower than in simpler fields like chemistry, where a finite number of elements take on well-behaved forms in specified combinations under controllable conditions.

But even in the social sciences, there's been progress. Part of it is the recognition that however powerful are the selfish promptings of our natures, we humans are also deeply *social* beings with innate tendencies of empathy, inclinations to cooperate, and concern about how we're viewed by one another. Our prodigious abilities to manipulate our physical environment could easily lead to ecological disaster, but properly directed, they might instead allow us to live lives of material comfort and security in sustainable relation to nature. Many of us seem to find irresistible the pleasure of owning a gigantic flat-screen TV and enjoying all of the car chases, fiery explosions, celebrity gossip, and escapist drama it can throw at us. But a thirst for moral purpose and a fulfilling life animates enough of us sufficiently to give grounds for hope.

The hope that, as we learn more and study our history more carefully, we might somehow make our world better can of course be questioned by a pessimist who asks whether humanity ever collectively controls its destiny. Individuals or groups may come up with ideas for social amelioration, but each idea can be opposed by others, and all proposals tend in the end to be overtaken by events. There are those, moreover, who argue that there's no real "us" to control things—only the interaction of myriads of people each with his or her own goals, outlooks, and interests.

Maybe so. Yet the claim that humans lack joint influence over their destinies is belied by the histories of both failed and successful experiments, ranging from the American experiment with democracy in the eighteenth century to the European experiments with welfare capitalism and Russian and Chinese experiments with state socialism in the twentieth. Signs of human progress (i.e., trends in the organization of society that bring it closer to our higher aspirations and to the shared moral visions of so many of our cultures) are numerous. Slavery, taken for granted in ancient societies and throughout much of the world until the nineteenth century, can no longer be openly defended, even if it lingers on in certain forms and places. The ideal of government as the tool of a country's people has spread, with colonial rule ending in dozens of countries in the decades after World War II and with mass movements successfully ousting unpopular or despotic rulers in recent decades in places as different and as distant from one another as South Africa, Haiti, East Germany, and Libya. One of the world's poorest countries, India, has managed to maintain a democratic political system, channel timely aid to famine victims, and safeguard the human rights of most citizens for more than half a century. Its huge neighbor, China, has emerged from a century of civil war, invasion, and swings in ideology to enjoy three decades of unprecedented economic growth. The notion of equal rights for women has gone from being a radical idea in the nineteenth century to a mainstream one in the industrialized countries of today. Notions of racial equality have also made headway both within countries and in international dealings. Environmentalism, the concern of only a handful of people as late as the 1950s, has grown to achieve widespread support today.

The attraction of moral values

There's plenty of evidence of attraction to uplifting ideals before recent history, as well. Doctrines positing a universal moral order and embracing virtues such as honesty, compassion, and charity have swept over virtually every world region during the past three millennia. Confucianism, which called on China's early emperors to acknowledge moral standards and gradually permeated east Asia after its beginnings in the fifth century BCE, was venerated for more than twenty centuries and remains an active force for social order in one of the world's most successful regions. Buddhism spread across south Asia during the sixth to third centuries BCE, stimulating the maturing of its parent tradition, Hinduism, before finding hundreds of millions of adherents in east and southeast Asia. Prophetic Judaism took root in the Middle East during the same centuries, later sending an offshoot—Christianity—across Europe and then much of Latin America and Africa and another offshoot—Islam—across the Middle East, north Africa, and Asia, into Africa, and as far away as Indonesia and the Philippines. These doctrines were often spread by violent means or were used for the benefit of rulers and religious authorities, but if people were entirely amoral creatures, why was it teachings of love, peace, and brotherhood that were adopted in place of cults of human sacrifice and the worship of capricious gods? Why did essentially the same "golden rule" arise in each of these philosophical and religious traditions?

"Do not unto others what you would not have them do unto you."
(Confucius, *Analects*)

"Hurt not others in ways that you yourself would find hurtful."
(*Udanavaga*, a Buddhist text)

"What is hateful to you do not do to your fellow man. This is the entire law.
The rest is commentary." (a saying of Hillel in the *Talmud*, a Jewish text)

"All things whatsoever ye would that men should do to you, do you even
so to them, for this is the law and the prophets." (*Matthew* 7:12, attributed
to Jesus)

"No one of you is a believer until he desires for his brother that which he
desires for himself." (*Sunna of Islam*, attributed to Mohammed)

More likely than not, humanity shares deep-seated moral sentiments
implanted in us by the evolutionary selection process discussed in Chapter 5, a
process that took place long before our ancestors dispersed to different parts of the
globe. Although the influence of rulers and their swords often helped to determine
which doctrines spread, rulers' senses of what could readily be disseminated and
what would promote order in their realms weren't accidental. More appealing
ideologies helped rulers to secure the allegiance of their subjects, to maintain
internal peace, and, sadly, to increase their subjects' willingness to fight on their
behalf. The appeal of such moral systems must have stemmed in large part from
the fact that they resonated well with human needs for senses of purpose and of
justice, with the shared recognition of human interdependence, and with admiration for those who serve the common good.

Something similar seems to be true of more modern drafts of moral doctrine. Democracy, civil liberties, and equality before the law are among the
modern virtues that have probably acquired momentum in part due to intrin-
sic consonance with deeper principles of fairness, as well as continuity with
moral ideas evolving in the cultural sphere. A phrase like "All men are created
equal" may have had rhetorical appeal to a generation of white male property-
owners in late colonial America partly for the same reason that it would later

inspire anti-slavery agitators and that its spirit, if not letter, would help to feed the movement for equality of the sexes and for freedom from discrimination based on sexual orientation. Of course, a cynic could say that one reason why Jefferson and his colleagues adopted the phrase was that they thought it might attract sympathy for their cause from the people of nations like France. But this hardly undercuts my argument, since it leads back to asking: Why would such sympathy be expected to be forthcoming, as opposed, say, to laughter or bewilderment? The answer, once again, probably includes the resonance of such declarations with the same evolved human moral nature that accounts for the consistency of the declaration's egalitarian premise with Jesus's declaration that "the meek shall inherit the earth," the Bible's admonition to "not wrong or oppress the stranger, for you were strangers in the land of Egypt," and similar strains not only in other Eurasian traditions, such as Buddhism, but even in quite independently developed moral traditions in some cultures of the Americas and Oceania.

Do markets constrain human potential?

The question of how capable we are of achieving a better world can also be posed in a more specific way. We've seen that private property, markets, and competition have been central to the economic and technological achievements of recent centuries, that their role was dictated by the centrality of self and family in the motivational make-up of human beings, and that they've come accompanied by some serious negatives—including *economic* ones, such as inequality, and *cultural* and *psychic* ones, such as the accentuation of acquisitiveness and of the use of earning power and possessions as yardsticks of self-worth.

Suppose that despite their negatives sides, property, markets, and competition remain indispensable to any plausible escape from poverty for the remainder of the world's people in the decades ahead. And suppose that, despite all the harm to global ecosystems that's already occurred as a byproduct of the lure of profits, market incentives are nevertheless crucial for the rapid development and deployment of technologies capable of easing the clash between an acceptable standard of living and a livable environment. The question would then be whether we can have sufficient checks on unwanted political influence by firms and whether we can alter regulations, tax rules, and the like in the ways needed to make broader social goals and the profit motive more compatible.

More broadly: If property rights, markets, and competition must be core elements of our social systems for the indefinite future, to what degree are we condemned to suffer the negative spillovers of a self-interest-based society as the cost of using them, and to what degree can we escape from those spillovers by appropriate adjustments of our institutions, of the way in which we educate our children, and of other correctives?

If history is a guide, there could in fact be much room for maneuver. The market economies of the advanced industrial countries have proven to be quite resilient and adaptable in the face of societal experimentation and intervention. Social insurance, health care, education, public sanitation, and workplace safety outcomes have been significantly better than what could be delivered by markets alone. Though the policies that brought about these results have been far from trouble free, and though reasonable people can debate details of the long-run viability of specific welfare state programs, there's no indication that market economies require a strictly *laissez faire* setting in order to accomplish what we want them to. In fact, no market economy has ever existed free of accompanying laws, norms, and institutions, nor is it likely that the twentieth century would have ended on a relatively triumphant note for markets had our economies not long since become complex interactions of private, public, and other players. Social acceptance of private ownership and markets was waning on both sides of the Atlantic until anti-trust action, collective bargaining, and the welfare state were introduced early in that century. The construction of the mixed economy allowed a more socially cohesive America to help extricate Europe from the grip of fascism in the first half of the 1940s. Afterwards, the variant of capitalism that arose in Europe exhibited to an even greater extent the interplay of public, private, and collective elements.

The resilience of Europe's welfare states is worth remarking on at greater length. Put under severe pressure by competition from low-cost Asian manufacturers and from a less-regulated United States, those countries have made some concessions and adjustments, but they show little sign of shifting towards the American version of capitalism. The big surprise in their experience over the past twenty-five years isn't the trimming of some welfare state programs by politically centrist governments, but the fact that the pressure they're under—due in part to the doubling of the numbers of people in the world's middle and upper income ranks by the economic ascent of Asia—*hasn't* brought about either the wholesale abandonment of social welfare systems or a sharp reduction in living standards in these high-income countries. As the size of the European Union has doubled and as its economic integration has deepened, Europe's mixed market and welfare state systems have both survived and remained prosperous. Although the recent debt crisis involving several EU member states may have exposed serious flaws in EU and monetary union institutions as such, there's still a Denmark where the average income per person is forty-eight thousand dollars a year, where taxes capture thirty-six percent of gross domestic product (GDP), and where the incomes of the poorest forty percent are substantially increased by transfer payments, rising to be about seventeen percent greater as a share of national income than would be the case without such supports. There's still a Belgium in which government revenue is almost forty-four percent of GDP, the income share of the poorest forty percent is raised through redistribution by some nineteen percent of national income, and income averages thirty-six thousand dollars a year. Guaranteed health care, retirement pay, and high quality public transportation systems are among the many benefits effectively provided by those and neighboring mixed economies.

Pecuniary values don't trump all others

Concern that the atmosphere and ethos of the market comes to dominate every dimension of life may be warranted by some social trends, but may also be overstated. We seem able, in fact, to operate social systems in which different values are respected in different domains, without private pecuniary values always trumping all others.

Consider our political institutions. The principles of self-determination and democracy are potentially at odds with the market logic that the highest bidder has the last word, since self-rule and democracy require that a country, city, or jurisdiction have a government elected by its citizens, with each (regardless of ability to pay) having an equal vote. If their rights to control the government were instead put up for sale to the highest bidder, the citizens might financially profit by selling those rights to wealthy individuals, companies, or actors either in or outside of their jurisdictions. Main Street America might literally be owned by Wal-Mart, and corporations might buy and sell entire Third World countries. Corruption does occur and money does influence politics, yet we continue to place the outright sale of votes off limits, and no one proposes abandoning political self-rule and democracy in favor of government-for-sale. The sphere of the market and the sphere of political choice and citizenship enjoy a degree of separation.

A second example is found in the area of relationships and the family.

Consider, for instance, how the right to play the parental role in the life of a child belongs by custom and law to the biological parents. If marriages dissolve, and market logic alone were left to dictate outcomes, the custody of children would be awarded to whichever parent demonstrated a greater willingness to pay more for that right. Rather than follow this market logic, though, our societies determine child custody through judicial proceedings where the exchange of money between judges and concerned parties is strictly prohibited. Although the wherewithal to provide for a child's financial needs receives consideration in this process, the court is more likely to order a transfer of funds from the parent better positioned to pay than to order a transfer of custody towards that parent on financial grounds. In short, the human dimension of the parent/child relationship takes precedence over economic considerations, and the fact that our economy is thoroughly based on property rights, markets, and competition shows no sign of threatening that dimension's decisive role.

As a third example, consider that the buying and selling of human beings has been legally prohibited in most market economies for a century and a half, and neither the triumph of market systems over Communist planning nor the increasing competition in global markets show any sign of eroding this principle in countries with effective governments. Intensifying global economic contacts appear to be strengthening pressures to ban remaining forms of child labor and slavery, though the process may take years to complete. A recent report by the International Labor Organization (ILO), for example, found an eleven percent drop in the number of child laborers in 2004 compared to 2000. The number of five- to fourteen-year-old children in what the ILO classified as hazardous jobs was also down by fully a third during that brief period. This report, tracking trends associated with campaigns against child labor led by first world consumer groups, human rights activists, and international institutions, bears the encouraging title "The End of Child Labor: Within Reach."

These are only a few of the examples one can cite to argue that a thriving market economy isn't incompatible with pluralism of societal values. The rule of competition when it comes to personal material advancement in economic life doesn't seem to drive out the possibility of inviolable rights that flow from alternative logics, such as the principle of human dignity and its equal application to all. The value societies attach to parent/child bonds, personal liberty, the sanctity of life, and principles of non-discrimination likewise seem relatively resistant to erosion. Perhaps, then, the market system needn't be a barrier to the strengthening of other values—from those relevant to the provision of basic health care to the poor, to those preserving the global environment for future generations and those fostering a balance between work and other aspects of life.

Helping the poorest

Does the plurality of our values and the complex human nature on which that plurality is based offer hope for addressing the problem of poverty? Substantial inroads into the problem *have* been made in some countries with the help of social insurance and other schemes, suggesting that the requisite values are possible to elicit and to sustain under at least some circumstances. A plausible interpretation is that impulses towards fair-mindedness, empathy, reciprocity, and the desire to think well of ourselves are capable of supporting considerable levels of redistribution and aid to the less fortunate, provided that taxpayers believe that the poor are not making suckers of them by living on assistance simply to avoid work of which they are otherwise perfectly capable.

Can the factors that sustain redistribution in small, prosperous, and homogeneous societies like Denmark's, and that seem to do so with somewhat greater difficulty in more diverse countries like the United States, possibly be applied on a global scale? We've seen that the circle of human empathy is rather flexible, expanding from the members of one's own foraging band alone before the Neolithic revolution to the ethnic group and nation-state in more recent times. As technology has shrunk the globe further during the last few generations, our sense of the human family has become more global, still. But the indications that support for redistribution declines even within a country or state as ethnic heterogeneity rises might translate into a limited taste for international aid.[2]

Willingness to support redistribution is undoubtedly also subject to an interplay between feelings of empathy and worries about the magnitude of the task. The most prosperous sixth of the world's people may be so daunted by the notion of taking responsibility for the forty or fifty percent who live in extreme poverty around the world that they keep their compassion in check unless confronted with the most visceral images of need. With an average 2006 income of almost forty thousand dollars in the United States, Canada, Western Europe, Japan, and Australia and New Zealand—combined population 836 million—and with a billion of the world's people estimated to be living on less than one dollar a day and another billion on less than two dollars, the richest fifteen percent would have to give up most of their existing after-tax incomes to bring the poorest two billion up to a common (and for the donors, much lowered) level of income.

With such massive transfers, those now in the world's bottom two billion and those now in the top fifteen percent could hypothetically share average incomes of about eleven thousand dollars—in the neighborhood of Chile's, Estonia's, and Malaysia's averages. But transfers that approach that magnitude are not only politically inconceivable. It's also economically inconceivable that taxable output in the rich countries would stay high enough to get to that eleven thousand dollar mark, since there would doubtless be a drastic incentive effect of a tax rate that cut the accustomed living standards of those in the now richer countries by more than two-thirds! Moreover, if not managed with unprecedented care, so much largesse would be likely to negatively affect incentives for productivity in recipient countries, and guarding against corruption would be a herculean task. Even achieving through redistribution the more modest fifteen dollar a day income level for the poorest, which one economist has suggested would be necessary to eliminate the kind of poverty associated with severe malnutrition, stunted growth, and high under-five mortality rates, would require rich country citizens to contribute thirty percent of their incomes over and above existing tax payments.[3] The likelihood that we'll see a burst of generosity so large that substantial majorities in developed countries vote to have their living standards slashed in this way is no greater than that of seeing millions (as opposed to the present handful) line up to donate their kidneys to strangers.

Suppose, however, that what was under consideration was not a thirty to seventy percent income tax (on top of taxes already paid) but only the better targeting of existing aid and the elimination of trade preferences and subsidies that harm developing country producers, accompanied by whatever domestic transfers or assistance are required to ensure that no group bears a disproportionate share of the impact at home. Willingness to pay for aid on this sort of scale is entirely imaginable, since official development assistance (ODA) has in recent years surpassed a full half of one percent of GDP in Norway, Sweden, the Netherlands, and other countries, more than three-tenths of a percent in Britain, Switzerland, and Belgium, and more than one-tenth of one percent even in the United States and Japan. Virtually every industrialized country spends at least one-tenth of one percent of its income on ODA.

Polls suggest a relatively strong willingness to help. In the United States, where much less than one percent of federal taxes goes to supporting foreign aid (only a part of which is humanitarian in nature), polls show substantial numbers of people believing that too much is spent on aid. But the average citizen also has the exaggerated sense that vast sums are already being spent. When asked what share of the federal budget went to foreign aid, the median response in a 1995 survey was fifteen percent![4] When asked what an *appropriate* level would be, the average response was five percent—more than thirty times the actual US level. For a majority, then, willingness to help the world's poor, at least at present levels, seems to be indicated. In European countries, where aid levels as a percentage of GDP are in many cases much higher than those of the United States, a poll conducted in 2004 showed that only eleven percent of twenty-five thousand respondents said these levels were too high, while thirty-three percent said they were too low, thirty percent said that they were about right, and twenty-six percent said they didn't know. Responses from the included countries with the highest aid shares, Sweden and the Netherlands, were in the same range.[5]

A more important point is that outright transfers are one of the least efficient ways to attack problems of persistent poverty, so increasing the size of transfers isn't the most pressing requirement for addressing global poverty. What's needed most are ways to raise the productivity of people in poor countries, an achievement shown to be well within the realm of possibility by the emergence of roughly a half billion people from the most extreme poverty—some four hundred million of them in China—between 1970 and 2000. Among other steps, removing trade barriers that make it difficult for poor countries to export to rich ones could increase the incomes of developing country farmers by billions of dollars.[6]

An important implication of Chapters 8 and 9, however, is that not every country has the same capacity to take advantage of opportunities in world markets as have recent success stories like Taiwan, South Korea, and China. Inequality of capacity is likely to run deep, since in the societies just mentioned, cultures were evolving during many hundreds of years in ways helpful to the operation of large-scale political structures and to the possibility of trusting relationships with relative strangers, while in others, there's been little experience of trust beyond the clan. Those societies acquired large state structures only recently from former colonial powers, making it easier for leaders to turn their countries into personal fiefdoms. The message I draw from this is that strengthening human and institutional capabilities should be a top priority of international development programs.

Helping poor countries to establish better functioning institutions would almost certainly be one of the best ways to achieve large medium- and long-term effects at a modest cost. This could be done on the basis of global organizations working with regional ones, such as the African Union, which already shows encouraging signs of a growing capacity to help individual member countries. International support of the African Union's efforts to prevent the overruling of the November 2010 presidential election results in the Ivory Coast provides a partial illustration of the desired synergy, although internal armed conflict still played a major role in determining that the winner ultimately took office. Building institutions capable of promoting norms of good government and respect for human rights so as to prevent future cases of abuse of their own populations by rulers like those of today's Sudan and Zimbabwe would be among the goals of such collaborative efforts.[7]

If the political and economic climates were improved sufficiently in some poor countries, more of their best educated and most productive citizens, who now often reside abroad, could begin to invest their resources and energies back home, contributing to a build-up of know-how critical to attracting investment from both domestic and foreign sources. The Chinese and Indian overseas diasporas played major roles in their countries' recent economic growth, and similar parts could be played by African, Caribbean, Arab, and other populations that have acquired skills of every kind while living abroad. With citizen's interests better protected by accountable and well-functioning governments, investment inflows to poor countries from richer ones, including Asian countries' increasing investments in African and Latin American extractive industries, might yield more dividends to the local people.

Flows of development assistance that might realistically be offered by international donors can still help, if they are well targeted. Assisting the growth of education and the retention of educated cadres of people in critical fields like medicine, engineering, and public administration is an area deserving priority because it can contribute to raising the targeted countries' own capabilities. Programs to make critical medications available to the poor and to fund more research on the diseases that afflict them are other ways in which the proceeds of progressive taxes on the wealthiest countries could be well spent, both from a humanitarian standpoint and from that of productivity. Putting credit and savings tools into the hands of the poor, a growing movement in recent years, could also be fostered.

Rich countries' people need economic security, too

Although average incomes are far higher and poverty tends to take much less extreme forms in rich than in poor countries, inequality of income and wealth, along with widespread economic insecurity, are rightly viewed as failings of their economic systems by many rich country residents. Median income—the income of the individual earning more than exactly half and thus also less than exactly half of the population—has failed to rise in the United States for decades. Almost all income gains have gone to the top few percent, and inequality measures like the Gini coefficient have seen a steady increase. Beginning in 2007, the US economy went through a wrenching economic crisis, causing large-scale and thus far persistent unemployment, home forfeitures, and near-universal declines in personal wealth, mainly due to the carelessness, hubris, and, in some cases, outright deceit by actors in its financial sector. All of this suggests that something is seriously wrong with America's economic institutions, if not with capitalism as such. How can anyone believe that markets are efficient, much less fair, after the events of the past few years?

A few reasons for the recent rise in inequality were discussed in Chapter 7. A point to be added here is that even if this trend were mostly a byproduct of market forces, and if some of those market forces are simultaneously having beneficial effects—say, lifting millions of Chinese workers from poverty—its severity has been greater than need be due to the increased influence of the rich and the declining influence of countervailing forces in terms of government policies, labor markets, and the managerial compensation practices of businesses. The success of conservative ideologues in altering popular perceptions and beliefs through the spread of misinformation is perhaps the single greatest cause for alarm and pessimism about the marriage of the market economy with democracy.[8] There's more than enough evidence, both from looking at the past and at market economies with less extreme degrees of inequality, that earnings ratios far lower than those recently seen in the United States are quite adequate to motivate high levels of skill acquisition, effort, and risk-taking. If market forces alone fail to keep inequalities within socially and morally acceptable bounds, an informed citizenry can add constraints through public policies, including progressive and loophole-free income taxes, without need to fear large impacts on efficiency, if empirical analysis rather than ideological propaganda is to be believed.

One more remark about the economic institutions of contemporary society seems critical here. I've repeatedly endorsed the idea that markets and property have shown themselves to be effective—and for the indefinite future indispensible—elements of an economic system capable of delivering decent standards of living. They're also required for the technological progress needed to address our environmental problems and will be part of the recipe for delivering further advances in medicine. But to say that markets and property are necessary is far different from asserting that they're the only institutions required for a well-functioning economy. On the contrary. For centuries, well-functioning markets have always co-existed with well-functioning states, families, schools, religious institutions, and civic organizations, among others. The elaboration of mixed economies exhibiting a reasonably well-functioning government-market symbiosis from roughly the 1930s to the late 1970s may have saved capitalism from either total collapse or total rejection by citizens. That the unlearning of this lesson by too many in the 1980s had a disastrous impact on our social well-being should be the take-home message of the recent crisis.[9]

Lives more worth living
What about the less narrowly economic parts of the "better world" vision? If it's markets, competition, and investment that will gradually eliminate the gulf between the world's rich and poor nations, what will prevent the end result from being a future of limitless job hunting, investment managing, and shopping? With millions upon millions of businesses competing to sell billions of human beings their products, and with the increasingly educated people of dozens of once-poor countries all competing to sell their labor more cheaply, won't we find ourselves on an endless treadmill of hard work, self-promotion, and maneuvering to afford the latest goods being spread before us by marketers (whose ranks we might even feel compelled to join), with each year's latest gadgets being quickly consigned to heaps of toxic landfills as they're rendered obsolete by new and better models? Won't this world of marketing, marketing, and more marketing continue to mold us into one-dimensional customers lining up for surgical makeovers to refashion ourselves after our latest pop idols?

Maybe so, but recall again that our fears that the atmosphere and ethos of the market inexorably dominate every dimension of life may be overstated. Values, such as the inviolability of the franchise and democracy, the importance of parent/child bonds, and the anathema of slavery, as we've noted, show little sign of falling prey to the contending logic of "for sale to the highest bidder." Other examples might include constraints on advertising to children, now a well-established principle in the United States and other countries, and the continuing importance of non-market institutions, including schools and churches. Consider, too, the ability of multiple genres of music, art, and literature to remain vibrant, sometimes alongside better-funded, mass-marketed alternatives, thanks to the enthusiasm of artists and their audiences. Or the relative autonomy of intellectual life in universities and other settings. Or the flourishing and sharing of diverse opinions facilitated by the Internet. Or the emergence of new value orientations—such as environmentalism—not as a result of, but despite, the profit motive.

Anti-consumerist and anti-elitist ideas have even been spread by popular culture itself. While the trends in question might so far be superficial ones—middle class men no longer wear ties and jackets to take the trash out—there are areas in which they appear to run more deeply. The notion has spread in some circles that one of the rewards of prosperity can be that one needn't pursue the most lucrative, or even the most prestigious, career, that self-exploration, self-expression, and other dimensions of work and life may also be important. The appeal of "careers for the common good" mentioned in Chapter 4 is one indication of this. Another illustration is that thousands of middle-aged Americans from Taiwan, India, Hong Kong, and Korea, people who succeeded economically through their intense efforts to enter good schools and study engineering, medicine, and computer science, have woken up in America's suburbs in recent years to find that a bright and well-behaved child is not willing to study round the clock for his or her math exams, but has dreams of becoming a pop musician, a dancer, or a film-maker. Such "going to seed" by the offspring of the affluent may to some extent reflect the principle (popularized by psychologist Abraham Maslow) that after "lower order" needs like food and shelter have been met, there may be a hunger to satisfy "higher order" ones that for some will mean something other than engineering, computer programming, or marketing.

Could non-consumerist and other life-balancing values come to have the consensus status enjoyed by the idea of democracy, the protection of votes from dollars, and the prohibition of slavery? If there's something in our natures that gives us basic needs of affection, affiliation, and a desire for purpose and meaning, then the answer is probably "yes." But even a less-optimistic observer might concede that a swing of the world cultural pendulum towards an extreme and uniform consumerism would likely set off opposing forces due to the heterogeneous and complex nature of human beings. At worst, the pendulum will always be in motion.

Placing bets, or taking action?

In the book *Non-Zero*, Robert Wright explored the possibility that history has an inherently positive trajectory. Despite the principle of entropy, which implies the ongoing dispersal of energy and thus the breakdown of structure, the unfolding of time has seen the formation of galaxies, suns, and planets, the self-organizing of inert matter into life, and the variegation of life-forms, including the appearance of social and intelligent creatures. And it has seen humans, the most complex and social of those creatures, obtain an ever greater understanding of their surroundings and achieve progress in at least some aspects of their social, political, and economic arrangements.

With mental powers sufficiently developed for our ancestors to invent improved tools and domesticate crops and animals, human technological and social evolution accelerated. The rate of technological progress in recent centuries has been breathtaking, and while our record of social achievement is far more mixed, we might think we see traces of progress, such as the winding down of colonization, slavery, and political despotisms. Are we, then, destined also to see a still better human society some day?

No destiny can be inevitable unless there's a benevolent and all-powerful protector watching over us. There's nothing to rule out the possibility that tomorrow will bring thermonuclear, biological, or astronomical disaster. We might also see economic growth stall, the poor "break all the windows" of the global economy, a hundred years of war between modernity and religious fanaticism, and other nightmares.

There are grounds for maintaining hope in the face of all of the tragedies and disappointments of the past century. My two main reasons for optimism are that *human beings have considerable potential for goodness and cooperation* and that *human beings are capable of enormous intelligence* and have made great strides in discovering how their world and they themselves work. Perhaps the next few decades will see still more progress, with advances in our understanding of our social world and of our own natures, including our moral natures, better keeping pace with improvements in our understanding of chemistry, biology, and physics. Perhaps adding such understanding to the other factors working in our favor will help to tip the balance towards the better world that we'd like to see.

My two main reasons for pessimism are that *human beings have considerable potential for viciousness* and that *human beings can be enormously stupid.*

It would be fascinating to sit back, with detachment, and watch the spectacle as these opposing forces play themselves out. But if we care about the outcome and want to see things get better for those who follow us, we can't afford to sit back. Educating ourselves and our children about the reasons we're finding it so hard to achieve our dream of a better world is one of the things we can do to try to help tip the balance towards a better outcome.

One of the worst mistakes our society could make would be to adopt measures and institutions that would work well for angels but that fail to account for the pernicious sides of human nature. But an equally bad mistake would be to adopt policies and institutions that assume self-interest to be all that people are capable of. The human inclination to think and act socially is real. There's much evidence that it's innate. When wisely summoned into use, it flourishes. And we dismiss it at our peril.

Notes:

1. The incomes mentioned are those before subtracting taxes paid or adding transfer payments received.

2. A number of recent studies by economists find evidence that in jurisdictions that are more racially or ethnically heterogeneous or that have larger immigrant populations, there is less support for redistribution.

3. The fifteen dollar a day standard is proposed in: Lant Pritchett, "Who is Not Poor? Dreaming of a World Truly Free of Poverty," *World Bank Research Observer* 21, no. 1 (2006): 1-23. In annual terms, it translates into an income of $5,475, about half the $11,000 that I estimated for the case of complete equalization between the richest 15 percent and the poorest 2 billion.

4. Program on International Policy Attitudes, University of Maryland, "Americans on Foreign Aid and World Hunger: A Study of U.S. Public Attitudes," 2001.

5. Reported in European Commission/Eurobarometer, "Attitudes towards Development Aid," February 2005.

6. A 2003 paper from the International Food Policy Research Institute (IFPRI) in Washington put gains at $8.3 billion in Latin American and the Caribbean, $6.6 billion in Asia, and $2 billion in sub-Saharan Africa. See Xinshen Diao, Eugenio Diaz-Bonilla, and Sherman Robinson, "How Much Does it Hurt? The Impact of Agricultural Trade Policies on Developing Countries," MTID Descussion Papers 84, IFPRI, p.3. World Bank economists have also forecast large gains, but the subject is complicated, since the potential beneficiaries are usually not among the poorest developing country farmers, since some citizens of poor countries could be hurt rather than helped by rising food prices, and since effects on employment and investment are difficult to predict with any precision. Contrary to suggestions that the benefits from eliminating First World agricultural subsidies would dwarf the scale of existing official aid, the numbers just mentioned are in the neighborhood of annual aid flows to Latin America but substantially smaller than those to Asia and Africa.

7. Economist Paul Collier's book *The Bottom Billion: Why the Poorest Countries are Failing and What Can Be Done About It?* (New York: Oxford University Press, 2007) discusses numerous suggestions as to how international institutional regimes can be strengthened to reduce corruption and the likelihood of civil wars in the poorest countries. Examples include better monitoring of restrictions on leaders' placement of funds in "First World" (e.g., Swiss) banks, better mechanisms to track exactly how aid funds are used, reducing arms flows, tracking revenues from oil sales (as has already been fairly successfully done with diamonds) to prevent unsavory rebel movements from profiting from illegal seizure of national resources, and agreed international standards for identifying and isolating particularly corrupt national leaders.

8. This is the main theme of George Soros's thought-provoking *The Soros Lectures at the Central European University* (New York: Perseus Books Group, 2010).

9. On the 2008 crisis, needed reforms, and problems of "economic doctrine," I highly recommend: Joseph Stiglitz, *Freefall: America, Free Markets, and the Sinking of the World Economy* (2010). Other interesting reading includes: Robert Reich, *Aftershock: The Next Economy and America's Future* (2010) and his earlier book: *Supercapitalism: Transformation of Business, Democracy, & Everyday Life* (2007).

Acknowledgments

In this book, I've drawn on a number of collaborative research projects, especially ones with David Weil, Toby Page, Avner Ben-Ner, Areendam Chanda, Stephen Atlas, Olivier Bochet, Matthias Cinyabuguma, Arhan Ertan, Bruno Garcia, Kenju Kamei, Ting Ren, Jean-Robert Tyran, and Bulent Unel. My collaborators deserve credit for whatever is valuable in our joint work, but they share no responsibility for the interpretations I've freely added, and they should not be blamed for any defects in the ways in which I've used our work here.

The projects drawn on also benefited from the help of research assistants too numerous to mention in full. I'm especially indebted to Yaheng Wang for her work on developing the world migration data and to Cary Anne Trainer for her work on developing the agricultural transition data, both of which are used in the research discussed in chapters 8 and 9; to Rob Letzler for helping to launch the experimental research with Page and others discussed in chapter 6; to Nilay Patel for help in completing the agricultural transition paper mentioned in Chapter 9; and to Joshua Wilde, Ishani Tewari, Isabel Tecu, Federico Droller, and Momotazur Rahman for their work on the paper with Weil that I discuss extensively in the same chapter. I apologize to those not mentioned either due to oversight or because they worked on projects not featured in the book. No doubt, whatever merit the book has reflects the influence of many other wonderful students, colleagues, teachers, and intellectual mentors whom I've also not mentioned by name but who are fondly in my thoughts as I write this.

In the investigations that I undertook for the book on topics beyond the scope of my usual research, I benefited from the help of several able research assistants, especially Robbie Corey-Boulet, Bruno Garcia, and Joel Soltman. I'm grateful to Brown University for the funding that supported their work.

I could not have completed arrangements for the book's publication without the supportive and experienced advice of Stephanie Lawyer and the encouragement and suggestions of my close friend Rick Shor. I also benefited from the editorial advice of Tershia d'Elgin, the editing work of Erin Roof, and assistance on matters including indexing from Nina Joyce. I also want to thank Jane Mansbridge for taking the time to go through the manuscript and offering a great many helpful suggestions.

Most important of all, my wife Vivian, our daughter Serena and our son Mark have contributed their funny, earnest, warm, inquisitive, infinitely interesting and lovable selves as the otherwise missing pieces of the work/life balance that made it possible for me to complete this and so many other projects in recent and not-so-recent years. I'm grateful to my daughter Laura for her gifts of unalloyed joy, love and inspiration, and I give special thanks to those who care for her with loving devotion and are an inspiration to me, as well. Last but not least, I thank my parents, Eileen and Milton Putterman, for making the leap of faith that brought me into this world and for setting remarkable examples of what being human is all about.

About the Author

Louis Putterman is a long-time professor of economics at Brown University in Providence, Rhode Island. Following his childhood in suburban Long Island, he spent three years doing farm work in *kibbutz* communities in Israel before returning to earn undergraduate and graduate degrees at Columbia and Yale universities. While in graduate school, he learned Kiswahili and carried out field research among peasant farmers in rural Tanzania. As a young faculty member, he then studied Chinese and pursued similar research in rural China. His edited Reader on the organizational economics of business enterprises (*The Economic Nature of the Firm*) was adopted in leading universities and business schools. As an expert on China's economy and an authority on workplace organization, he was elected president of the international scholarly organization, The Association for Comparative Economic Studies, in 1999. Mid-career, he developed new areas of expertise on the evolution of human economies over the millennia and on the behavioral and experimental economics of human social interaction. He has published more than one hundred scholarly articles in peer-reviewed journals and books and authored, co-authored, or edited seven books, including *Economics, Values and Organization* (1998) and *Dollars and Change: Economics in Context* (2001).

Louis lives with his wife, attorney Vivian Tseng, in Concord, Massachusetts. He is the father of two college-aged children and is the parent and guardian of an older daughter dependent on nursing care as a result of profound brain damage. He enjoys playing Beatles and other tunes on the piano for her amusement and his.

INDEX